Leading for All

Leading for All

How to Create Truly Inclusive and Excellent Schools

Jennifer Spencer-Iiams

Josh Flosi

Foreword by Paula Kluth

FOR INFORMATION:

Corwin

A SAGE Company

2455 Teller Road

Thousand Oaks, California 91320

(800) 233-9936

www.corwin.com

SAGE Publications Ltd.

1 Oliver's Yard

55 City Road

London EC1Y 1SP

United Kingdom

SAGE Publications India Pvt. Ltd.

B 1/I 1 Mohan Cooperative Industrial Area

Mathura Road, New Delhi 110 044

India

SAGE Publications Asia-Pacific Pte. Ltd.

18 Cross Street #10-10/11/12

China Square Central

Singapore 048423

Publisher: Jessica Allan

Senior Content Development Editor: Lucas Schleicher

Associate Content Development Editor: Mia Rodriguez

Project Editor: Amy Schroller

Copy Editor: Shamila Swamy,
 QuADS Prepress Pvt. Ltd.

Typesetter: Hurix Digital

Proofreader: Dennis W. Webb

Indexer: Integra

Cover Designer: Candice Harman

Marketing Manager: Sharon Pendergast

Printed in the United States of America

Library of Congress Cataloging-in-Publication Data

Names: Spencer-Iiams, Jennifer, author. | Flosi, Josh, author. | Kluth, Paula, writer of foreword.

Title: Leading for all : how to create truly inclusive and excellent schools / Jennifer Spencer-Iiams, Josh Flosi ; foreword by Paula Kluth.

Description: Thousand Oaks, California : Corwin Press, [2021] | Includes bibliographical references.

Identifiers: LCCN 2020031002 | ISBN 9781071827925 (paperback) | ISBN 9781071827901 (epub) | ISBN 9781071827895 (epub) | ISBN 9781071827871 (ebook)

Subjects: LCSH: Inclusive education. | Children with disabilities— Education. | Educational leadership. Classification: LCC LC1200 .S69 2021 | DDC 371.9/046—dc23

LC record available at https://lccn.loc.gov/2020031002

This book is printed on acid-free paper.

20 21 22 23 24 10 9 8 7 6 5 4 3 2 1

Contents

Foreword

By Paula Kluth

"Is anybody actually doing this?"

I was finishing a presentation on inclusive education to a group of about 300 administrators when I was approached by a young principal who was really interested in the message. Holding an open notebook, he asked a lot of questions about implementation, discussed some of the barriers he faced, and mentioned the strategies he was going to try when he got back to his district. As we spoke, he took notes and nodded with gusto. It was a great conversation, and as it drew to a close, I felt nothing but excitement about his energy, enthusiasm, and clear commitment to creating a school for all.

He started walking away, but after a few steps, he turned and asked one last question—the one that so many leaders have asked me over the years—"Is anybody actually doing this?" I took a deep breath before answering.

I knew exactly what he meant because I have been asked the same question literally hundreds of times. I've been asked by parents who are desperate to move to a place that will educate their child in an inclusive classroom. I've been asked by teachers who want to do this work but feel thwarted by their own administrators. I've been asked by school board members who want to advocate for inclusion in their communities. I've been asked by teacher educators, learning coaches, therapists, lawmakers, mediators, and lawyers. Mostly, however, I've been asked by administrators.

So many school and district leaders want to create more equitable, responsive, and inclusive educational experiences for their students. In many cases they have the resources to do so. They may even have some of the know-how, but they often do not have the one thing they desperately need—a model and clear evidence that it can be done effectively across an entire district and community.

So what was my answer to this principal? My response was an emphatic "Absolutely!" Then I told him the rest of the truth, which is that many schools were doing phenomenal work in inclusive education but not nearly enough of them. When he pressed me to tell him about places he could visit to "see it," I sighed. I could not name a single K–12 district or community within driving distance with a strong inclusive philosophy and inclusive placements for a wide range of learners—including those with significant disabilities. They do exist, certainly, but they are few and far between. I could, however, name fantastic elementary schools, a few wonderful middle schools, a great high school district a few towns away, and a team doing incredible work in early childhood a mile down the road. I also knew of some administrators who were doing a bang-up job including kids with learning disabilities and emotional needs but not those with intellectual disabilities or complex support needs. I knew of a district that had a long history of supporting students on the autism spectrum in general education classrooms, but they only provided those opportunities for students considered "high functioning." And so on.

I never want my honest response to "the question" to be discouraging. Instead, I hope it will be seen as a positive challenge, as in "This is the work we need to do." But I know it often *is* discouraging, as well as frustrating and deeply disappointing.

Over the years I have spent as an inclusion facilitator, teacher educator, university professor, and advocate, I have met countless educators who want to create truly inclusive schools, but they don't have mentors to get them started and help them over the barriers they will find along the way. When I picked up *Leading for All: How to Create Truly Inclusive and Excellent Schools* and read the first few pages, I started thinking of every one of those educators. As I read the first chapter and then the second, I started calling some of them I knew personally! I couldn't wait to tell them what I'm sharing with you in this foreword, which is "Your mentors have arrived!"

Dr. Jennifer Spencer-Iiams and Dr. Josh Flosi don't just explore the "why" and "how" of inclusion in this book. They discuss what inclusion actually means and help readers understand why discussions on disability can't take place outside of those related to school culture, equity, and student agency. There is plenty of practical advice in this text as well, and readers will be adding many a sticky note to the chapters on teaching strategies and behavior support. For leaders, however, I think the most earmarked section will be the one on "leadership moves," as it is filled with creative ideas and thoughtful, change-related questions. My favorite chapter is the last one, because it challenges us all to look forward and to realize that what is progressive today will not be so tomorrow. To serve all students well, it is indeed critical to always be asking, "What's next?"

I am just so grateful for *Leading for All*. I'm aware that it sounds dramatic, but it is absolutely true. This is the book the field of inclusive education has waited for. Administrators and advocates alike have had plenty of helpful "how to" articles and texts they could access on the topic, but we have never before had a K–12 story like this one to use as a guide and as a reminder of all that is possible for all of our students. So the next time I'm at a conference or visiting a school and I'm asked, "Is anyone actually doing this?" you can bet I will be sharing this book so the hopeful questioner can take from it what I did—yes, it's happening in Jennifer and Josh's district, and it can happen *everywhere*!

Acknowledgments

The Students. This is the story of the amazing students who continue to rise to new opportunities, who persevere through challenges, who take action every day to be more inclusive. The students, above all others, have earned our deepest admiration. The students bring us hope for the future—not with a rose-colored-glasses optimism but in a "I see what they are doing and the ways they value inclusion and excellence, and I really believe our world will be improved by them" way.

The Educators. This is the story of *special education teachers* who completely changed the way they work, who embraced new challenges outside of their expertise, who shared their successes, who carried the torch with a "We got this" spirit as we moved into uncharted waters, and who learned and led as they went. This is the story of *general education teachers* who looked past their old schema of which students belonged in their class, who became collaborators with special educators for the good of the children, who planned their lessons differently to create entry points for all learners, and who created classroom communities where everyone is "in." This is the story of *specialists* (occupational therapists, speech language pathologists, physical therapists, school psychologists, social workers, school nurses, transition specialists, school counselors) who embraced All-Some-Few thinking and universal ways of doing previously siloed work, who compassionately did whatever it takes for individual students while creating systems that work, and who helped us find the miracles in creating access for each student, every student. This is the story of *paraeducators* who dedicated themselves to learning new ways of supporting all students, who became facilitators of learning, and who continue to take on the whole variety of tasks that make it possible for all students to be at school with dignity and independence. This is the story of *school administrators* who fearlessly championed the belief that every student in their building belongs, who courageously led professional development that enabled teachers to have the tools for the work, who rearranged their physical spaces and schedules with equity in mind, and who navigated through the millions of small details that are required in systemic change. This is the story of *district office leaders* who practiced what they preached by standing in circles together and committing to inclusion and excellence, who engaged in public and private conversations about why our schools need to be inclusive, who allocated the resources to support all students, and who bravely moved forward with programs, architecture, and hiring that supported inclusion. This is the story of *school board members* who set goals about closing opportunity gaps and valuing inclusion that made our work public and aligned, who approved hiring staff to make this work possible, who bravely listened and responded when some citizens brought forward complaints without having all of the information about school climate, and who truly brought their heart to supporting all students in the district.

The Parents. This is the story of parents who challenged us, who asked the hard questions, who pushed us to be better, who celebrated successes with us, and who demanded what we all want for our children. Parents have partnered with us through every step—sometimes in strong collaboration, sometimes through difficult conversations. They have all been important because inclusive and excellent schools can never happen without deep respect and understanding of the unique and vital role that parents play in the educational process.

We can never name all of the people who have inspired and facilitated the journey that you will read about in this book. We hope each one of them will see the words above and know that we mean "Thank you!" to them personally.

There are a few names that we must specifically mention. Deepest thanks to Dr. Kathy Ludwig, who is a true warrior for inclusive and excellent schools. Her leadership and partnership are at the core of everything reflected in this book. Her district theme, "Leading for All," encapsulated the vision for our work and provided the title for this book. Also, Dr. Bill Rhodes gave us the inspiration and mentorship to start this work, starting with his first district theme in 2012, "Mindset and Miracles." Carolyn Miller was our assistant director in the first two years of this journey, and her leadership helped us put down the first goals on paper and begin the process of change. Special thanks to Dr. Elaine Fox and Dr. Candace Pelt for their shared commitment to inclusion and learning together. We have had the partnership of so many great leaders in our community, including Jean Hansen from Special Olympics Unified Champion Schools, Roberta Dunn from FACT Oregon, and Angela Jarvis-Holland from NWDSA. Our administrative assistants over the years, Ruth Zollner, Brenda Hogan, Sara Harmon, Maria Swanson, Karina Archibald, Connie Zollner, and Lisa Marti, worked behind the scenes to create the conditions for change and helped us keep our sanity. Our unending thanks to our Core Team (special education instructional coordinators) over the years: Jennifer Ziolko, Cathy Smith, Mark Lapides, Lori Prater, Zach Deets, Marian Wattman Oshima, Stephanie Clawson, Jason Hobson, Kathy Versteeg, and Patrick Kelly. You are amazing leaders of change and are truly at the heart of our work. Our deep appreciation to Paula Kluth for the inspiration she has been to so many in support of the work of inclusion and for her encouragement and mentorship to us in this project specifically.

Josh wants to personally thank Corrie and Mark Dunkerton for their faithful friendship and for modeling advocacy for inclusion. Thanks to Jeremiah Hubbard for reading an early draft of this book and even more for being an amazing teaching partner and for challenging me to think in new and provocative ways. To Mom, Dad, Chris, and Todd for always believing in me and supporting my dreams. To Jake and Becca for inspiring me with your creativity, curiosity, and kind hearts. And, finally, to Laura for being my constant—I am thankful every day for your passion, faith, and joyful spirit of service to your family, your students, your community, and the world.

Jennifer's personal thanks to my sisters, Linda, Ellen, Ingrid, Becky, and Miriam; to Bonnie and Sarah, my forever besties; and to Dr. Sara Deboy and Dr. Suzanne West for their constant friendship and educational push. To my mother, Kathleen Forsythe Wysong, for modeling strength, activism, and grace. To McCartney, Shelby, and Landon, for letting me be the mom to three of the most wonderful people on the planet. And of course, to Carl, the love of my life, who has supported me every step of the way.

PUBLISHER'S ACKNOWLEDGMENTS

Corwin gratefully acknowledges the contributions of the following reviewers:

Peter Dillon, EdD

Superintendent of Schools

Berkshire Hills Regional School District/Shaker Mountain School Union

Stockbridge, Massachusetts

Dr. Anthony Mays

Senior Director of Schools Division with the Harris County Department of Education

University of Houston Downtown

Houston, Texas

Linda R. Vogel

Professor and Program Coordinator

University of Northern Colorado

Greeley, Colorado

Ronald D. Wahlen

Director of Digital Teaching and Learning

Durham Public Schools

Durham, North Carolina

About the Authors

Dr. Jennifer Spencer-Iiams is Assistant Superintendent for Student Services in the West Linn-Wilsonville School District near Portland, Oregon. She has been a teacher and educational leader for 32 years. She has led significant transformation in her district in the movement to a full inclusion model that honors student strengths and promotes belonging. Jennifer has served as an adjunct professor in the areas of special education and emerging bilingual education. She has presented on models of inclusion at numerous conferences, served on statewide leadership groups focused on improvement in special education, and collaborated to support national educational reform efforts for higher education and educator standards. Jennifer is a triple Duck, earning her bachelor's, master's, and doctoral degrees from the University of Oregon. She is the child of educators, and her mother was always active in improving her community. Jennifer is a younger sister to five strong women. Jennifer and her husband live in West Linn, Oregon, spending time with their three grown children and their dog, Gus.

Dr. Josh Flosi has been an educator for 25 years in public, private, and international schools. He currently leads Student Support Services at the International School of Tanganyika, an inclusive school in Dar es Salaam, Tanzania. Before that, he spent 10 years as a building administrator and then as Assistant Director of Student Services in the West Linn-Wilsonville School District near Portland, Oregon, where he helped lead the transformation to a profoundly inclusive model of education. He spent 14 years as a high school English and social studies teacher. He has also been an adjunct professor in a teacher preparation program and is a regular presenter at conferences.

Josh is committed to promoting inclusive and excellent schools, believing that we all have the capacity to learn and we all have the right to belong and contribute to a community. He earned his bachelor's and master's degrees from Stanford University and his doctorate in educational leadership from the University of Oregon. He enjoys traveling with his family, reading, coaching soccer, and crafting homemade ice cream.

Introduction

A few years ago Jennifer received a call from Susannah Frame, an investigative reporter from a Seattle TV station. Her heart froze, wondering whether there had been a student tragedy or some other ominously bad event. What would cause a television news journalist from another state to call the head of Special Education in a medium-sized suburban school district in Oregon? Ms. Frame began to ask about our approach to supporting students with significant disabilities in our schools—did we *really* include them in their neighborhood schools and general education classes? Jennifer affirmed this, still wondering why the reporter was calling. Ms. Frame proceeded to ask more questions about why and how we came to be an inclusive school district.

Sometimes when you are deep in the work of changing systems and beliefs, you can forget to step back and reflect on the journey. What were those moves that we made? What was the initial decision point when we realized that things had to change? What successes and failures have informed us along the way? Were we really so unusual in that our whole district was committed to the beliefs and structures of inclusion?

Ms. Frame traveled to our district to interview some teachers, parents, and administrators about this journey. She said she was passionate about inclusion because of a personal connection in her family and because of the shock that some people feel when they first learn that the vast majority of children in U.S. schools who experience intellectual disability are in separate classes or schools for all of their educational years. She is an investigative journalist, so her lens is different from ours as educational leaders. She may have phrased her questions differently from how we would, but her inquiry was authentic.

The investigative report was seen by many people in her state, and clips of her work were shared widely on the internet. People who saw this and were eager to learn more about inclusion—or to understand how it could work on a districtwide level—began to reach out to us.

Every superintendent, principal, teacher, or parent who called or emailed us about our journey first heard this honest disclaimer: "We are on a journey; things are messy; nothing is perfect. We will share our experience with you, but we also want to learn from your experience."

With that disclaimer clearly stated, we opened our doors. We opened our doors for visits, for learning walks, for long conversations with parents who were frustrated, for inquiries from state departments of education, for conference presentations, and for talking about inclusive practices with anyone who would listen.

People mostly asked us the same cluster of questions: How did you get started? What have you learned along the way? Do you really mean *all* children? How did teachers adapt to their changing roles? What about parents who want their child in a self-contained classroom? Won't the rigor for other students suffer? How do you deal with challenging behavior? Are there hard data to show you've been successful? What's next?

During one of those visits, we took a group of administrators from Tennessee to see our incredible teachers and students at work on a typical Tuesday. After visiting classrooms and sharing the answers to all of those questions, Jennifer turned to Josh and joked, "We should just write a book." We both laughed. Like all district administrators, we are extremely busy, and we never thought we could find the time to write a book.

A few weeks later a man called us from upstate New York. His son was on the autism spectrum and spent almost all of his day in a self-contained classroom. This father believed that his son could be so much more successful if he could be included in a general education classroom with the right support. We spoke with this father about how to advocate in a way that would build partnership with his Special Education department. We directed him to parent resources and advocacy groups in his area. At the end of the conversation he said, "My son doesn't have time to wait. I think we are going to move to your district." We laughed and again encouraged him to work with his current school team in New York.

The next month we received another call from this father. He was at a rest stop in Colorado. He and his family had packed their belongings into their van and were moving to Oregon to enroll in our district.

Families make decisions to move based on schools all the time. In our own district many families move here for the strong college preparatory focus, the arts programs, the science opportunities, or the athletics. So it is natural that a family may choose to move to a new district seeking new opportunities for a child who experiences disabilities. We were, of course, happy to welcome this family, and they are now a valuable part of our community.

However, this story reveals some deeply concerning equity issues in the state of American education. A family should not have to move (across town or across the country) for their child to have the opportunity to be included in their general education class. A zip code should not determine a student's sense of belonging.

When we reflected on this family's journey, and thought about families all over our country who do not have the means to move to an inclusive school district, we felt compelled to dedicate late nights and weekends to writing this book.

Superintendents, principals, and teachers all over our country want to do what is best for students. They deeply want all children to be successful. We hope our journey in this book may be part of the inspiration for, or confirmation to continue on, their own journey toward inclusive and excellent schools.

Stories are one of the best ways to learn, so we share many stories in this book. We hope that you will feel our deep respect and care for these students, parents, and educators who have bravely created a new paradigm for inclusive and excellent schools. Throughout this book, we use pseudonyms rather than student names. All of the student stories are true. We recognize that other people who know the students may have different interpretations of these stories. And we recognize that a single story does not capture the complex reality of any individual student's journey through school. We hope that these collections of stories help to illustrate the real work and the real impact of creating inclusive learning communities.

We humbly hope that by sharing our stories, beliefs, and frameworks, and by owning that our mistakes and flaws are many, we will provide an opportunity for school districts to become more inclusive. It can be done, and our children don't have time to wait.

CHAPTER 1

Finding Our Why

Meeting Raj in first grade, his passion for learning was so evident—he was filled with curiosity about the world around him. His dinosaur knowledge was encyclopedic, and he had never seen a Lego set that he couldn't assemble to perfection. Raj spent most of his day in a small supported classroom for children with autism spectrum disorder (ASD), working to develop the social and executive functioning skills that were elusive to him and that created barriers to his interactions with others. Our goal was always to have him spend more time in the general education classroom when he was ready. We surrounded Raj with adults and carefully controlled the variables in his environment, trying to teach him these skills in a context that was wholly different from the cheerful hubbub of a typical first-grade classroom. The academic expectations in this specialized setting were predictable but in no way rigorous, emphasizing rote skills and fluency rather than application and comprehension. We would have Raj join, or more accurately visit, the typical first-grade classroom for a small portion of each day.

Raj's difficulties with social interactions and his need to make sense of his sensory world in unique ways contributed to daily evidence that he "wasn't ready" to be in general education. Raj and his first-grade classmates learned this message and internalized it.

Raj developed a deep sense of being a visitor in that classroom. He did not feel that he truly belonged in that community. He would often be taken back to the special classroom sooner the more pronounced his behaviors became. Without intending to, we had created a cycle that reinforced the very behaviors that we said we were working to change. A sense of belonging is in many ways the deepest human need. Raj felt that sense of belonging in a small segregated classroom with many adults, and if vocalizing in unusual ways helped him get back to that place, then that is what he would do.

At the same time, the classroom teacher and other students were learning the message that Raj was a classroom visitor. He wasn't *really* part of the class. His name was not on the first-grade teacher's attendance list. When he showed up, he sat at a table in the back of the room instead of having a desk like everyone else.

He wasn't part of the frequent child-to-child negotiations that happen among first graders on the playground. Rather, Raj came into the class in orchestrated ways—with adults always near him—being given different tasks rather than reading books like the other students during reading time. Even though we may have made explicit statements about Raj being part of the class, the message was clear to the teachers and students that Raj was a visitor rather than a true community member. This message led to an implicit lack of ownership in his education from the classroom teacher. The teacher was aware of Raj's learning differences far more than all the sameness that he shared with first graders everywhere. And if the adults don't behave in a way that clearly communicates that "Raj belongs," how can we expect the children to not embody the implicit or explicit "othering"?

We thought about Raj and other students in similar situations, with so many adults working to teach skills first in a separate setting and then have those students gradually earn their way into general education classrooms. We realized it almost never happened. Students educated in special (segregated) classrooms, grouped with other children with similar learning challenges, did not move on to general education classrooms. Almost all students in these classrooms maintained a parallel educational track through their public school career. This parallel track was separate and clearly not equal, in terms of richness of academic curriculum and diversity of social experiences. This parallel track came at a great cost to the culture of the school as a whole. In an age where educators are, rightfully, thinking deeply about how to interrupt patterns of inequity and eliminate bullying behaviors in schools, we needed to take a long hard look at ourselves and our actions. If we want students to value diversity, deepen understanding of differences, and develop qualities such as empathy and compassion, how can we continue to draw lines between who belongs and who doesn't?

We realized that it was time to examine our beliefs and assumptions, time to think and act differently. We knew it would not be easy or smooth and that we would be incredibly imperfect in the journey. Yet we knew it was the right thing to do. We knew we would continue to have individualized schedules and supports—not a one-size-fits-all approach to inclusion. When your starting point is that everyone is *in*, everything changes. This book is about that journey: what we have learned, where we have stumbled, and what we are still questioning. But when our basic paradigm shifted to truly believing that all children belong, we knew our journey was the right one.

> When your starting point is that everyone is *in*, everything changes.

As for Raj, his trajectory changed as we lived into our model of inclusive practices, eliminating self-contained programs and educating all students in general education classrooms in their neighborhood schools. We saw him six years later when we were visiting a language arts classroom in one of our middle schools. The class was sitting in small groups, three or four students to a table. The teacher introduced an activity to help the students dig deeply into a novel. The activity involved some elements of a game, some visual and textual supports, and academic discourse between students. When we had selected that class to visit, we hadn't known that Raj was in that class—and he certainly didn't stand out when we entered the room. He was working at his table group with his peers, carefully following the rules of the game, referring to some of the visual supports as needed, fully engaged in the academic conversation. When his peers started to engage in a side conversation, he reminded them of the task at hand. The peers sighed, as one might from a reminder from a sibling, then smiled and got back to the work in front of them. The teacher (a general education language arts teacher) came around and provided feedback to Raj and his table, as he did to the others, but perhaps a bit more often. The social and academic learning for Raj, as for the other students in the classroom, was complex and rigorous. Raj still experiences ASD. He still interacts with the world in some ways differently than his peers. But that difference is now seen as part of the fabric of diversity in the classroom, where it is our responsibility to find ways for Raj to maximize his strengths alongside his general education peers.

The shift that is embodied in Raj's story happened over time and with great intention. We used to have a fairly traditional model of general education and special education—including "resource rooms," with mostly pull-out supports, and self-contained "program classes" in areas like behavior, life learning, and social communication. We had resource rooms at every school, but program classes were clustered at a few schools. Students were bused from their neighborhood to the self-contained classes in order to receive the program level of support.

In our new model, every student is at their neighborhood school, every student belongs in their general education classroom, and we bring individualized supports to them. Because every student is different, it is not a one-size-fits-all model. The Individualized Education Program (IEP) team still grapples with times when a student may need some instruction in a small-group setting or different types of modifications to their schedule or curriculum. But by and large, we have changed how we set up our general education classrooms and deliver instruction in the first place to make our schools more inclusive, more focused on the needs of the whole child, and more intentional about creating multiple access points for all learners. Thousands of small moves, conversations, strategies, structures, and details have moved us along in this journey of inclusive practices. It is not perfect; it is hard, and it is in process.

And it is the right thing to do.

Why Inclusion?

Comedian Michael Jr. (2017) has a video on YouTube where he talks about the importance of understanding "The Why." During a stand-up routine, he pauses to ask a man from the audience to sing a song. The man happens to be a high school choir director, so he confidently starts into a stately version of "Amazing Grace." It is a solid, respectable performance. Exactly the sort of thing a choir director hopes to hear from his students.

After a few bars, Michael Jr. stops him, and the crowd gives a genial cheer. Then the comedian gives the singer some context: "This time, imagine your uncle just got home from jail, you got shot in the back when you was a kid . . . give me the 'hood version' . . . if that exists."

The man pauses and then begins again, summoning up a profound and powerful mix of pathos, hope, and pure joy. As he works his way through the opening verse, the audience begins to be transported along with him to a transcendent place. People are standing, cheering, dancing, shouting "Amen!", and mock fainting. The camera cuts to Michael Jr.'s face, and his eyes bulge in disbelief.

During the first rendition, as Michael Jr. explained, the man knew "The What"— sing us a song. Simple and direct. Effective. But nothing that would leave a lasting impact on his audience. When he sang the song a second time, he knew The Why. He was able to draw on stores of emotion and passion that he may not have even known he had. And you know his audience would be talking about it for weeks. Michael Jr. sums it up for his audience: "When you know your Why, your What becomes more impactful because you are walking toward, or in, your purpose."

When we think about creating inclusive cultures in our schools, it is important to know *The What and The How*. Much of this book is dedicated to The What and The How of one school district's journey toward greater inclusion.

However, if we do not explore The Why, we will be missing out on deeply powerful internal resources. The work is hard at the start—changing mindsets and overcoming deeply ingrained institutional habits. And it will get harder as you get deeper into the work. So building your sense of The Why is critical at the start, and it is indispensable as you move deeper into the experience of inclusive school communities.

Leaders need to know their Why deeply (TED[X], 2009). And we need to help each individual at each layer of the system to know their Why too. We need to recognize that your Why and my Why may not be the same. And we need to learn to tell the story of our Why and provide opportunities for others to tell their stories too.

Academic Research Supports Inclusion

As educators, we are charged with making decisions that are grounded in research. For many of us, this part of our Why is particularly important in public education. Educational research is a broad and varied field of academia where there are many different values, approaches, and conclusions to be drawn. Yet when one compares the preponderance of research studies over the past 35 years on students with disabilities educated in inclusive settings in comparison with students educated in specialized classrooms, it is clear that inclusive education leads to better outcomes (SWIFT, 2014, 2014–2020).

ACADEMIC ACHIEVEMENT

The primary barometer of school success over the years is academic achievement, and here there is great clarity about the benefits of inclusive education. Achievement outcomes for students served by special education in both reading and mathematics are significantly higher in inclusive settings (Agran et al., 2018). There may be multiple factors at play in considering how inclusion leads to improved academic achievement.

> Achievement outcomes for students served by special education in both reading and mathematics are significantly higher in inclusive settings.

First, the role of teacher expectations in student performance is well recognized. According to a report from the Brookings Institution, "teacher expectations do matter as they have a causal effect on student performance" (Papageorge & Gershenson, 2016). When students are separated from grade-level peers because of their learning difference, educators may subconsciously adjust their expectations for the level of work students will produce. The learning difference or disability becomes the defining feature of those students in segregated settings, and the expected learning is almost always reduced in depth, breadth, or complexity.

The social nature of learning means that the connection and conversation with peers in the learning process are embedded in the positive academic impact of inclusive education on students with disabilities (Darling-Hammond et al., 2020). The underlying assumptions of constructivism (Bruner) and social learning theory (Bandura) are evident in what is generally considered best practice in classroom instruction today. The Center for Educational Leadership (CEL) developed a model of the key elements of effective instruction, known as The 5 Dimensions of Teaching and Learning™ (Fink & Markholt, 2011). This model includes many components, yet the heart of the instructional framework is students interacting with one another and engaging in rigorous academic discourse, with entry points that make those tasks accessible and meaningful to each student. With this understanding of what effective instruction looks like for all students, it is not surprising that when students with disabilities gain meaningful access to this same sort of instructional approach, their outcomes would improve as well.

Additionally, John Hattie's (2008) research highlights that students' belief in themselves as learners is one of the most important factors in educational success. This self-efficacy has a significant impact on achievement (Yusuf, 2011). When students are taken out of general education classes and removed to an alternate setting, what self-talk occurs for those students? The message many students internalize is that they are not capable of learning the content or not capable of learning with peers who they may perceive as more capable. By creating inclusive learning communities, we have shifted the classroom culture. Expectations are higher for all students, and different ways of learning are normalized. Students served by special education can develop authentic self-efficacy and a deep sense of belonging.

SOCIAL, PROBLEM-SOLVING, AND SELF-ADVOCACY SKILLS

School is about so much more than developing academic skills. In his powerful TED Talk "Disabling Segregation," Dan Habib asks his audience to think about a memory from school. Almost no one selected a memory of learning an academic skill. Instead, people reflected on the people they were with, the friends they made, the adventures they had (TED[X], 2014). Why would we ever assume that this would be different for students with learning differences?

We know that learning is a social activity. Dr. Patricia Kuhl, from the University of Washington's Institute for Learning and the Brain, notes that from infancy, humans are always trying to figure out what those around them are doing, and this deeply influences learning (Merrill, 2018). Understanding this strong social component of learning has deeply influenced what is considered best practices in teaching, with high levels of student-to-student academic discourse being considered a strong indicator of rigorous learning. Students learn with and from their peers, and wise teachers use this peer learning in positive ways.

Some students may have challenges in peer interaction connected to their area of disability, as is often the case with students on the autism spectrum. Yet for students with ASD, it may be even more critical to be surrounded by peers with strong social skills. Woodman et al. (2016) found that inclusion in school decreased antisocial behaviors, improved independence skills, and led to more positive long-term social gains. We have certainly seen a dramatic increase in age-appropriate skills for students with ASD in our district when they spend a major part of their day in typical settings with a wide variety of peers.

> Students learn with and from their peers, and wise teachers use this peer learning in positive ways.

In many districts students who have complex communication needs are often segregated into schools or classrooms where curriculum is "functional" and peers are unable to model language. With no peers engaging in language, should we be surprised when students in these settings do not grow in their communication skills? When students with complex needs are included along with peers in typical classrooms, and appropriate access plans are in place, they make meaningful gains in social skills, self-advocacy, and independence (Haber et al., 2016).

An important consideration in the move toward inclusive classrooms is the academic impact for students who are not served by special education. Will the outcomes for other students decline, due to a decrease in academic rigor, pacing, or other concerns? This question goes to the very heart of concerns that some administrators, teachers, and parents may be wrestling with as they consider fully committing to inclusion. It is a worthy question and one for which we share our two responses, which are likely interrelated: (1) research outcomes and (2) teachers' deeper understanding of instruction.

Analysis of research shows that inclusion has a positive or neutral impact overall on the academic achievement of students without disabilities (Dessemontet & Bless, 2013; Kalambouka et al., 2007; Ruijs et al., 2010; Ruijs & Peetsma, 2009). These studies vary in the specific outcomes that they examined, from results of standardized tests in reading and mathematics to measures of student engagement during class time. The common thread throughout is that there is no negative impact on academic outcomes for students without disabilities at the macrolevel. At the same time, we are keenly aware that at the specific-classroom level, our obligation is to ensure that *all* students are learning. If we gather evidence that some students are not engaged, are not increasing their understanding, or are not challenged, it is absolutely our responsibility to address it—whether that student has an intellectual challenge or a different home language or whether that student qualifies for Talented and Gifted services.

Inclusive practices make teachers *better* teachers. In the model of education that many of us grew up in, the teacher presented information and the student learned it, or not. Now teachers are charged with ensuring that students are actually learning. As teachers consider the range of learners in their classrooms, they must think deeply about what the essential learning target is and where it fits in an overall learning trajectory. This consideration allows the teacher to create different pathways toward the same essential learning target, for students who need significant support to engage with the topic as well as for students who may already understand the topic at one level but need to extend or deepen their learning. As teachers work in this inclusive way, their own skill at designing and refining instruction deepens.

Inclusive practices make teachers *better* teachers.

One analogy that we like to think about is the technique of professional bowlers. Most amateur bowlers aim straight toward the center pin. If they are consistent, they will have a good chance to knock down seven or eight pins in the middle. But the corner pins (the outliers) are less likely to be impacted. Professional bowlers often do not aim toward the center of the pin cluster. Rather, expert bowlers often send the ball down the edge of the lane, curving their balls toward either side of the pin configuration. They are secure in the knowledge that by effectively considering the outlying pins, they increase their probability of hitting both the outliers and the pins in the middle.

Like the bowler aiming to knock down all of the pins, teachers need to design lessons and activities to reach *all* learners. Sometimes this means we don't start by bowling down the middle. Thinking about learning targets through the lens of many, diverse learners is challenging. That is one of the reasons why having teams to share expertise and codevelop strategies is so critical to the success of inclusive practices. Future chapters will delve more deeply into this.

INCLUSION AND THE WHOLE-CHILD MOVEMENT

Wise people in our district who came before us established several *vision themes* as values to guide our educational strategies and commitments. One of these vision themes is "Educate the Whole Child." Having this commitment to the whole child and ensuring that this value was realized for students caused us to think deeply about the role of special education.

Published in the Association for Supervision and Curriculum Development Info Brief, the tenets of whole-child education are as follows (McCloskey, 2007)):

- Each student enters school healthy and learns about and practices a healthy lifestyle.

- Each student learns in an environment that is physically and emotionally safe for students and adults.

- Each student is actively engaged in learning and is connected to the school and broader community.

- Each student has access to personalized learning and is supported by qualified, caring adults.

- Each student is challenged academically and prepared for success in college or further study and for employment and participation in a global environment.

These are the goals that we have for every student. We do not see any exceptions in these statements, qualifiers that imply that students with disabilities aren't a part of "each student." And if on the front end, we plan for learning environments where "each student is actively engaged in learning and is connected to the school and broader community," we interpret that as a charge to make our classrooms work for each student, every student. We do not see any justification in these statements for sorting some students into separate classrooms. Rather, the goal of personalization means that we need to make our classrooms work for every student—that we should expect learning differences and plan for them. A commitment to the whole child is a commitment to inclusion.

EQUITY AND SOCIAL JUSTICE

> Some argue that the social justice occurring in . . . inclusive education is not the responsibility of schools. But if not, then whose responsibility is it? A country's systems and institutions teach by example what the country, state, or community values: either inclusion or segregation or exclusion. (Villa & Thousand, 2016, p. 9)

Children spend the majority of their days in public school classrooms from age 5 to 18 years. These are formative years, when young people are making sense of the world, deciding their values, and developing habits of mind that will influence their ways of being for the rest of their lives. Our community understands this formative power of schools. This is one of the reasons why parents and other community members get so involved in debates about topics such as sexual health education. Advocates on both ends of what should be taught in schools will emerge at school board meetings around the country where sexual health curricula are being adopted. Though the content these advocates are espousing may be vastly different, both sides agree that this is the moment in life when children are forming their values and what the school presents or doesn't present may influence behavior.

Grouping children by perceived ability, even to the extreme where some students are forever removed from interaction with other students in a school setting, clearly sends a strong message to all children about who belongs and who doesn't. In their most formative time children experience an "othering" that has been wholly constructed by the adults around them. It is not reasonable to think that experiencing this would not affect children's belief about who belongs in our communities. Students who are segregated into self-contained classrooms experience a clear message that they don't belong with "typical" peers. Perhaps just as impactful on our society, students without disabilities who are in those typical classrooms experience a lack of learning diversity. They come to believe that this is "normal" and that students who are not there are "others." This leads to a lack of understanding that disability is in fact a normal and predictable part of the human experience (Snow, 2013). The unknown becomes scary, and so the segregation of human experience continues.

> In their most formative time, children experience an "othering" that has been wholly constructed by the adults around them.

A recent powerful example of this occurred at one of our schools. Several new students enrolled with very different learning profiles from what staff at that particular school had experienced for a long time. It led to a busy time for staff, trying to learn more about these students' strengths, needs, and communication styles. Some of the staff were frustrated because they had to significantly readjust their schedules to meet the needs of these students, along with the needs of all of the others. One staff member, in a moment of frustration when asked to work with a student who had limited verbal communication and significant personal care needs, told the learning specialist, "I'm not here to babysit"; she resigned her position the next day. This came at a very human low point for all involved and certainly did not reflect the deeper belief that all children can learn and it is our responsibility to find out how to engage each student. Yet we were encouraged when the learning specialist told us,

> See? This is exactly why we need inclusion. Folks of our generation were raised in a segregated world, and when situations are tough, many fall back on the beliefs of that time. When our students are grown, they will understand that disability is natural and everyone belongs.

Her commitment to equity and inclusion was strengthened, rather than lessened, through this challenging experience.

The Perspective of Families

When starting the work in our district, we began to meet with families of children served by special education to hear about their hopes and dreams for their children. Not surprisingly, "I want my child to be happy" and "I want my child to be successful" were some of the universal themes we heard. These themes would likely be the same for parents of any children. In addition, there were things that other parents may take for granted, such as "I hope someday my child is invited to a birthday party," "I want kids in the neighborhood to know my child and say hello," or "I just want my child to be at the same school as all the other kids on our block." In our model of inclusion, these hopes and dreams that used to seem very hard to attain are now just the norm.

Families know their children best and are able to understand their broad range of strengths and challenges. One of our families chooses to introduce their daughter this way: "Kara is funny, loves to run, is incredibly passionate about fairness, hates loud noises, is a fan of Taylor Swift's music, enjoys hands-on learning. Oh, and she is on the autism spectrum." This description captures a critical point: autism is an important part of Kara, but it is not all of her. Placing her in a class for students with ASD misses so much. What if we placed her in a class with only fans of Taylor Swift? Or if we placed her just with funny students? Why does autism have to be *the* defining feature? We talk more about how individuals with disabilities choose to identify themselves in the section about the power of language in Chapter 4.

In our old system, where some students were sent to segregated classrooms in a different school, families that already had to navigate the challenges of having a child with significant learning disabilities were then expected to balance having their children sent to multiple schools. Here is an experience recently shared with us that poignantly illustrates the impact of noninclusive school systems on families:

> A good friend in our neighborhood [in a different school district] has kids the same age as my own kids. Their son is one of the most physically gifted people I know. He could ride his bike all over the neighborhood long before most boys his age were out of training wheels. He can climb trees with feline agility. He is strong. He has a huge smile and a great laugh. He also has an intellectual disability.
>
> He was in my son's class in elementary school and developed friendships with other boys in the neighborhood. But when it was time for middle school, the district decided to send him to a self-contained classroom in a school across town. The special ed team tried to convince his parents that this would be the best place for him, that he would receive better academic support at his level, and that he would develop a community of friends in the self-contained class. His mom understood all of these things, and maybe even believed them. But when she told me he was slated to attend a different school than all of the neighborhood friends he had grown up with, her eyes welled up with tears.
>
> Those tears have stuck with me. She was heartbroken because her son would be torn away from the community he knew and from the friends he belonged to. He would have to ride a specialized (short) bus rather than ride his bike to school like the rest of the kids in the neighborhood. He would have different experiences and inevitably grow apart from his friends.
>
> Now that his sister is in middle school (at the neighborhood school), the parents are split between two schools. Two PTAs to attend. Two school carnivals. Two fund-raisers to donate to. Two bell schedules to learn. Two sets of administrators to meet.
>
> The siblings don't get to ride to school together. They don't get to see each other at lunch and talk about school drama together. They don't get to cheer for the same sports teams or wear the same school colors on spirit days.

These may seem like small things in the grand scheme of life. But in many ways, these shared experiences are the things that form the foundations of a family. They are the things that cannot be replicated in other ways. Of course, some families choose to send their children to different schools, but this family didn't have a choice. The district had a program—a self-contained classroom at only one middle school. The boy had no choice but to go. And it left his mom in tears.

The voices of families have been absolutely critical to our journey. We will share more stories about specific family experiences in future chapters. We have also learned with and from families outside our district through organizations such as Family and Community Together (FACT) and Northwest Down Syndrome Association's All Born (in). Both are groups of parents who have courageously fought for inclusion and access for all in our state, and they have been amazing leaders and partners in this work. When we listen to families, the need for inclusion, the need for belonging, the need to value every child is clear. As John Dewey (1899) declared in *School and Society*, "What the best and wisest parent wants for his child, that must we want for all the children of the community. Anything less is unlovely, and left unchecked, destroys our democracy" (p. 19).

All parents want their children to be valued, to belong, to be challenged, to succeed. Inclusion, done well, is the path toward fulfilling this for all children.

MOVING FROM *WHY* TO *WHY NOT?*

There are so many reasons for inclusive education: the basic human need for belonging, improved outcomes for students with and without learning differences, improving instructional practices for all students, consistently implementing ideas of social justice and civil rights. Thinking through these powerful reasons, the question shifts from why we should create inclusive schools to why we wouldn't do this.

Inclusive education does require change. It requires uncovering assumptions and beliefs; it requires different roles; it requires trust, innovation, collaboration, and capacity building. Becoming an inclusive school district requires intention. With intention, being an inclusive school district is a completely achievable goal.

Our purpose in writing this book is simply to lay out the ideas and structures that worked for us. You may do things differently. You may discover more effective ways to move forward. What is important is that we are all on the path to becoming more inclusive every day. Our children deserve this.

References

Agran, M., Spooner, F., Brown, F., Morningstar, M., Singer, G., & Wehman, P. (2018). Perspectives on the state of the art (and science) of selected life-span services. *Research and Practice for Persons With Severe Disabilities*, *43*(2), 67–81. https://doi.org/10.1177/1540796918769566

Darling-Hammond, L., Flook, L., Cook-Harvey, C., Barron, B., & Osher, D. (2020). Implications for educational practice of the science of learning and development. *Applied Developmental Science*, *24*(2), 97–140. https://www.tandfonline.com/doi/full/10.1080/10888691.2018.1537791. https://doi.org/10.1080/10888691.2018.1537791

Dessemontet, R. S., & Bless, G. (2013). The impact of including children with intellectual disability in general education classrooms on the academic achievement of their low-, average-, and high-achieving peers. *Journal of Intellectual & Developmental Disability*, *38*(1), 23–30. https://doi.org/10.3109/13668250.2012.757589

Dewey, J. (1899). *The school and society*. University of Chicago Press.

Fink, S., & Markholt, A. (2011). *Leading for instructional improvement*. Jossey-Bass.

Haber, M. G., Mazzotti, V. L., Mustian, A. L., Rowe, D. A., Bartholomew, A. L., Test, D. W., & Fowler, C. H. (2016). What works, when, for whom, and with whom: A meta-analytic review of predictors of postsecondary success for students with disabilities. *Review of Educational Research*, *86*(1), 123–162. https://doi.org/10.3102/0034654315583135

Hattie, J. (2008). *Visible learning*. Routledge.

Kalambouka, A., Farrell, P., Dyson, A., & Kaplan, I. (2007). The impact of placing pupils with special educational needs in mainstream schools on the achievement of their peers, *Educational Research*, *49*(4), 365–382. https://doi.org/10.1080/00131880701717222

McCloskey, M. (2007). The whole child. *ASCD INFO Brief, 51*. http://www.ascd.org/publications/newsletters/policy-priorities/fall07/num51/full/toc.aspx

Merrill, S. (2018, July 25). *Learning and the social brain*. Edutopia. https://www.edutopia.org/package/learning-and-social-brain

Michael Jr. (2017). *Know your why* [Video]. YouTube. https://youtu.be/1ytFB-8TrkTo

Papageorge, N., & Gershenson, S. (2016, September 16). *Do teacher expectations matter?* Brookings Institution, Brown Center Chalkboard.

https://www.brookings.edu/blog/brown-center-chalkboard/2016/09/16/do-teacher-expectations-matter/

Ruijs, N. M., & Peetsma, T. (2009). Effects of inclusion on students with and without special educational needs reviewed. *Educational Research Review*, *4*(2), 67–79. https://doi.org/10.1016/j.edurev.2009.02.002

Ruijs, N. M., Van der Veen, I., & Peetsma, T. T. D. (2010). Inclusive education and students without special educational needs. *Educational Research*, *52*(4), 351–390. https://doi.org/10.1080/00131881.2010.524749

SWIFT. (2014, December). *The bibliography of research support for K–8th grade inclusive education.* The School Wide Instructional Framework for Transformation. http://www.swiftschools.org/sites/default/files/Bibliography%20of%20Research%20Support%20for%20K-8%20Inclusive%20Education_1.pdf

SWIFT. (2014–2020). *Resource shelf: Research and journal articles.* http://www.swiftschools.org/shelf

Snow, K. (2013). *Disability is natural: Revolutionary common sense for raising successful children with disabilities* (3rd ed.). BraveHeart Press.

TED^X. (2009, September 28). *Start with why: How great leaders inspire action* (Simon Sinek, TEDxPugetSound) [Video]. YouTube. https://www.youtube.com/watch? v=u4ZoJKF_VuA

TED^X. (2014, April 22). *Disabling segregation: Dan Habib at TEDxAmoskeagMillyard* [Video]. YouTube. https://www.youtube.com/watch?v=izkN5vLbnw8

Villa, R., & Thousand, J. (2016). *Leading an inclusive school: Access and success for ALL students.* Association for Supervision and Curriculum Development.

Woodman, A. C., Smith, L. E., Greenberg, J. S., & Mailick, M. R. (2016). Contextual factors predict patterns of change in functioning over 10 years among adolescents and adults with autism spectrum disorders. *Journal of Autism and Developmental Disorders*, *46*, 176–189. https://doi.org/10.1007/s10803-015-2561-z

Yusuf, M. (2011). The impact of self-efficacy, achievement motivation, and self-regulated learning strategies on students' academic achievement. *Procedia: Social and Behavioral Sciences*, *15*, 2623–2626. https://www.sciencedirect.com/science/article/pii/S187704281100704X. https://doi.org/10.1016/j.sbspro.2011.04.158

CHAPTER 2

What We Mean by Inclusive Education

The focus of this book is inclusive education in relation to special education. However, when we say "inclusive education," we mean *all* learners. In our district inclusive education is not just about special education. It is also about students who are emerging bilinguals, it is about students with diverse racial or ethnic backgrounds, it is about students who are excelling academically, and it is about students from diverse socioeconomic backgrounds. Inclusive education means that everyone belongs, diversity is a strength, and demographics should never be predictors of outcomes. There may be some specific structures or areas of expertise that support growth among these different student groups, but we continue to find that our approaches are more alike than different.

We support high expectations for all, while allowing individualized pathways to get there. We believe that everyone wants to, and deserves to, belong. We believe that all children should see their perspective and story reflected in their educational materials and experience and all children should be learning about perspectives and experiences that are different from their own. We believe that implicit biases and deeply held beliefs are difficult to uncover yet we must remain committed to this work. We believe that identity matters and that voluntary affinity groups can help build understanding. We believe that our language is powerful, and we continue to adapt our terminology as social constructs and understanding of people's experiences become clearer. We believe that all children can learn and that we can be the district where each child, every child, succeeds.

Michael Giangreco and Mary Beth Doyle (2007) explained the importance of inclusive classrooms for all students:

> What matters most is not only standards from the district or state curriculum framework, but also values such as tolerance, kindness, and fairness.

An inclusive classroom that embodies these dispositions forms a strong foundation for teaching students the lessons of history and the tools of modern scientists, historians, writers, healers, and artists. With these tools, all students, including those with a label of "disability," can be successful learners and citizens in their communities. (p. 228)

In terms of special education it is important to clarify what we mean by inclusion. Words are powerful and can create mental pictures and assumptions based on the schema and experience that each person brings to an interaction. *Inclusion* is one of those words that can bring with it stories and references that may vary significantly. For some, inclusion is the rallying cry of civil rights. For others, inclusion harkens back to a classroom experience where a student with significant learning differences was physically present in a general education classroom with no entry points for meaningful participation in the learning.

For us, inclusive education is about belonging, equity, and instructional practices. Every child belongs in their neighborhood school and in their grade-level classroom with their peers. That is always our starting point. We no longer have any self-contained classrooms; we no longer bus students to another school in our district to access the services they need. Because we believe students belong in their neighborhood school, we are committed to developing the resources and support for each student at their school. They belong at their school, so we need to bring the support to them, in their general education classroom.

FIGURE 2.1   Exclusion-Segregation-Integration-Inclusion Diagram

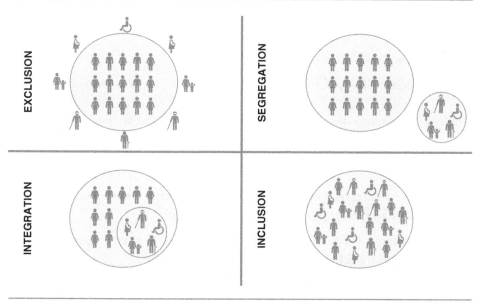

IMAGE SOURCE: iStock.com/Sudowoodo

Exclusion. Figure 2.1 is a picture of the history of children with learning differences. In the United States, prior to Public Law 94-142 of 1975, many students were simply excluded from public school altogether. This historic law, reauthorized in 2004 as the Individuals with Disabilities Education Act (IDEA), provides the basic rights for students with disabilities to receive a free, appropriate public education. The concept of least restrictive environment (LRE) is made clear in the IDEA, and the law explicitly states that removal from the general education classroom cannot be solely based on the need for curriculum modification.

Segregation. More commonly, segregation for children with learning differences has occurred at the classroom rather than the school level. There are separate classes, often called "self-contained" classrooms, in most school districts throughout the country even today. There are many acronyms and euphemisms for these classes, such as Social Learning Center, Behavior Support Class, Life Skills Center, Structured Learning Program, Medically Fragile Class, and Applied Academics Program, to name a few. Generally, these classrooms are centralized, to be most efficient with district resources. For example, there may be students with cognitive learning differences living throughout a school district, and when a determination is made that a student needs significantly modified curriculum, and things like learning to do laundry independently are more important for that student than learning grade-level content, that student will then be bused to another school in the district where the Life Skills Center is located.

There is certainly a logic to this model. It is efficient. It is systematic. Most important, it is familiar. Most of us attended school and began our careers as educators in this kind of model. There are a few arguments in favor of segregated, self-contained classrooms:

- We can capitalize on the talents of teachers who have expertise working with students with significant cognitive differences.

- We can teach relevant life skills.

- Students will spend time with peers who share similar characteristics.

But look deeper into these assumptions, and some provocative questions emerge:

- Don't all young people need to learn life skills, not just students with disabilities?

- If we espouse axioms like "All children can learn," are we adding an asterisk and really saying, ". . . except those children"?

- How do we know what a student is learning if they have significant challenges or differences in how they communicate?

- When we assume that children who share a common characteristic (e.g., a disability) are the children who will be friends, what does that say to our axiom about valuing diversity?

- These same beliefs—that "those children (or people) should be together"—have led to segregation and ghettoization throughout U.S. and world history. How many of us grew up in schools where all we knew about the children in those segregated classes was that they were different, "other," and not worthy of being in our classrooms?

Integration. Early attempts at inclusion were actually much like the integration visual in Figure 2.1. Students with learning differences may have been present in the classroom, but that was all. The curriculum, the learning tasks, the adults with whom they interacted, these were all different from what was occurring for the other students in the class. Often, there was a physical separation in the classroom, where the student with learning differences was placed at a table in the back of the room with a paraeducator or instructional assistant. The goal was to have learning activities that did not "interfere" with the learning of other students or get in the way of the general education teacher. For many students this model can have all of the negative aspects of a segregated classroom but without the benefits. This can even be considered a more restrictive model as there is often very little interaction with typical peers and no interaction with other children with disabilities. The general education teacher may not feel empowered to engage with or teach this student, and therefore, there may be no real learning and embracing of diversity.

Inclusion. Imagine a classroom where students are all learning together, learning targets are clear and rigorous, and all children are engaged in the learning. Engagement can look different for different students. But it is a learning community where differences are accepted and diversity is valued, several adults are moving around to meet the needs of the learners in the classroom, access to content may come in different ways, and wherever you look you see evidence of the belief that all children can learn.

Equity. Equity means that every student gets what they need to access rigorous levels of learning but what each student needs is not the same. Therefore, our commitment to equity means recognizing that though every student belongs in their class, the ways they access their learning or represent their thinking may be different. If a student needs to be pretaught key vocabulary words in a less distracting setting so that the student may access an important social studies lesson with peers, then that is exactly what needs to happen. Our commitment to equity allows us to be okay with some students getting more teacher attention, different sorts of scaffolds to access learning, or additional opportunities to practice.

Inclusive education means that all teachers are changing the way they teach. Years ago, the prevailing attitude was that the teacher presents the material and the student has the opportunity to learn it. Some students may seize that opportunity, while others may choose not to work hard to learn. The dramatic shift that has occurred in the past 20 years, is that we are now committed to student learning (outcomes) rather than simply teaching (inputs).

> We now understand that there is, and always will be, a range of ways in which all students learn in every classroom.

Educational leaders Richard and Rebecca DuFour note that the focus in public education as a whole has shifted to being clear about what we want all students to know and be able to do, assessing if they have learned it, and then having clear ways of responding if they haven't (DuFour et al., 2010). The responsibility has shifted from teaching (or presenting the material) to student learning. This radical shift is in perfect alignment with inclusive education. In the old model, if a student needed a different style or pedagogy, no one would have thought to ask the general education teacher to change their methods. Instead, the student was pulled out to receive this "special" education in another setting. We now understand that there is, and always will be, a range of ways in which all students learn in every classroom. If classroom teachers plan lessons through a lens of Universal Design for Learning (UDL), allowing multiple ways for students to access and represent their learning, we can inclusively support the learning of all students in the classroom. The role of the special education teacher then shifts to the role of collaborator, coplanner, and "access expert," working with the general education teacher to create lessons that engage all learners to move toward rigorous, meaningful learning.

A Continuum of Inclusive Practices

Early in our journey toward more inclusive learning communities, we learned that the binary construct of segregation versus inclusion is not authentic or useful. Rather, there is a rich spectrum. There are steps that we can take to be more inclusive wherever we are, while keeping our eye on the target of what inclusive practices in their most developed form will look like. The title of Richard Milner's (2010) insightful book about equity in education provides a helpful word of encouragement here: *Start Where You Are, But Don't Stay There.*

Figure 2.2 shows a continuum that describes a range of student experiences in schools. In our district we can look at this continuum and see where we have been. We can reflect on and celebrate the steps we have taken and their impact on students and the school community. And we can still see goals ahead in the distance.

We have formatted this continuum with "Segregation" at the bottom and "Inclusion" at the top. However, we know that the continuum of inclusion—from separate classrooms and schools to meaningful leadership and true friendships among all students—is not a direct, linear path. Researchers Danforth and Naraian (2015) affirm this idea, framing inclusive education as a process where we can always find ways to be more inclusive. Each school and district will need to chart their own direction as they work within their unique historical and cultural context. There will certainly be overlays of racial and linguistic equity that will influence how you

FIGURE 2.2   Inclusion Continuum

```
Inclusion         True Friendships
                  Meaningful Leadership
                  Meaningful Contributions to Classroom Community
                  Entry Points for Collaborative Meaning-Making
                  Access to Rigorous, Standards-Based Curriculum & Instruction
                  Constructed Opportunities for Student to Lead Activities in Class
                  Peer-Mediated Instruction
                  Working in the Classroom on Separate Content with 1-to-1 Adult Support
                  On the Roster—Desk in the Gen Ed Classroom
                  Joining a Gen Ed Class for Music & PE
                  Buddy Classes
                  Separate Classes within Neighborhood Schools
                  Centralized Separate Classes within Cluster/Magnet Schools
Segregation       Separate Schools
```

NOTE: Gen Ed, General Education; PE, Physical Education.

proceed toward greater inclusion. The nature and quality of your relationship with parent groups and teacher unions will inform specific leadership moves and modes of communication. Nonetheless, there are certain markers or signposts that can help guide the way toward true equity and inclusion for all.

Here are brief definitions of the terms in the continuum of inclusion. These are intended to help school leaders reflect on their own successes and identify opportunities for future leadership.

Separate schools: This is the oldest model of special education, where students with learning differences were not allowed to attend the same schools as students who were not labeled with a disability. Most districts have eliminated separate schools, but they do still exist. In particular, some districts house a cluster of segregated classrooms in a former school building that no longer serves a general education population. The only students in the school are those served by specialized programs.

Centralized separate classes within cluster/magnet schools: Many districts use a structure of centralized classes as a way to pool resources and expertise by bringing the students to the resources rather than bringing the resources to the students. This is an efficient model, but it values efficiency over student outcomes, including belonging and peer interactions and even academic progress. This is the most common model in Oregon (and many other states) for serving students with significant learning differences. There are students with and without disabilities in the same school, but their educational experience is still predominantly segregated.

Separate classes within neighborhood schools: In this model, students are allowed to attend their neighborhood school, but students with more complex needs are housed in a self-contained classroom, where they have limited opportunity to interact with peers or engage in grade-level curriculum. These are often multi-age classrooms based on ability (or disability).

Buddy classes: A self-contained class will often partner with a general education class for a specific activity or project. The gen ed buddies drop in for brief encounters. These may be joyful interactions for both the students in the self-contained class and their gen ed buddies. But they are not sustained and are not likely to lead to a deep sense of belonging or true friendship. In addition, the academic rigor is vastly different between the two class settings.

Joining a general education class for music and physical education (PE): Students in a self-contained classroom sometimes "get out" for specials or electives like music and PE. Ideally, they should join their grade-level classmates, but due to the multi-age nature of many self-contained classes, students are often paired with a general education class that does not match their age/grade level. Sometimes this results in fourth or fifth graders from the self-contained class grouped for PE with kindergarten or first-grade classes because of their similar functional skills. Or sometimes K–1 students from a self-contained class get grouped with older elementary students who can be role models. Either way, students are often not with their same-age peers.

On the roster and with a desk in the general education classroom: Students with significant disabilities may receive a substantial amount of their daily instruction in a separate setting. However, they are listed on the general education teacher's roster and have a dedicated space in the classroom. Wherever possible, that space should be a desk just like any other student's. If the student needs a more specialized work space, it should be provided in the most typical way possible. This is a significant first step that districts can take to break the model of segregated self-contained classes.

Working in the classroom on separate content with one-on-one adult support: The student is physically in the classroom but not interacting with peers or engaging in the same content or learning activities. All interactions (with peers and with the classroom teacher) are mediated through an adult assistant. An outside observer stepping into the classroom would immediately recognize that this student is not fully part of the classroom community. This is described above as "Integration."

Peer-mediated instruction: In addition to being present in the classroom, the student has specific, intentional connections to peers, both socially and academically. Peers can also help the student follow routines and manage behavioral expectations. Peers are often trained with specific strategies and language to support the student.

Constructed opportunities for a student to lead activities in class: The teacher designs activities to give the student a prominent place in the classroom community. For example, a student who communicates with an augmentative communication device could be the person who asks their classmates about the weather during the morning circle each day.

Access to rigorous, standards-based curriculum and instruction: The purpose of special education is to provide services that help students learn the skills to access grade-level curriculum. Some students with significant functional and learning challenges may need significantly modified curriculum. However, whenever possible, the target should be connected to the work their peers are doing in class. Over time, this should result in measurable academic outcomes, including improved graduation rates.

Entry points for collaborative meaning-making (including structures for student talk): When teachers use specific strategies and structures to enable students to contribute to the conversation in small groups or the whole classroom, it increases students' status and emphasizes that they are colearners with their peers. In Chapters 5–7 we will talk more about the power of student talk for collaborative meaning-making and the impact this can have for students with significant learning needs.

Meaningful contributions to the classroom community (social-emotional and academic): Belonging is one of the most powerful factors in any individual's sense of well-being. Many of the earlier stages in this continuum address the need to belong. In addition, all people need to feel that they are making a *meaningful contribution* to their community. Students are much more engaged learners if they know that their participation in the class is helping their classmates make sense of the content and learn more deeply. If they are always receiving support from adults and peers, the classroom community is missing the opportunity to experience unexpected richness.

Meaningful leadership: In most classrooms, most of the substantive decisions are made by adults. In high-functioning classrooms teachers incorporate student voice in meaningful ways. In truly inclusive classrooms all students have authentic opportunities to take the initiative and assume leadership roles.

True friendships: The mark of a true friendship is that both participants contribute to and benefit from the relationship. They both need each other, and together they are better than they are as two separate individuals. While we cannot measure friendship with standardized assessments, some signs that we are planting the seeds of true friendships are that students spontaneously play together on the playground, laugh together at inside jokes, stand up for each other in challenging situations, and invite each other to birthday parties and sleepovers.

This continuum is not linear, and we may never feel that we have fully arrived. But these signposts may be helpful for your school and district leaders as you dream together and set targets and aspirations for your school community. You may have additional or different steps along your inclusion continuum. What is most important is to keep moving, keep questioning, and keep improving. Our children are counting on us.

A Summary of Changes Over the Past Eight Years

The 2011–2012 school year is a useful demarcation for the start of the inclusion journey in our district. That is the year we identified inclusion as our goal and began actively disrupting our status quo. In truth, there were many important beliefs and structures in place prior to that, setting the stage for the work of the past eight years.

Previous superintendents of our district greatly influenced the culture in ways that laid the groundwork for inclusion. *The Relentless Pursuit of Excellence* chronicles the work of Dea Cox, our district's superintendent from 1978 to 1994 (Sagor & Rickey, 2012). Cox led a transformation in the district through commitments to hiring the very best teachers and continuous responsive professional development. These commitments were critical to our district moving forward with inclusive practices. Having teachers with high levels of professionalism who value continuing to learn is foundational to implementing this sort of deep and comprehensive reform.

Superintendent Roger Woehl (1994–2011) followed with, among other things, a commitment to inquiry and well-rounded education. Dr. Bill Rhoades (2011–2016) led the district next, with an emphasis on equity and closing achievement and opportunity gaps. When Dr. Kathy Ludwig became superintendent in 2016, she built on these previous ideas and currently inspires our district with a commitment to "Leading for All" with a steadfast commitment to inclusive practices.

What Inclusion Looks Like

Throughout this book, we will share stories of teachers and students in our schools. The stories will illustrate specific elements of our frameworks or specific leadership moves that we have made over the years. They will also help create a composite picture of what inclusion looks like. We could not fit all of the stories in the next few pages. So we will end this chapter with two examples of what inclusion looks like in our district.

We don't pretend to have it all figured out. We know that on any given day, there are students who are struggling in our schools. We know that we have a lot more to learn about how to support each student's needs in an inclusive setting. We know that it is really hard work. But we also know that it is the right work. Here are two reasons why.

The first example of what inclusion looks like is one of the most basic measurable outcomes: graduation rates. When we began our journey toward inclusive practices, the graduation rate for students served by special education in our district was 68%. Our overall graduation rate for all students was 90%. Over the past six years, as our classrooms have become more inclusive, the graduation rate for students served by special education increased to 83.8%. This is higher than the overall graduation rate (for all students) for most districts in the state of Oregon. (Oregon's average graduation rate is 80%.)

This is only one measure, but it is an indication that inclusive practices have been beneficial for students served by special education. In addition, during the same six-year span, the district's overall graduation rate has improved to 94.7%.

FIGURE 2.3   Graduation Rates and Inclusive Practices

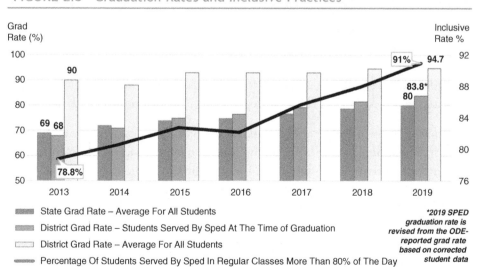

NOTE: Grad, Graduation; SPED, Special Education.

SOURCE: Used with Permission from West Linn-Wilsonville School District.

As we have become more inclusive, students who are not served by special education are also experiencing benefits. During this span, both graduation rates have increased. And more important, the gap between the graduation rates has been cut in half from 22 to 11 percentage points.

We are proud of the growth in graduation rates and the progress we have made toward closing the achievement gap. These numbers don't just represent trends and scores. They are reflective of the hard work and commitment of teachers, paraeducators, specialists, administrators, and families. They represent the lives of individual students who will have a greater range of opportunities in the future because of their inclusive school experience.

We are even more proud of the transformation of our school communities and the impact of those transformations on individual students with and without disabilities. This is illustrated by a powerful story that one of our parents shared about her daughter's class. We were presenting at an educational conference, telling the story of our district's journey toward inclusive practices. A parent from another district asked about the need to protect students with significant disabilities. "I like what you are saying about inclusion," she said. "But I'm afraid that if my daughter leaves her self-contained classroom, she will be bullied by all of the other kids. How do you prevent that in an inclusive school?"

Before we could begin to respond, another parent stood up from the audience. We recognized her as the mother of a fourth grader in our district who experiences significant developmental disabilities. The mother, Shannon, answered the other parent by telling the story of her daughter, Stella.

Stella began her school career in a self-contained Life Learning classroom in our district. Over the course of her first few years, we were working on breaking down the Life Learning program and moving toward more inclusive opportunities. By third grade, we no longer had a segregated Life Learning program. Stella was on the roster of her classroom teacher and spent most of her day in the general education setting. She still received significant support—for academics, communication, and behavior. Because she was part of her class, she began to develop relationships with her peers.

Shannon told the audience at our workshop session that day about how she used to worry about Stella being bullied—and how she might react aggressively toward students who were making fun of her. But over time, Shannon realized that Stella was becoming part of her classroom community. One day, a new student joined the class, moving from another district. This new boy hadn't been in an inclusive classroom before. He had never had classmates who learned and communicated in unfamiliar ways. He didn't know Stella. When she began vocalizing in unexpected ways, he started to laugh at her. He looked to his new classmates for encouragement, and he made rude jokes about Stella.

At that point the coolest boy in the class stepped forward and confronted the new boy. "Hey, stop that," he said. "You don't treat Stella like that. She's our friend."

References

Danforth, S., & Naraian, S. (2015). This new field of inclusive education: Beginning a dialogue on conceptual foundations. *Intellectual and Developmental Disabilities, 53*(1), 70–85. https://doi.org/10.1352/1934-9556-53.1.70

DuFour, R., DuFour, R., Eaker, R., & Many, T. (2010). *Learning by doing: A handbook for professional learning communities at work.* Solution Tree Press.

Giangreco, M., & Doyle, M. (2007). *Quick guides for inclusion: Ideas for educating students with disabilities* (2nd ed.). Brookes.

Milner, R. (2010). *Start where you are but don't stay there: Understanding diversity, opportunity gaps and teaching in today's classroom.* Harvard Education Press.

Sagor, R., & Rickey, D. (2012). *The relentless pursuit of excellence: Lessons from a transformational leader.* Corwin. https://doi.org/10.4135/9781483350547

CHAPTER 3

The Foundations of Inclusive Education

Putting Our Goals on Paper

There is no denying that creating real change in schools is an extremely challenging task. In many ways it may be harder in schools than in other large bureaucracies or organizations. We assert this because people's schema of what schools should be like is not primarily formed in their adult career years, as it would be for, say, a large health care system. Rather, every educator's experience in schools began when they were five years old, as a student. These formative experiences set the stage for what adults will expect schools to be, whether consciously or not. Very few of us experienced positive inclusive schools as children, so it makes it difficult to envision a truly inclusive learning community.

An important first step for us was to listen to teachers, parents, and students about their experiences, their hopes, and their dreams. We had many one-to-one conversations with staff. We listened to the concerns of parents in group meetings as well as in IEPs. We collectively looked at the research. Out of these listening sessions and conversations, we crafted three areas of focus and specific long-term targets. Then, we wrote them down.

Putting the long-term targets on paper was a critical step. Seeing them written down pushed us to move from the dreaming stage to the doing stage. At the same time, we did not at that time have a clear path or timeline; we just knew these were the goals we were working to achieve. Putting our goals on paper invited action and accountability. Dr. Rob Horner, a University of Oregon researcher who focuses on systemic education reform in the areas of behavior and academics, frequently reminds us how important it is to focus our most important ideas in groups of three to five (Algozzine et al., 2010). We knew that we needed three rich and compelling areas of focus that could be broad enough to move us forward across grade levels, schools, and years yet specific enough that all members of our district could relate to them. The three areas that we chose are the following:

- Creating Inclusive Cultures
- Improving Instructional Practices
- Increasing Student Voice

These three focus areas remained consistent throughout our years of change, though we have revised the areas of subfocus and specific targets under each focus area to be responsive to our evolving context. Each of these focus areas has a strong research base behind it. And there are places in these focus areas where everyone in our system can find motivation and connection to their work. *Creating inclusive cultures* includes the ways students and adults interact with one another in an inclusive way. This includes structures and strategies such as co-teaching and Unified Sports, with the goal of cultivating a true appreciation of diversity. *Improving instructional practices* is a critical area of focus because it recognizes the work that we have to do as educators to get better at understanding and engaging every learner. We are constantly engaged in an inquiry cycle that includes planning, engagement strategies, and assessment, while recognizing that there will always be great diversity in the background knowledge, communication skills, and interests of our students. *Increasing student voice* means ensuring that every student has an effective way to communicate, students drive their own IEPs, and students are authentically included in the big-picture work of school reform.

In Chapters 4 through 7 we will outline specific strategies and structures that have helped move us forward in each of these three focus areas.

GUIDING PRINCIPLES FOR OUR WORK

PRINCIPLE #1: BUILDING CAPACITY—WE CAN ALL DEVELOP EXPERTISE

Embedded in the traditional model of special education are fundamental beliefs about expertise. The general education teacher is trained to work with "typical" students. Students who learn in ways that are determined to be "other than typical" must need instruction from a teacher who has specialized training and expertise. Within special education the specialization and expertise model moves into various subsets of learning differences and areas of pedagogy. Often, there are teachers who have expertise in working with students with ASD and different teachers who specialize in working with students with behavioral challenges, students who struggle with reading, or students who use augmentative communication and assistive technology. There is a logic to this model as there is great complexity in each of these educational areas. And expertise in these areas is absolutely necessary to help students become successful learners. However, there are also unintended consequences that result from this model.

The first challenge is that children just don't fit neatly into the categories that we create. In a district where one of us worked previously, there were two types of classrooms where students with significant needs were sent: the Structured Learning Program—Academic (SLPA) and the Structured Learning Program—Behavioral (SLPB). Teachers and paraeducators with expertise in these areas were assigned to these classrooms, and professional development had a clear focus for staff. Yet children are complex and whole. Their strengths and challenges are multifaceted and often do not align with our labels. Imagine the difficulty in deciding in which class to place a student who displays both significant academic and significant behavioral challenges. We might hear SLPA staff say, "This student with behavioral challenges really shouldn't be in the SLPA," or SLPB staff might say, "I don't really know much about adapting content for a student with developmental delays."

Over time, teachers met more students who did not fit neatly into the program boxes we had created (SLPA and SLPB). The district decided that the "solution" was to create an SLPBA, an additional segregated classroom at another school for a smaller subset of students. Not too long after, the district determined that students experiencing ASD didn't fit the traditional profile of SLPA or SLPB (or the hybrid SLPBA). So they created another centralized program focused on ASD strategies at another school. The larger the district, the more common is this phenomenon. This can become a never-ending process of sorting and grouping children. And it may never achieve the intended outcome of fully matching students with professional expertise. Meanwhile, this process of sorting and separating impacts the children in so many negative ways by limiting the range of peers and by establishing a child's learning challenges as the biggest factor in their schooling environment.

An additional challenge of the expert model is how to manage consultation. When there is one person who is the autism expert, another person who is the behavior specialist, and a third person who is the instructional expert for students with cognitive delays, imagine the experience of the teacher of a student who requires support in all of these areas. Often these experts are spread thinly across many schools, so they may only be able to drop in and provide suggestions every other week. Typically, these are highly skilled professionals with a strong heart for children. Yet in our experience when an expert consultant provides suggestions without a strong understanding of the context of that individual student and that particular classroom, their guidance may not be as helpful as intended. Even worse, the teacher may receive completely different suggestions from each specialist for the same student. This can lead to a sense of frustration for the teacher and an experience that may be disjointed for the student.

In our previous model (when we had different specialists spread across many schools), we often had dilemmas like this. A teacher came to us in tears, unsure of how to proceed with a student demonstrating unexpected and sometimes unsafe behaviors in her classroom. "I just don't know what to do," she shared. "The behavior specialist tells me to have more collaborative, problem-solving conversations, but the autism specialist says to emphasize visuals and limit verbal interactions." Both of these may have been valid strategies. In a perfect world, the teacher would have called a multidisciplinary team meeting where all of the specialists could sit down together and generate one comprehensive plan for the student. In real life though, where there is often just one behavior specialist and one autism specialist serving many schools, they are often not available to be present at every meeting.

As a result, we have worked to create a model where one specialist, the IC, can bring an understanding of a range of best-practice strategies, like visual supports and collaborative problem-solving, while at the same time knowing the school and classroom teacher. These ICs are limited to serving two to three schools so they can get to know administrators, special education teams, classroom teachers, students, and parents. They develop relationships and become strong partners in the work, and we believe relationships are in many ways just as important as expertise. We will talk more about the role of the IC in later chapters.

Often, when there are many different experts working with the student, we can forget to think holistically about the student's experience. A few years back we attended an IEP meeting for a student who was receiving special education services under the category of Hearing Impairment. In this meeting the teacher raised a concern about the student's lack of progress in reading. Team members wondered if perhaps there were deeper learning challenges to be explored—maybe even an intellectual disability. What we found, however, was that this student was receiving reading instruction from four different experts, using four different approaches to reading.

His classroom teacher was working with him on the basal reading instruction, just like with the other students in the class. But he was only present for about a third of the time that the other students received this instruction because he was pulled out for other services. The special education resource teacher was using a direct-instruction reading curriculum for 30 minutes each day. The teacher for hearing impairment used a very visual, whole-word approach to reading when she came in to work with the student twice per week. Finally, because the student qualified for Title 1 services, a paraeducator pulled this student twice a week using a totally different approach to reading. Each expert brought their best thinking. But the expertise was siloed, and the experience for the student was completely fractured and ineffective.

We need expertise, and we will always have some areas of less common disability where we need to bring in specialists, such as visual impairments, orientation and mobility challenges, significant orthopedic impairments, and so on. But if it is our stance that all students can learn, we hold the same stance that all adults can develop expertise to support

We believe relationships are just as important as expertise.

diverse learning in the classroom. Children don't fit into the boxes of disability categories that we have created, and experts who are spread across many buildings for consultation often can't provide contextual and coherent advice. When each expert thinks through their own lens, the experience of students may be disjointed. We need expertise, and we can all develop expertise.

By developing a range of expertise among specialists who work in a smaller number of schools, we lay emphasis on relationships with teachers, students, families, and principals. By knowing the people and the context of each school really well, we can create more effective systems of support for students.

PRINCIPLE #2: MINDSET

During the first year of our journey of inclusion, our superintendent placed a strong emphasis on the concept of *growth mindset*, as defined by the research of Carol Dweck (2008). Embodying a growth mindset became absolutely foundational to us as an organization, to each of us as individuals in this work, and to the beliefs and expectations of our students. Dweck's theory of growth and fixed mindsets, rooted in the neuroscience of brain plasticity, describes the underlying beliefs people have about learning and intelligence. When people believe they can get smarter, they understand that effort makes them stronger. Therefore, they put in extra time and effort, and that leads to higher achievement.

As an organization, we had to adopt a growth mindset. We needed to believe that *our* abilities were not fixed, that we could learn, grow, and achieve things we had not tried before. We had seen examples of individual schools that were experiencing great results with inclusive practices. But we did not know of districts our size that had implemented inclusion successfully. We did not have a formula to make this happen. We knew that we needed to innovate, to learn, to adjust. We were very sure that we would make mistakes along the way.

Each educator's growth mindset was critical to our work. Teachers moved into new, and sometimes uncomfortable, roles. For example, one of our learning specialists who was extremely skilled in the resource model of special education (focusing on mild reading and mathematical disabilities) was now working with all students in the fourth and fifth grades, including students with complex cognitive and behavioral needs. The learning specialist began experimenting with co-teaching in a fifth-grade class. Neither the learning specialist nor the classroom teacher had co-taught before. Their growth mindset allowed them to be open to trying new instructional practices, to learning from their experiences, and to making significant adjustments to their co-teaching model. By the end of

We needed to believe that *our* abilities were not fixed, that we could learn, grow, and achieve things we had not tried before.

the first year, they had found such benefit from co-teaching for one hour a day that they proposed a model to double their co-teaching time the following year.

One of our middle schools was doing terrific work in supporting students inclusively for several years. Yet during that time, it happened that the range of learners they were supporting did not include students with the most complex medical and developmental needs. A few years later, that changed as five of the incoming sixth-grade students had more complex academic, behavioral, and communication needs than the staff had experienced before. We thought we had done a thorough transition process, but when the school year started, we learned right away that the teachers and paraeducators were not as prepared as we thought to meet the needs of those particular students. The team recognized that they had a lot to learn in a short period of time and that they needed to build expertise.

The team reassigned the duties of the paraeducators to support the needs of other students on IEPs for the first month of school. Each of the learning specialists spent the bulk of their time with these five students, building relationships and getting to know their strengths and needs. Speech language pathologists (SLPs), instructional coordinators (ICs), occupational therapists, and physical therapists brought in materials and provided job-embedded professional learning opportunities. At the end of that month, the students were experiencing more success, and the school team had developed greater expertise in supporting students with complex learning differences. The learning specialists were then able to plan more effective lessons and support. Eventually, they were able to readjust schedules, with the general education teachers and paraeducators taking up a larger role in working with these students. The following year, a new group of sixth graders arrived with complex needs. And the school team was able to jump right in with strategies and structures to meet their needs.

GROWTH MINDSET IN STUDENTS

Cultivating a growth mindset in our students was also key to creating more inclusive schools. All of our classroom teachers were explicitly teaching the idea of growth mindset. Students were invited to reflect on their own beliefs about what was possible for their own growth in learning. Conditions were created for students to take on big challenges. For example, a student who had not previously excelled in the arts was encouraged to take a sculpture class. A student who was learning English as a second language had the opportunity to excel in the science fair. A student with Down's syndrome engaged in a project comparing the Odyssey to his own personal journey. This pervasive culture of growth mindset encourages students to challenge perceived labels and limitations.

Hiring in our district is a multistep process, culminating in a final interview with the superintendent for every new teacher we hire. One of the superintendent's favorite questions to ask is "Share something that you did that made a student believe in themselves more as a learner and how that impacted the student's success."

By asking that question, we communicate the value of teacher efficacy (*something that you did*) as well as student efficacy (*that made a student believe in themself more*), with a clear emphasis on outcomes (*that impacted the student's success*). By asking that question, we are communicating that growth mindset is not just what some may call the power of positive thinking, but it is grounded in reflection on real action and struggles and how we can intentionally learn from those situations to develop more confidence and more competence for the future.

PRINCIPLE #3: COMMUNICATION, COMMUNICATION, COMMUNICATION

System change requires communication that is coherent, compassionate, and constant. A coherent approach to communication is not easy to achieve yet is one of the most important factors in successful change. Compassion requires being authentic, bringing our true selves to the work, and being willing to listen deeply to the experiences of others, particularly when the work gets challenging. Finally, remember the old adage that you cannot overcommunicate? Well, we found that to be totally true.

Communicating coherently across an organization takes time and intentionality. Having a common framework helps ground our thinking in common language. We explore our district's common frameworks ("The 7 Components of Inclusive and Equitable Learning Communities" and the Student Services Focus Areas) in later chapters. Common frameworks also provide visual artifacts to help us express and explore shared values (Fullan & Quinn, 2016).

Coherence is not a top-down message that is simply adopted by members of the organization. That sort of directive communication will not result in true coherence. Rather, as each member of the organization works with the ideas of the framework, through a lens of common values, each member constructs meaning. For example, when we first brought forward the idea of *increasing student voice* as a key focus area, we worked to construct shared meaning about the role of the student in their IEP process. One of our colleagues in district leadership helped us connect the student's role in the IEP to Ron Berger's concept of students being captains of their own learning (Berger et al., 2014). Because we each made sense of it in our own way, we were able to own that part of the message and see how these two ideas were interconnected. As we bring new ideas to people, we have to allow the time and structures for people to make sense of those ideas, so that each person can build their own sense of connection and commitment. This is the path to coherence, where the thinking and the messaging are unified throughout the organization.

As we bring new ideas to people, we have to allow the time and structures for people to make sense of those ideas.

District leaders frequently remind us of the need for *planned redundancy* in communication.

As we bring forward an idea to a group of educators, each person has a different schema or framework for receiving, analyzing, and synthesizing that information. If the message is important, we need to communicate it in multiple ways, multiple times. Individual experiences continue to influence the context in which people receive and process information. For example, we sometimes lead teacher workshops about planning for students who use augmentative and alternative communication (AAC) devices to engage academically and socially in their classroom. A teacher who has never had a student who communicates with a device may not deeply attend to this content. The following year, that teacher may be working closely with a student who uses AAC. The next time this topic comes up in a teacher workshop, it is now deeply relevant to that teacher, and the teacher brings more comprehensive schema to the conversation.

Another reason to commit to planned redundancy in our communication is that education has traditionally moved way too quickly to that next great idea or new shiny thing. Many teachers prefer to adopt a "wait it out" mentality rather than deeply investing in new learning. This is particularly true in districts that experimented with mainstreaming or other attempts at inclusion in the 1990s. Veteran teachers may have experienced "initiative fatigue." This will likely be part of the schema that they bring to the sense-making process related to inclusion. Planned redundancy gives people the opportunity to reframe their previous expectations and build a common understanding. Everyone in the system needs to hear again and again that this is who we are, this is what we do: we are inclusive.

In addition to coherently communicating our ideas, we have to be open and compassionate listeners. People need to feel heard in times of stress and change. Eliminating segregated classrooms and serving all students in their neighborhood school is a significant shift in school culture. In the process, we are asking people to take on different roles and learn new skills. There may be educators who feel a real sense of loss even as they embrace new roles and responsibilities. We need to listen openly to people's experiences and concerns. We need to consciously determine that we will not react defensively when they raise questions.

We listened to learning specialists who had taught in self-contained classrooms in the past. They definitely missed the small communities they had developed over many years. We listened to paraeducators who felt confident working with students with reading difficulties but were struggling to now learn how to support students with social communication challenges. We listened to SLPs who were working through the idea of incorporating language goals into the student's literacy block or social studies class rather than pulling students out for small-group language instruction. These listening sessions provided an important emotional opportunity for educators to let the very real challenges of change be known. Equally important, we learned so much from these listening sessions that informed what types of professional development were needed, when we may need to provide more support, and how to adjust on-the-ground implementation of the principles of inclusive education.

In addition, listening is important because many of the brilliant ideas and creative solutions that we need are already present within our organization. There are times when external expertise is necessary, but we have found over and over again that the best solutions emerge from dedicated teams of teachers and specialists working together. Allowing for both scheduled and spontaneous times to listen is thus absolutely critical to this work.

We never pass up an opportunity to communicate our vision of inclusive school communities by sharing the successes of our educators, students, and families. We also invite our community to share their stories. We know that everyone in our community has been affected by our creating more inclusive schools. But we never really know who will have a story of success to share. So we look for every opportunity to talk with members of our community who are not directly connected to the classroom, including school secretaries, our operations department, our bus contractors, and parent groups.

We also partner with community organizations to keep the conversation going. We share success stories with our local news organizations. We present at professional conferences. We talk about inclusion around our own dinner tables and at parties. Even more important, we create opportunities for learning specialists, general education teachers, paraeducators, students, and parents to share their *why*—their successes, their passion, and their conviction that everyone belongs in this imperfect, messy, and absolutely critical world of school.

PRINCIPLE #4: START AND GET BETTER

A few years ago, we ran into some colleagues from another school district who we knew shared our values about inclusive education. We were excited to chat with them because we knew they were in their second year of a large grant through a national technical assistance organization that supported inclusion. We wanted to hear about the changes that were happening in their district. They told us that they had flown staff to a national conference on inclusion and that they had led several professional development days in their district. These are great things! Giving professionals time to learn together to support students' learning in new ways is totally critical to substantive change. However, as we continued to talk, we learned that in the two years of working with this grant, they had not reduced the number of students in segregated classrooms or increased students' time in general education classrooms. They said they were committed to inclusion but they felt like they needed to learn more and get more people on board before they were ready to actually make changes for students. Unfortunately, there is always more to learn. If we were to adopt this stance—waiting until we have it all figured out and have everyone on board—we would never make substantive change.

Michael Fullan (2010) describes the concept of "Ready-Fire-Aim" (which he attributes to Peters & Waterman, 1982) as critical in leading transformative change. This means that it is prudent to do some preparatory learning (getting ready) but then you must get into the work (fire). After you have spent time engaging in the work, you learn what else you need to know. You follow that initial work with critical reflection and adjustment (aim). This was certainly the stance we adopted. At each decision juncture we did the best that we could to prepare and anticipate challenges; then we jumped in. We continued to reflect on our process, examine student outcomes, and make necessary adjustments. We learned the work by doing the work. One example of "Ready-Fire-Aim" is the way we worked with our middle schools in the first year of our journey.

We met with the middle school principals about halfway through year 1. At that point we had resource-level support in all middle schools, and we had three self-contained program classes (Applied Academics, Behavior Support, and Life Learning) clustered at one middle school. With the principals we looked at the academic and behavioral data for the students in these programs, as well as enrollment trends over the past few years. We saw that the academic outcomes for the students in these programs were generally not great. We also saw that many of the students in these classrooms (particularly the Behavior Support program) were eighth graders, so there was likely to be a large drop in enrollment in these classes the following year.

We saw an opportunity to do things differently by disbanding the Applied Academics and Behavior Support programs for the next year and working to make sure the appropriate levels of support for those students would be available at each middle school. (We decided we needed an additional year of preparation to make the shift for the Life Learning program.) Once we made these decisions, we were in the "Ready" phase. We conducted planning workshops and gathered input from students, parents, and teachers. We held informational meetings, reviewed curriculum needs, and assessed our physical spaces. We facilitated many IEP meetings and listening sessions. We had a clear direction, but we did not have a clear answer to every possible question. We worked hard to develop trust, and we knew that we would likely need to meet often the next fall.

> We had a clear direction, but we did not have a clear answer to every possible question.

Before the start of the school year, we gave all students who had previously been in the centralized middle school Applied Academics and Behavior Support classrooms the option to be in their neighborhood schools. Most of them chose to transfer to their neighborhood schools. We would provide a similar level of support to what they had in the segregated class, but now that support would be based in the general education classroom. That fall, we were deep in the "Fire" phase. We kept moving forward, propelled by our passionate educators, our strong collaborative culture, and our deep commitment to stay very close to the work. We learned so much. By the middle of the year, we were in the "Aim" phase, as we made some staffing adjustments, scheduled targeted professional learning opportunities, and learned more about the needs of the general education teachers.

It is simply not possible to completely plan your way through this work. There is so much innovation that happens when great educators work together in the midst of complex and uncertain challenges. So much of the learning that happens is specific to the unique context. We had to learn the work by doing the work. We had to start, dig in, try new things, and learn together through it all. This is a critical principle. There are resources available to guide the work (including this book). But there is simply no way to learn it all, except by diving in and engaging in the work—breaking apart structures that segregate, increasing engagement for all students, and listening closely to the journeys of students, parents, and educators.

PRINCIPLE #5: THE MAGIC IS IN THE TEAM

Make no mistake, becoming an inclusive school district is challenging work. There were moments, many moments, when we were stymied, flummoxed, at a loss. There were many nights when we couldn't sleep as we wondered, "What do we do now?" As leaders, there were difficult meetings where all eyes turned to us to ask, "How are you going to make this situation better?" People seemed to be looking for the program, curriculum, or model that provided consistent answers to all questions—a silver bullet or magic wand to fix the situation. What we learned again and again is that there *is* magic—and the magic is in the team!

Team processes are at the heart of everything we do in education today. Improvements in classroom instruction are led by professional learning community (PLC) teams. Innovations in schoolwide culture are led by Multi-Tiered Systems of Support (MTSS) teams. Specific student behavior supports are led by functional behavioral assessment (FBA) teams. In special education, team processes are specifically codified through the federal requirements of the IEP, where general educators, special educators, parents, students, and district representatives are called to work together to support the success of the student. Teamwork in some form is critical to improvement and change.

Yet simply having teams is not enough to create change. Most of us have been part of IEP teams that simply go through the motions of fulfilling their legal requirements. Many of us have been part of PLCs that have sat together to "admire" the problem of low student achievement without impacting classroom instruction. We have participated in Behavior Support team meetings that did not create positive change for the student or help the teachers feel inspired and supported.

So what makes the difference? What leads teams to be a catalyst for positive change?

First, make sure the right people are in the room. Not just people who are filling the legally prescribed roles (as in the IEP process) but people who are passionate about students and committed to working through messy situations to find creative solutions. Whenever possible, hire great people, people with varied backgrounds and expertise who share a common work ethic, optimism, and belief in students. Our building principals, teachers, paraeducators, and specialists are outstanding professionals who truly care. We are always looking for people who dream big, stay focused on what is best for students, and want to do this work linking arms closely with others. But as we learned in the previous section (Ready-Fire-Aim), we can't wait until we have hired an entirely new staff to engage in transformative change. So we need to work to build teacher efficacy—teachers' belief in the mission of inclusive schools and in their own ability to learn and adapt their systems and structures to meet the needs of all students. We know that people become educators because they want to affect the lives of children. We are committed to continuing to nurture and support them in their work. We take every opportunity to build community and understand that all of our work is built on relationships.

When we say, "The magic is in the team," we mean that we believe in the collective wisdom, experience, and capacity of the team members. The people who know that particular student, the people who know that specific curriculum content, and the people who know that unique classroom context—those are the people who are the most equipped to solve that problem. External resources, including curriculum materials and guidance from specialists, can be critical in helping us dig deeper, but the people who make it happen are our teams.

> We believe in the collective wisdom, experience, and capacity of the team members.

It is essential to give people the time, tools, permission, and guidance to work effectively in teams. Time is a precious resource, and there never seems to be enough time for everything teachers want to do. We choose to invest in prioritizing team time because we believe in the power of teams.

Some teams are set up with regular meeting times and structures, such as PLCs and co-teaching partners. Other times, when new challenges arise, we bring teams together to authentically solve specific problems. Whenever possible, we use clear protocols to help teams carefully examine data, understand the student's perspective, identify key variables, brainstorm solutions, and commit to action steps. When team members know that they are empowered to work through the problem—and they all have a mindset that it can be solved—and that they are the right people to be at the table to solve the problem, amazing things happen. And if the problem persists, the answer is almost always to bring the team back together to look at new data, consider things in a different way, think about what they may have missed, and recommit to their students.

Our journey toward inclusive schools began with putting our goals on paper. We have built on the foundational principles of building capacity, growth mindset, communication, getting started, and the power of the team. The next chapters will dig into more specifics about our focus areas and the leadership moves to make it happen. But before we dig into those areas, we want to share the story of one student, where you can see all five of these guiding principles at work.

Kortney's Story

Kortney moved to our district as a seventh grader. She had been in a self-contained classroom her entire school career, with no opportunity to be exposed to grade-level general education curriculum. We anticipated that the transition to a seventh-grade science class would be challenging.

As the school team got to know her over the first few days of school, it was clear that her stamina for academic tasks was very low. She demonstrated that she was not yet able to sit in a classroom for 55 minutes like her grade-level peers. After gathering some baseline data, the team decided to start with 5 minutes of class time followed by a chunk of choice time (her current favorites are colored strings and Peppa Pig videos).

During Kortney's five minutes in science class, she sat at a table with three other seventh graders (along with a paraeducator). The teacher was asking the students about the difference between the independent and dependent variables in an experiment they were preparing to do later in the period. She then directed the students to move across the room and find a partner to complete the next stage of the assignment together.

As the seventh-grade scientists began to engage in the task, the teacher came over to Kortney and said, "Can you come help me measure something?" Kortney asked for string, and the teacher turned to the paraeducator to check the timer, then replied, "Three more minutes in science class. Then you can have string. Come over here, and help me measure some water."

The teacher pulled two beakers from a cabinet and brought them over to the sink. She filled one with water and handed it to Kortney. Pointing to a line on the other beaker, she asked, "Can you fill it up to here?" Kortney poured the water. The teacher refilled her beaker and asked her to pour more water.

When Kortney was done pouring the water, the paraeducator showed the timer to the teacher. The teacher said, "Good job helping me measure. It looks like your timer is done. You spent five minutes in science class. Thanks for coming to class. See you tomorrow."

Kortney and the paraeducator walked out the door and down the hall to a quiet classroom where she could watch an episode of Peppa Pig before venturing into another class for another five minutes.

At first glance, Kortney's school day at that time may have looked like a traditional segregated special education experience. She spent most of her time in a specialized setting, and most of her interactions were mediated through an instructional assistant. But there were key differences that are worth highlighting and celebrating.

First, this schedule (five minutes in class followed by a longer chunk of time on a preferred task) was designed to be temporary. It was based on her present level of academic and functional performance at that time. She did not yet have the stamina to engage for the whole period. The key word there is "yet." The team was intentional in increasing her stamina. By the end of the week, they were planning for her to attend each class for eight minutes.

Second, Kortney's task while in the science classroom was substantively related to the work her classmates were doing. The other seventh-grade scientists were performing experiments to master the concepts of independent and dependent variables. Of course, measuring water in beakers is significantly simpler in depth, breadth, and complexity. But it is still related to the same grade-level standard.

Finally, and most important, Kortney's time in the science class included direct interaction with the highly qualified science teacher. The paraeducator could have guided Kortney in the activity of measuring water into a beaker. But the fact that the classroom teacher took charge of Kortney's learning in her classroom is extremely powerful. It conveys to Kortney—and to her classmates—that Kortney is a member of the classroom community and that Kortney is there to learn science along with the rest of the class. The teacher's actions dignified Kortney's learning experience in a way that could not have been done in a self-contained classroom or by a paraeducator alone in the back of the general education science class.

The classroom teacher took charge of Kortney's learning in her classroom.

Another part of what makes this possible is that the teacher had established clear classroom routines. The other students in the class knew how to begin working independently, so the teacher felt confident spending three minutes focused directly on measuring water with Kortney.

Throughout the rest of seventh grade Kortney worked to build stamina but continued to spend very few minutes in class. When she was there, the teachers worked hard to create meaningful learning activities connected to grade-level learning targets (like her science teacher did). But we had not yet helped her find an effective way to communicate, and the result was that she still had a lot of challenging behaviors, including biting, hitting, scratching, and throwing things at adults. She continued to spend much of her time in a separate classroom doing preferred activities. She had very little verbal communication and showed little interest in learning to use her communication device.

By November of eighth grade, Kortney was spending much more time in her classes. A major impact was the role of peers. The learning specialist showed peers how to communicate using Kortney's device, so she has much more consistent interactions with peers throughout the day. She showed more interest in learning to use her device so she could talk with other eighth-grade girls. As a result, she also developed more interest in going to class. In some classes with peer support, she would attend for most of the period without additional support from a paraeducator.

Another challenge Kortney experienced is that she had limited skills in using the toilet. She wears a pull-up and often has significant chafing and rashes on her skin. The learning specialist and paraeducators have hypothesized that part of her challenging behavior may result from being in a constant state of discomfort—and being unable to tell anyone about it. After intensive work by the SLP and the learning specialist, the team experienced a major breakthrough when Kortney used her device to say, "Underwear hurt." Kortney's independence in self-care continues to grow. But the fact that she can now communicate her needs is a significant step in helping her gain a sense of control over that fundamental element of her life.

Kortney's story is a reminder that the path for some students will be extremely complex. It takes a dedicated team, constantly asking questions, reviewing data, and trying new things. It also takes a steadfast belief in the power of inclusion.

Kortney is not in her general education classroom every moment of every day. In fact, she spent a lot of time out of the general education classroom for most of seventh grade. But remember, when she came to us, she had never been out of a segregated self-contained classroom from kindergarten through sixth grade. Her time in general education continues to grow, and so do her ways to meaningfully engage in the learning and with her peers. The key thing that didn't change is our belief that she belongs with her peers and that (with the right skills and supports) she will get there. As we continue to build capacity, maintain a growth mindset, communicate consistently, start and get better, and value the magic in the team, we know Kortney's success will grow, and all of the other students in her classes will continue to benefit as well.

References

Algozzine, B., Horner, R. H., Sugai, G., Barrett, S., Dickey, S. R., Eber, L., Kincaid, D., Lewis, T., & Tobin, T. (2010). *Evaluation blueprint for school-wide positive behavior support*. National Technical Assistance Center on Positive Behavior Interventions and Support. https://www.pbisapps.org/Resources/SWIS%20Publications/Evaluation%20Blueprint%20for%20School-Wide%20Positive%20Behavior%20Support.pdf

Berger, R., Woodfin, L., & Rugen, L. (2014). *Leaders of their own learning: Transforming schools through student-engaged assessment*. Jossey-Bass.

Dweck, C. S. (2008). *Mindset: The new psychology of success*. Ballantine Books.

Fullan, M. (2010). *Motion leadership: The skinny on becoming change savvy*. Corwin.

Fullan, M., & Quinn, J. (2016). *Coherence: The right drivers in action for schools, districts, and systems*. Ontario Principals' Council; Corwin.

Peters, T. J., & Waterman, R. H. (1982). *In search of excellence*. HarperCollins.

CHAPTER 4

Creating Inclusive Cultures

A panel of high students spoke to our principals and district administrators recently. In response to a question about inclusive practices in their schools, one of the students said, "Of course, all students should be in our schools. When they get out of school, there aren't separate places for them. It's not like there's a special ed Target." Another student said simply, "Segregation is bad. Just don't do it."

In Chapter 3 we outlined the three focus areas that have guided our work for the past eight years: *creating inclusive cultures, improving instructional practices,* and *increasing student voice.* This chapter will address the first focus area.

When we are working toward creating inclusive cultures in our schools, the first step is having all students together in the same building. Then, the next logical step is to have all students together in the same classrooms.

But being physically included is only the beginning. To create a truly inclusive school community, each student needs to feel a sense of belonging—connected to their classmates and to the spirit of the school.

True belonging begins with a seat at the table. It develops with access to the same rigorous content and thinking routines. And it becomes truly inclusive when all students make a valuable contribution to one another and to the classroom and the school community. All students have opportunities for meaningful leadership, and true friendships develop that are not predicated on one student always in a helping role.

This is how we envision the pathway toward inclusion. Our district has eliminated separate classes (both in centralized locations and within neighborhood schools). All students are listed on the general education class rosters. Special education case managers (we call them learning specialists) work closely with students, but the starting point for each student is the general education classroom with the general education teacher. The classroom teacher owns and connects with every student in their class. Every student receives the support they need (regardless of whether they are officially identified as a student with a disability).

One simple, but important, practice we have committed to is that all students have a desk in their general education classroom. If there are multiple students with complex needs at a grade level, we generally do not assign them to the same classroom. This is something we learned through experience. When we eliminated the Life Learning classroom in one of our primary schools, we had three second graders who needed significant support. We knew it would be more efficient to have one highly skilled paraeducator support the three students in the same classroom. So we initially assigned all three students to a single teacher's classroom.

The teacher was eager for them to be there. When she created her desk arrangement and seating chart, she set up all three students at a table together near the back of the room, with a desk and a chair for the paraeducator to sit with them.

This was efficient. And the students were out of the segregated setting of the Life Learning classroom. But we discovered that in practice, there was a bubble that developed around these three students in the classroom. The classroom teacher and other students often referred to them as a group ("the Life Learners"), rather than individual students with individual and different learning needs.

Because there was always a paraeducator with the three students, the classroom teacher often did not work directly with the students. And because the students were clustered in a table group by themselves in the back of the room, they rarely had the opportunity for meaningful peer interactions. Most peer connection was mediated through the adult who was always in close proximity to all three students.

Over time we recognized that this model of clustering students with significant disabilities in the same general education classroom was not the most inclusive practice. It was efficient and it was more inclusive than the segregated self-contained classroom, but it perpetuated structural barriers that prevented the students from truly engaging in their classroom community.

So the next year the principal courageously and intentionally assigned these three students to three different third-grade classrooms. We knew this would stretch our resources, but we knew it would be the right decision for those students and for all the third graders. We found that the classroom teachers began to take more

> True belonging begins with a seat at the table. It develops with access to the same rigorous content and thinking routines. And it becomes truly inclusive when all students make a valuable contribution to one another and to the classroom and the school community.

ownership of each student's learning experience—like they were just another student in the class. And the students began to build more meaningful peer connections.

These students still received intensive supports, including adult assistance for significant portions of their day. But breaking up the cluster of students with significant disabilities allowed their classmates and teachers to view each student as an individual who can contribute to the classroom community rather than as a trio of kids who were defined by their disability and segregated in the back of the classroom.

One of the greatest benefits of inclusion is the way natural relationships can form between students. This can also be a powerful pathway for providing support for students with complex needs. Here are a few examples of peer support that we have witnessed over the years.

- During recess MacKenzie, a kindergarten student with ASD who does not yet have a method for expressive communication, ran from the playground and headed across the field toward the regional park next to the school. The paraeducator who was overseeing several students with intensive needs was not able to chase her. Unprompted, another kindergarten student, MacKenzie's classmate, ran across the field, calling to her. After running about 50 yards across the grass, MacKenzie stopped; the classmate grabbed her hand, and they walked back to the playground holding hands.

- A fifth-grade class was working on ratios during the Math Workshop period. Esther was working on a significantly modified worksheet (counting objects and practicing writing the numbers 1–10). The teacher spent a few minutes helping Donaldo (Esther's table partner) make sense of ratios. Then, the teacher moved on to confer with another student across the room. Esther was stuck on a problem, so she started wriggling in her chair and looking toward the teacher for support. The teacher continued working with students at other table groups. Donaldo looked up and noticed Esther's agitated body language. He calmly asked, "Do you need help?" Then he shifted his chair to sit beside her and helped her count items and write numbers. In previous years when Esther faced academic challenges, she would create significant disruptions (including screaming, removing her clothes, and urinating on the floor). The school team has worked intensely to help Esther develop coping skills to be able to participate in her classroom more successfully. And peer supports have played a huge role in that transition.

- Micah is a kindergartener who uses an eye gaze device to communicate. He has become quite proficient with his device, but sometimes peers want to have conversations with him involving words that are not yet programmed in his device. On the day before Micah's birthday, he and a friend were talking about how he was planning to celebrate. The friend asked, "What kind of birthday cake do you want?" Micah's device did not include options for flavors of cake. So his friend held up his two hands, palms facing out. He looked to his right hand and said, "Do you want pink raspberry . . . ," then looking to his left hand, ". . . or blue raspberry?" Micah stared at him with a blank look on his face, as if to say, "Seriously? Those are my two options of cake flavors?" A paraeducator suggested the friend give more conventional options. When he tried again with "chocolate" or "vanilla," Micah selected chocolate, and the conversation continued.

- Jennica is a seventh-grade student who had spent her entire education in self-contained classrooms until she moved to our district in sixth grade. She had very few academic behaviors and minimal expressive communication skills. Despite hard work from teachers and paraeducators, she spent most of her time in a separate setting during her first year with us. But in seventh grade, the learning specialist worked to promote intentional relationships with her peers. Over the course of the first few months of seventh grade, Jennica was spending nearly all of her time in general education classes. Instead of having constant support from a paraeducator, Jennica was generally accompanied by peers who helped her engage in her learning and connect to modified versions of the grade-level content. When Jennica's family moved midway through seventh grade, her classmates were devastated to have to say goodbye.

- When Ahmed moved to our district in eighth grade, he experienced inclusive classrooms for the first time. He desperately wanted to be friends with the popular and athletic boys and hang out with the girls, but he had limited social communication skills, and he struggled to understand appropriate social boundaries. The speech language pathologist and learning specialist worked closely with classroom teachers, counselors, and school administrators to find ways for Ahmed to connect with peers in a structured and predictable manner. Through formal and informal means, he began to develop the social skills to match his relentless enthusiasm and school spirit. Ahmed became the captain of the Unified Basketball team and took on other leadership roles. By the time he was a senior, he had developed genuine friendships with his classmates, and he was elected to the Associated Student Body (ASB) leadership team as part of the rally committee.

One concern that parents and teachers sometimes raise is the question of how students with "typical" learning needs will be affected by having students with more intensive needs learning alongside them. Nearly 40 years of education research has shown that students without disabilities who are in inclusive classrooms have equal academic outcomes to students who are in segregated classrooms, and often even better outcomes. Erik Carter's (2019) recent summary of the research demonstrates that peers benefit academically, socially, and in their understanding of others.

We have seen plenty of examples of this in person. For example, in one eighth-grade mathematics class, the daily lesson was about systems of equations. Colby, a student who had previously been in a Life Learning classroom, was in this algebra class with his peers. His entry point to the lesson was far simpler: He was working on basic number sense.

The paraeducator and several of the students near him were asking him to count out play money for them. He would count a few dollars and hand the money to a friend. Then, Colby would use his communication device to ask for a different number of dollars from another classmate.

While this was happening, the teacher was leading a lesson on the elimination method of solving systems of equations. At one point the teacher asked a question. One of the students who was very engaged with Colby's play money activity raised his hand and answered the teacher's question correctly.

When asked about whether Colby's presence in the classroom was distracting, a girl in his class looked at us like we were crazy for asking and said, "Colby is just another student. He deserves to learn math too."

This kind of acceptance in class seems so remarkable to adults who grew up in segregated school systems. It is even more remarkable because it seems so *unremarkable* to our students. Inclusive communities are what they know, so they don't see why it would be any other way.

For example, Yuji is a first grader who uses a device to communicate. One day, a substitute teacher was calling roll at the beginning of class. Students were responding by raising their hand and saying, "Here." The teacher called Yuji's name. When she didn't hear an immediate response, she began to mark him absent, saying to herself, "Yuji's not here." One of Yuji's classmates called out, "Wait! You have to give him time!" After a few moments of wait time, Yuji used his device to say, "Here." Another student explained to the substitute teacher, "This is the way he talks."

Consider this example of when the values of an inclusive culture are truly internalized by students. Franklin is a third-grade student with significant health and communication barriers who also uses a wheelchair for mobility. At one point during the school year, a substitute teacher walked the class to their music classroom, taking a shortcut across a stepping-stone path through the grass. As they walked across the stones, some students noticed that Franklin had to go the long way around the courtyard, with only an adult assistant by his side. When they discussed this with their teacher the next day, the class agreed that they would never leave their friend on his own without a classmate or group of peers.

A few months later the class took a field trip to the Bonneville Dam. The tour guide led the way for the students, while the teacher was at the back of the line. Suddenly, the whole line of students stopped. The tour guide was starting to lead the class down a stone staircase from the parking lot toward the dam, and the students immediately realized that Franklin would not be able to follow this path in his wheelchair. The students asked the tour guide to stop, and they advocated for an alternate route for the class to ensure that their classmate would not have to be on his own.

The group problem-solved together and decided to have a few students ride the elevator with Franklin. When the teacher asked for volunteers, almost every student in the class raised their hand.

True Friendships

When Alsea started first grade in our district, her mom shared with the teacher that she wasn't sure if an inclusive setting was the right place for her. Alsea had come from a self-contained kindergarten in a different district. Before that, she had been in a segregated preschool classroom to receive Early Childhood Special Education (ECSE) services. She had never made any friends, and her mom was afraid she would be isolated and bullied in a general education classroom. The classroom teacher encouraged Alsea's mom, the school staff worked hard to create entry points for Alsea, and her classmates wrapped their arms around her. A few months later, Alsea's mom came to the teacher in tears of joy because Alsea had been invited to a friend's birthday party for the first time.

McKenna and Mario were high school juniors, both with outgoing personalities and a huge love for soccer. They played on the same soccer team for their high school, which happened to be the Unified Soccer team. Unified Sports brought them together. Mario has the label of intellectual disability; McKenna does not. McKenna and Mario were selected to represent the Portland Timbers for a Unified Soccer game as part of the Major League Soccer All-Star Weekend festivities in Atlanta. They traveled with a sponsor to participate with other high school students from around the country. These types of experiences (playing on a team together, sharing interests, going on a trip together) often create friendships, and this is exactly what happened for McKenna and Mario. As they saw each other as teammates, they saw each other's strengths and moved beyond the labels. Their friendship is authentic.

Providing Supports in the General Education Classroom

People often wonder if it would be better for the student to work with a specialist in a separate setting rather than in the classroom. Wouldn't the student benefit from a quieter space where they can focus directly on the instruction? Wouldn't the student feel self-conscious if an adult is working closely with them in the classroom, where other students can see them? Occasionally, it is better for a student to receive intensive, explicit support in a separate setting before returning to practice those skills in the classroom. But we are finding more and more that this kind of intensive support often works really well in the general education classroom.

For example, Cho is a kindergarten student who experiences ASD. He is working on developing fine motor skills and receives weekly support from an occupational therapist. At the beginning of the year, the occupational therapist pulled Cho out during writing time to help him focus on his pencil grip and letter formation. By mid-October, the occupational therapist and the classroom teacher asked themselves why he needed to receive this support in the hallway.

He was doing tasks that approximated the same work his classmates were doing. While they were working independently, the classroom teacher and an instructional assistant were moving through the room and providing support. It would look perfectly natural for another adult to be working closely with Cho during that time. So they moved his slant board and chunky pencils into the classroom, at a desk near his peers.

While the other kindergarteners were working on letter formation (writing the letter *B*), Cho was tracing lines, practicing the vertical and horizontal strokes that would eventually lead to more complete letter formation. He and his curious classmates could see that he had the same worksheet and was approximating the same task.

When he had finished his writing work, the occupational therapist brought out a reward activity—using oversized plastic tweezers to pick up poofy cotton balls and place them in a bottle. Other students started coming over and wanted to play too. Isabella stood by his desk, taking turns in the game. The occupational therapist prompted Cho to say whose turn it was. He alternated between "Cho" and "Isabella" until the bottle was full. Isabella helped demonstrate how to screw the lid on the bottle, and then Cho did it himself.

As the class was cleaning up from the writing task, Isabella led Cho across the room (unprompted) to show him the in-basket for his writing work. Before he put it in the basket, he took a detour to show the teacher the large *B* he had written on the back of the page. She praised him for his straight vertical line and two curving arcs.

For a student with ASD, these natural peer interactions are critical for developing strong social communication skills. Peer support and modeling are more effective than a paraeducator providing one-to-one support to the student (Carter et al., 2016). Cho could have practiced writing in the hallway, but he would have missed out on the social play time with Isabella. He would not have seen his classmates writing the letter *B*, so he might not have been inspired to do it himself. And Isabella would have missed out on the opportunity to play with a new friend.

Students are also intensely aware of the status implications of being "pulled out" to receive services. A few years ago (when we were still in the early stages of our inclusion journey), one of our principals was walking through the hall when she saw a third-grade boy heading back to his classroom from a pull-out reading group. She knew the class was engaged in Readers Workshop at the time, so she asked, "What are you reading in class?" He paused with his hand on the door handle, looked at her with a puzzled expression, and said, "Oh, I don't read in there. I read out here." The principal wondered what message we are giving our students about their status as readers (and as classmates) if we are pulling them out during this critical period of learning.

Shared Ownership and Co-Teaching

Building a culture of inclusive practices among school staff is both easier and harder than it should be. When we talk about creating a culture of belonging and eliminating segregation based on disability, it is easy for people to say, "I'm in!" But when it comes down to the practical day-to-day aspects of the work, it is often much more difficult. In particular, general education teachers and other school staff often feel unprepared, unequipped, or unskilled to provide instruction and support to students with complex needs.

It should be no surprise that general education teachers say, "Isn't there some-place else that would be a better fit for his learning needs?" or "I don't have the training to teach a student like her." For 40+ years, we have been telling teachers exactly that. We have said, "This special ed teacher has specialized training and expertise that you don't have" or "If we move him to this specialized classroom, we will have the curriculum and physical equipment to teach him better."

The special education establishment has essentially told general education teach-ers, "Don't worry about this kid. We'll take care of him. You can focus on the rest of your class." So it is no surprise that general education teachers are feeling dis-equilibrium when we now say, "Actually, every student belongs in your class. We are going to build your expertise and bring specialized support to your classroom."

The first step we took to build shared ownership of students was to make sure all students were on classroom teachers' daily rosters. In the older, "mainstreaming" model, students who spent most of their day in a self-contained classroom were on the class roster of the special education teacher. They might have a buddy class that they joined for PE or music. They may have been welcomed and even loved by the students in the general education class. But they were fundamentally outsiders.

In the old model a classroom teacher might have had 30 students in their class—then they needed to find room for a few extra kids whenever the "buddies" from the Life Learning class showed up. But with all students on the class roster, the 30 students in the class now include 1 or 2 students with more intensive needs. When the teacher arranges their classroom, they make sure there are desks for all their students.

Listing all students on the class roster or making sure every student has a desk in the classroom may seem like very small changes. But they open the door to more substantive changes that, over time, have a tremendous impact.

Listing all students on the class roster or making sure every student has a desk in the classroom may seem like very small changes. But they open the door to more substantive changes that, over time, have a tremendous impact.

For example, in the old model two of our primary schools had a self-contained Life Learning program for students with significant cognitive disabilities. Students from across the district would be bused to these programs and segregated for most of their school day.

At the end of the year, when fifth-grade teachers were putting together the program for the graduation/promotion ceremony, the fifth-grade students in the Life Learning class were often inadvertently left off the list. So the Life Learning teacher would host her own promotion ceremony for three or four fifth-grade students. It was a quiet affair, isolated from the rest of the school.

When we eliminated the Life Learning class and moved all the students into their general education classes, students began to develop genuine peer relationships. During a recent fifth-grade promotion ceremony, students who had formerly been served in the Life Learning program were among the stars of the show. Every student shared something about their memories of elementary school or dreams for the future—even students who speak with an augmentative communication device. After the ceremony ended, one parent of a student formerly served in Life Learning jokingly complained that she couldn't get her son to leave the celebration because there were too many friends who wanted to take pictures with him.

Our general and special education teachers now share roles in the classroom, coplanning and co-teaching as much as possible. As with all teachers, more time to collaborate and coplan would be better. Yet even with the limitations of their daily schedules, teachers are finding ways to coplan and co-teach. Building administrators have supported this in important ways. At the high school level, aligning general and special education teacher prep periods is a concrete way to show the value of and provide the opportunity for coplanning. In our primary schools some building principals align the specials schedules or even cover teachers' classes for a time each week to allow for coplanning.

A visit to one of our high schools exemplified the power of co-teaching and coplanning. We popped into a biology class with the intent of seeing the learning specialist who co-taught that period of biology. When we came in, the learning specialist was out of the room at that moment. As we turned to leave, the general education biology teacher called us over. "Want to look at my unit tests?" he asked enthusiastically.

He proceeded to show us three versions of the test for the end of his unit on evolution. The first was the standard version he had used for several years. The second version was of the same content and level of rigor, but it was streamlined and shortened—what we might call an accommodated version to support students who may have learning disabilities to show their knowledge without distraction. Then he showed us the third version. It covered the same general concepts of genetics and evolution, but it was a modified version. In other words, it addressed the same basic standards but with the depth and complexity of the items significantly adapted. The teacher excitedly shared that the two students with significant disabilities who were in his class would be taking the modified version of the test, and he was hopeful they would do well. After all, he said, they had been part of all the labs and had been studying key vocabulary terms with flash cards and their communication devices.

This was a transformational moment. By co-teaching together, the learning specialist and general education teacher had both developed their capacity and beliefs. The general education teacher had taken ownership for the students with significant disabilities in his class, and the opportunities to learn biology had increased in powerful ways for all students.

> By co-teaching together, the learning specialist and general education teacher had both developed their capacity and beliefs.

CHANGES IN THE DAY-TO-DAY EXPERIENCE OF SPECIAL EDUCATION TEACHERS

The shift to eliminating segregated special education classrooms and promoting more inclusive school communities has had a profound effect on the day-to-day experience of classroom teachers. It has also shifted the role of special education teachers. Learning specialists who previously taught a self-contained class serving a narrow profile of students are now working with a broader caseload. They used to plan their day around creating a small, nurturing classroom community with an intensive focus on specialized skills. Now they spend most of their time providing push-in supports for students and consulting with general education teachers and related service providers.

At the other end of the spectrum, the learning specialists who used to serve students in a "resource room" are now working with the full range of student needs. Teachers who used to spend their day leading reading groups for students with a mild learning disability now also support students with significant sensory barriers, cognitive disabilities, or behavioral challenges.

When we made this shift, some of our most experienced teachers expressed concerns about how their role would be changing. They wondered if their expertise would be underutilized or go unrecognized. We have found that the opposite is true. We have seen a greater need (and appreciation) for the expertise of teachers who formerly taught in self-contained programs for students with significant cognitive, functional, and behavioral needs.

One of the highly experienced teachers who moved from a self-contained program class to a general education learning specialist role recently reflected about the transition. She said she sometimes misses having her own class. She loved being able to nurture her kids. She appreciated the simplicity of her clearly defined role. And now she sometimes finds herself exhausted from running all around the school instead of being confined to a single, self-contained classroom. But she said that she has seen so much growth in academics, social-emotional skills, and functional independence among her students that she knows she could never go back.

Our challenge as leaders was to create structures that allowed these experienced teachers to share their knowledge and strategies, building capacity in the other learning specialists and the general education teachers who would now be taking greater ownership of the learning of all students. We created teacher workshops and PLCs within schools and across the district that allowed for this explicit sharing of knowledge and experience. For example, one of our teachers has deep expertise in working with students significantly affected by ASD. We set up a workshop for this teacher to lead other teachers, specialists, and paraeducators in learning strategies and routines to help students develop independence in the bathroom. We will talk more about these structures for professional learning in Chapter 9.

The Power of Language

One of the most powerful (and most subtle) changes we have made over the past few years has been a change in the language we use to talk about the work of creating inclusive learning communities. We have placed a big emphasis on student-first language (Centers for Disease Control, n.d.; Snow, 2009). Instead of defining a student with an adjective, we try to focus on the student first.

For example, instead of "SPED kids" or "IEP kids," we try to refer to "students served by special education." Instead of "behavior kids," we talk about "students who demonstrate challenging behaviors." Instead of "He's a runner," we try to say, "He has a pattern of leaving the class when unsupervised."

Often these student-first phrases are wordier than the shorthand descriptions. But they also help reframe the way we think about students. Our language both reflects and affects our beliefs. The way we talk about students affects the way we think about students—which can affect our beliefs about a student's capacity and motivations. And those beliefs can have a fundamental impact on our actions.

We have been working on making systemwide shifts in our language in both direct and indirect ways. On our website, in our newsletters, and when speaking in front of principals, staff, students, and families, we always try to use student-first language. By modeling the language we have seen shifts in the kinds of phrases people use.

At times we are also explicit about the way we use language and the kind of language we expect staff to use. For example, during our orientation and ongoing professional development for new teachers and paraeducators, we lead activities for adults to reflect on the way language can affect beliefs and actions. We provide note cards with specific terms (*behavior kid, aspy kid, runner, spitter*) and then ask them to think about the connotation of the terms and how they could reframe the terms to be more respectful. We often share a cartoon by Michael Giangreco (1999)—an educational researcher and leading proponent of inclusion—that illustrates the importance of person-first language. The cartoon shows a person asking a young man in a wheelchair, "So, what do you prefer to be called? Handicapped? Disabled? Or physically-challenged?" The person in the wheelchair replies, "Joe would be fine." The caption to the cartoon says, "The most appropriate label is usually the one someone's parents have given them." Sharing this cartoon with our teams helps them reflect on their language with a little bit of humor.

> Our language both reflects and affects our beliefs. The way we talk about students affects the way we think about students—which can affect our beliefs about a student's capacity and motivations.

Whenever we talk about reframing language, it is natural to encounter questions. Most people don't intend any harm by their words, and they may feel like they are being accused of being insensitive or discriminatory if they are told that they are saying things "wrong." Even if they don't feel personally attacked, they will most certainly experience disequilibrium. Language shifts over time, and words that were not intended to be harmful can develop negative associations and pejorative connotations. Our purpose is not simply to label language as "right" or "wrong" or to call people out for saying the "wrong" thing. But if we recognize that someone is using a word or phrase that can be insensitive or hurtful, we want to help people understand the power of their words and consider ways for them to reframe their language.

We recognize that there is considerable disagreement within the disability community about person-first versus identity-first language. (Even labeling a vastly diverse group of individuals as "the disability community" is a questionable use of language.) Individuals with intellectual disabilities (and their families) are more likely to advocate for person-first language, while there are prominent individuals with autism and hearing impairments who prefer to place their autistic or deaf identity at the center of their language. In an article on person-first versus identity-first language, Cara Liebowitz (2015) says,

> There's no way to see the person *without* the disability. A person is not a blank canvas that other things are added onto. From the moment we're born, perhaps even from the moment we're conceived, our experiences shape us and make us who we are. My disability, among many other things, is integrated into who I am. There is no way to separate me from my disability. It's not as if "person" is a standard action figure, while "disability" comes in the accessory pack designed to make you spend more money.

Currently, we start with person-first language as our general rule but always honor the language a student selects for themselves.

In addition to the question about what we choose to put at the center of a person's identity, some people may assert that this kind of language shift eliminates our ability to talk directly and honestly about students with significant learning differences. We want all students to experience a sense of belonging, but that doesn't mean that we should ignore the fact that all students have unique learning needs. Indeed, the purpose of special education law is to protect the right of all students to access their education in the LRE. We need to recognize individual differences to make sure we are meeting individualized needs. That's why some students need an IEP.

The key is that we want our language to recognize and respect that individuality. Grouping students can be helpful for organizing systems and aligning resources. But language that groups students can also limit the way we talk about (and think about) their individualized needs. One example we have seen at several of our schools is when we have same-age siblings who happen to be served by special education. It is very easy for staff to refer to them as "the twins" or "the triplets," even if they present with different individual needs.

Another place where we have seen a significant language shift is in the way students and teachers talk about students with significant cognitive or developmental disabilities. Students with this kind of learning profile were previously segregated into self-contained Life Learning classrooms located at two primary schools in our district. Students from the Life Learning programs would occasionally spend time in their buddy classes, and teachers would refer to these peripheral members of their classroom as "life learners." For example, when organizing students into groups, a teacher might say, "D'Juan and Caitlin, can you work with our life learners today?" Or before heading to recess, the teacher might say, "Let's remember to include our life learners in your games today." The sentiment is honorable, but the unintended impact of the teacher's language may be to highlight the differences between students rather than create deeper bonds of community. And what is a "life learner" anyway? Shouldn't we all be striving to be life learners? Happily, what we hear now is more likely to be "Caitlin and Joe, you are partners today"—providing status and respect to both students.

A similar example arose in another school where teachers and paraeducators were in the habit of referring to students who had previously been in self-contained classrooms as "inclusion kids." For example, when coplanning for a mathematics lesson, a teacher might say, "This activity will work well for most of the class, but how do we modify it for our inclusion kids?" The intention behind this statement is great. We want general education teachers to be using a Universal Design lens to think about *all* students in their planning—and how they can provide access points for students with more significant learning needs. But the term *inclusion kids* carries with it an assumption that some students belong in the classroom and other

students are only there because of some districtwide inclusion program: "We are 'doing
inclusion' now, so I have 'inclusion kids' in my
classroom." *If we are truly committed to creating
inclusive learning communities, then all kids are
"inclusion kids."*

If we are truly committed to
creating inclusive learning
communities, then all kids are
"inclusion kids."

"SEGREGATED" VERSUS "SELF-CONTAINED"

We have chosen to explicitly use the word *segregated* to describe self-contained
classrooms because we recognize that the word contains power. And using powerful
words can help shift the way people talk about and think about the process of
changing schools.

In their influential chapter "Changing the Discourse in Schools," in the book *Race,
Ethnicity, and Multiculturalism: Policy and Practice*, Eugene Eubanks, Ralph Parish,
and Dianne Smith (1997) frame the way we talk about schools into two broad
categories: Discourse I and Discourse II. The first form of discourse is familiar and
comfortable. It is the language that is commonly used to talk about schools, teachers, and students. According to the Bay Area Coalition for Equitable Schools
(2003), Discourse I is about the way things are and replicating the status quo. It is
about identifying symptoms rather than causes, blaming students for not meeting
high standards, maintaining discipline and control over students, and reproducing
the current conditions in society.

Discourse II is about identifying and addressing the "uncomfortable, unequal,
ineffective, prejudicial conditions and relationships in a school" (Eubanks et al.,
1997, p. 154). Some of these factors create barriers or hindrances, lead to alienation
in students, and eventually push them out of the system.

When we choose to use the word *segregated* rather than *self-contained* we are consciously choosing to engage in Discourse II. We are using language that draws
attention to the underlying inequities that have historically been part of the school
system in general and the infrastructure of special education in particular.

A word like *segregated* can be inflammatory. It can make people feel uncomfortable. So we are also thoughtful about how we use it. When we talk about the historical systems and structures in schools, we want to draw connections between
segregation in special education and other forms of segregation that society has
deemed no longer acceptable. At the same time, it is critical to never minimize the
horrific and encompassing role race has played in unjust systems and outcomes in
our country, particularly in schools.

When talking to individual teachers who have created nurturing environments in
self-contained settings, we are careful about using inflammatory language. The

teachers did not create the underlying structure of segregation. They love their students and have worked very hard to care for them and teach them. They may genuinely believe that the self-contained setting is the best place for their students. It is small, familiar, and safe. Disrupting this nurturing environment may be necessary to transform the system, eliminate opportunity gaps, and create more equitable outcomes for all students. But there will be an affective impact for the teachers.

The challenge of transformational leadership is to draw attention to the fundamental inequities of the segregated system without alienating the people who have worked in the system and believed that they had the best interests of their students at heart. Careful attention to language allows us to disrupt the system while caring for the people whose emotional investment will be necessary for a successful transformation.

ALL STUDENTS PARTICIPATE IN COCURRICULAR ACTIVITIES

One of our goals in the focus area of *creating inclusive cultures* is that all students participate in cocurricular activities. This is an integral part of establishing a culture of excellence, personalization, and support for the whole child that extends beyond the classroom. Participation in cocurricular activities also has the benefit of improving student outcomes—including attendance, participation in class, sense of self-efficacy, and academic performance (Im et al., 2016).

Through participation in athletics, the performing arts, leadership, enrichment programs, clubs, and service activities, students served by special education can interact with peers in ways that benefit all participants and strengthen the overall culture of the school.

In addition to being a school district goal, student participation in cocurricular activities is a right protected by IDEA, Section 504 of the Rehabilitation Act, and the Americans with Disabilities Act (ADA).

One of our starting points for engagement in cocurricular activities was a partnership with Special Olympics to launch Unified Sports teams in our high schools. Our two comprehensive high schools were among the first schools in Oregon to receive the Unified Champion Schools national banner recognition from Special Olympics. This award recognizes excellence in Unified Sports & Activities, Inclusive School Leadership, and Whole School Engagement, along with a commitment to sustainable practices to promote a culture of inclusion.

Unified Sports brings together students with and without intellectual disabilities to compete on the same team. Over the past eight years, these activities have become among of the most popular events in our schools. At the Unified basketball and soccer games, the public address announcer calls out the players' names as they run through a tunnel of cheerleaders, the band comes to play the national anthem and fight song, and fans fill the stands. Unified teams have a page in the yearbook, teammates are eligible to earn varsity letters, and seniors are recognized with flowers and posters at the final home game of the season. Teachers and students have broadened the scope of Unified activities to include choir, band, and theater as well.

The Unified Champion Schools program promotes participation in sports and activities, but it also focuses on building inclusive opportunities for student leadership and promoting whole-school engagement. Starting with sports is relatively easy. Spreading the impact schoolwide requires more intentional action. Our schools have focused on increasing the role of students with disabilities in student leadership groups, including the Unified Club and the school's ASB student council. These groups have led whole-school activities to promote inclusive cultures, such as Respect campaigns (aimed at eliminating the use of the *R* word) and activities for Autism Awareness Week.

At one of our schools the Unified Club hosts a weekly board game gathering at lunch. Students come together to eat lunch, play games, and laugh together. At another of our schools the Unified Club organizes an annual Harvest Dance, which actively promotes the participation of students who experience heightened sensory awareness. One of our primary schools has a Recess Club, where students with and without disabilities come together to plan ways to make sure every student has someone to play with during recess that day.

For several years our middle schools have hosted tournaments for Unified basketball and soccer. This is one of the highlights of the year for students and staff. During the Great Recession funding for middle school sports dwindled across Oregon, and we eliminated our traditional school-based basketball teams. As a result, the Unified basketball team is the only basketball team in the middle school. Students feel a sense of pride that they are representing their school. There is a spirit of joy and cooperation on the court. But students also feel the intensity of competition. And the crowds who pack the stands feel it too. Twice in the past three years, the Unified Basketball Jamboree has ended with a student with an intellectual disability hitting a buzzer-beater shot and fans storming the court to celebrate.

These are examples of activities where teachers can create leadership opportunities for students to work together to build a culture of inclusion and belonging. Culture building is a long and complex process. It requires stakeholders (students) to feel a sense of ownership in charting the vision, planning the action steps, and valuing the outcomes. Our partnership with Special Olympics through the Unified Champion Schools program has helped provide a framework for this process.

Building a strong Unified Sports program has been fun for students and staff. The impact for the individual students who have an opportunity to participate in sports and represent their school has been immeasurable. But there is a broader impact that has been very clear as well. The schoolwide culture has shifted in all of the schools that have instituted Unified Sports & Activities. When students are playing and cheering together, it has the effect of breaking down some of the barriers, misconceptions, and prejudices that can affect students with disabilities. When students play together on the court, they are more comfortable sitting together in the cafeteria and learning together in the classroom.

In addition to the formal structures of Unified Sports & Activities, we have made a commitment to providing access to the broad range of sports and activities that students may participate in at school. We have had students with significant disabilities join our high school track, cross-country, swimming, and golf teams. In most circumstances the student is able to engage in the activity with minimal support. But when there is a need for additional adult presence, we partner with our principals or athletic directors to figure out the most effective (and least restrictive) way to provide that support. For example, when Brinna, a student who uses a wheelchair, wanted to participate in cross-country, we started by finding teammates who ran at about the same pace to be her training partners. During some practices and meets, we also needed to ensure that a coach was present to provide safety and supervision. As with additional instructional support in the classroom, it was important that Brinna's participation and interaction with the team were not limited to a single adult. During some training sessions, the head coach ran alongside her wheelchair to provide guidance and feedback, just as he would for any other athlete on the team.

Another significant component of this story was ensuring that we had the right equipment and facilities for participation. When Brinna expressed interest in cross-country, our head coach, athletic director, and physical therapist worked closely with Brinna and her family to find the right chair for trail running. Then we partnered with a local adaptive sports organization to acquire and maintain the equipment.

One ongoing physical barrier to inclusive participation in cocurricular activities was the design of our high school stadium and bleachers. During track meets, athletes tend to gather on the bleachers, protected from Oregon's spring rain. Wheelchair access to the bleachers is from the top of the bowl, not from field level. So Brinna often spent most of the meet sitting on the side of the track, sometimes alone. We worked with the track coaches to change the team norms to encourage students to gather on the track in addition to gathering in the bleachers so no student would need to be alone during the meet.

We have worked to create inclusive cocurricular activities at our primary schools as well. These include an after-school running club and more inclusive activities on the annual spring field day. In some schools principals and teachers have partnered with a traveling children's theater company to create access for students with more significant disabilities. The theater company adapted their program to include parts for students in a wheelchair and students who communicate with an augmentative communication device.

DATA COLLECTION FOR PARTICIPATION IN COCURRICULAR ACTIVITIES

As with other ambitious goals, we set the target at 100%. Our goal says, "All students participate in cocurricular activities inclusively, broadening opportunities for students with disabilities and promoting a culture of diversity and respect in all of our schools and throughout the community."

We said we expect 100% of students with disabilities to participate in a cocurricular activity. A goal with a lower threshold may be easier to reach. But when we talk about setting the target at 90% of students participating, we always ask ourselves, "Who are those other 10%? With which specific students are we ok if they don't get to build self-efficacy and foster peer relationships through participating in activities?" Who gets to choose who has the opportunity to participate?

When we ask these questions, we always come around to the conviction that our target should be 100%. Of course, this doesn't mean that every student will join the debate team. Or that every student will participate in robotics. Participation will look different based on the strengths, interests, and needs of different students. The degree of independence will vary, and we need to be prepared to support students in the most natural, least restrictive way possible.

As we think about data collection for this goal, we try to minimize the additional paperwork responsibilities for case managers. Our solution for this was to embed a question in our IEP software that requires case managers to note whether a student is participating in cocurricular activities and, if so, what kind of activity. To answer this question accurately, case managers are encouraged to directly ask about cocurricular activities during the IEP meeting or during the planning process in advance of the IEP meeting. If a student is not participating in cocurricular activities, the case manager can probe to find out more about the barriers and work on ways to eliminate those barriers.

ELIMINATING BARRIERS TO PARTICIPATION IN COCURRICULAR ACTIVITIES

Many students with disabilities would participate in cocurricular activities if they knew that it was possible. Some students and families believe that they are not eligible to participate because they learn differently, move differently, or communicate differently than most other students. They are often surprised to learn that they can participate and that we can make appropriate accommodations to provide entry points for access.

Other students may know that they can participate, but their disability may provide a barrier to initiating participation. For instance, many schools advertise their clubs and activities in the morning announcements. A student with auditory processing challenges or attention issues may hear the announcement and want to participate but may not fully comprehend the process for signing up and joining the club.

Think about the complex string of executive functioning skills necessary to sign up for a cocurricular activity. First, the student needs to attend to the announcement and comprehend what the activity entails. Then they need to remember to go to the office to pick up a permission slip, put it in their binder or backpack, bring the permission slip home, take it out of their binder or backpack, have their parents sign it, put it back in their binder or backpack, bring the form back to school, take it out of their binder or backpack, and turn it into the appropriate box in the correct office. If the permission slip or sign-up process requires recommendations from other teachers or payment of an activity fee, there are additional barriers that may trip up a student.

School staff may say, "Anyone can participate. They heard the announcement. We aren't keeping them out. They just didn't turn in the form on time. If they really wanted to participate, they would have found a way to get the paperwork done."

But what if we actively encouraged students to participate—especially students who may not have realized that they are eligible to participate? What if we helped students create a checklist or visual to guide them in the sign-up process? What if we sat next to the student as they wrote an email to their parents to help them remember to sign the permission slip that night? What if we helped the student pick up and fill out a scholarship form to apply for a fee waiver? What if we helped a student set a reminder alert in their phone so they remember to attend the club at lunchtime on Thursdays? What if we asked the student to tell us about the activity the next day?

Each of these supports could help a student get one step closer to engaging with their peers and discovering a new passion through participation. And each of these supports could be faded or removed easily as the student develops confidence and familiarity with the routine of participation. There are so many small ways we can help eliminate barriers to participation that do not involve additional staffing or any additional cost to the school.

When thinking about additional support for cocurricular activities, the services summary page on the IEP is a good place to start. However, it is also important to *consider the specific needs of the student and the demands of the task*. For example, the accommodations and support that a student needs at an after-school Anime Club may be much different from the support they need to access a writing activity in class.

Some guiding principles to consider when designing supports for cocurricular activities:

- *LRE:* We want students to participate in the most inclusive way possible with their peers without disabilities.

- *Natural supports:* Are there supports in place for all students that could be adjusted to allow access for students with disabilities?

- *Developing independence:* Can we establish support with the intention of phasing it out once students become familiar with the routines and structures of the activity? For example, rather than hiring an extra coach for the entire season to support a student with a wheelchair on the cross-country team, we could provide paraeducator support for the first few weeks of practice to help the student and coaches become familiar with the routines and to ensure that the student can participate safely.

- *Building capacity:* How can we help coaches, general education teachers, principals, and volunteers develop the knowledge and skills to be able to support access for all students to participate in cocurricular activities?

Sometimes a team will consider these factors and determine that a student needs additional support. The bottom line is that resources and materials should not be a barrier to access to participation in cocurricular activities for any student. Principals, coaches, and case managers have found these guidelines to be helpful as they work to promote greater participation in cocurricular activities in the least restrictive way possible. We want to break down barriers and ensure participation while also promoting independence, peer support, and student voice.

> We want to break down barriers and ensure participation while also promoting independence, peer support, and student voice.

PROMOTING STUDENT VOICE IN COCURRICULAR ACTIVITIES

As in so many other areas of effective educational practice, the best way to encourage student participation in cocurricular activities is to ask the student what they want to do. Many students have an interest that connects to activities that already exist in school, like theater, robotics, or the video game club.

Other students may have an interest that could be an inspiration for a new activity. For example, Arturo, a high school student with ASD, was fascinated with dominoes. He would watch YouTube videos of elaborate domino arrangements and even traveled to a nearby convention center to see a famous domino artist perform in person. Arturo's SLP knew his transition goals included building confidence to interact with people in informal, public, social situations. So she partnered with the neighboring elementary school to help him start a Domino Toppling enrichment class.

The elementary school purchased a few boxes of colorful dominoes and hired a paraeducator to supervise the class before school once a week. Arturo designed lessons with the SLP. During the first 10 minutes of the enrichment class, Arturo would demonstrate new techniques for arranging and toppling dominoes. Then he would encourage groups of elementary students to spend the next 45 minutes practicing the new skill as he circulated through the room admiring their creations and providing helpful suggestions.

The class was a hit! The paraeducator and SLP coordinated with Arturo to take the show on the road. At the end of the semester, the Domino Toppling Club took a bus to a local senior living community for a demonstration and participatory activity. With Arturo taking the lead, a group of about 20 elementary school students partnered with seniors to build (and destroy) elaborate, colorful domino creations.

This Domino Toppling Club was a success on so many levels. It helped Arturo develop leadership and social communication skills in conjunction with the post-secondary transition goals on his IEP. It provided a fun opportunity for elementary school students to connect in a creative, tactile experience. It was also a model of an inclusive activity.

Phillip, a student at the elementary school with significant cognitive and functional impairments, was working on IEP goals related to social interactions and fine motor skills. His SLP (who also worked with Arturo) wondered if he could benefit from joining the Domino Toppling Club.

When she asked if Phillip could participate in Domino Toppling, our answer was "Of course!" Then we talked about what supports would be necessary to help him access the activity alongside his peers. We eventually added an additional paraeducator to support the club. But we also emphasized peer support. Phillip enjoyed stacking dominoes in piles. This was not the same task that the other students were doing, but it was a close approximation that allowed him to participate alongside his peers and work on some of his IEP goals. Philip also really enjoyed knocking down dominoes. So his classmates would often let him knock over the first domino to set a chain reaction in motion.

Every school may not have a Domino Toppling Club. But every school can seek out and listen to student voices to help facilitate participation in cocurricular activities for all students.

PARTICIPATION IN COMPETITIVE COCURRICULAR ACTIVITIES

When people hear about creating universal access to cocurricular activities, they may wonder about competitive tryouts. Does this mean the varsity basketball coach needs to accept any player onto the team? Will other athletes be left out because we are making space for students with disabilities on the team?

It is important to make a distinction here between access to participation and legitimate competitive tryouts. For sports that have a limited number of roster spots, we should first ask whether there is a good reason for the limited roster. In some cases the answer is yes. There are only 5 players on the basketball court at a time, and there is an expectation that only the 10–12 best players will make the varsity team. Only a small number of students can participate in varsity basketball. And that is ok—as long as all students have access to tryout and the criteria for selecting the players is the same for students with and without disabilities.

For sports that can accommodate larger rosters, like track, cross-country, and swimming, all students should be able to participate, with appropriate supports and accommodations. For individual sports like tennis, golf, and wrestling, coaches may be able to include a student with significant cognitive or developmental disabilities to participate in daily training and practice. When choosing the top athletes to compete in matches, the coach would base the selection on performance in practice, just as they would for any other member of the team.

In some cases there may be structural barriers that are beyond the school or district level. Our athletic directors and coaches have worked with the Oregon School Activities Association to amend statewide policies to ensure greater access for athletes in competitions. These changes have included increasing the number of wheelchair races in the state track meet and changing the safety requirements for football helmets to allow a student with a visual impairment to play.

This whole book is about *creating inclusive cultures*. In this chapter we have focused on some specific strategies that we have used on our journey toward inclusion over the past eight years, including shifts in rosters, co-teaching practices, and participation in cocurricular activities. We did not make all of these changes at once. But we also didn't hold back when we knew that a current practice was inequitable or exclusionary. True to the spirit of Ready-Fire-Aim, we made some initial plans, then jumped in. We tried some things and learned along the way. We always asked ourselves how our strategies, systems, and practices were helping us become more inclusive as a whole, particularly how they were helping individual students experience a more truly inclusive education. And we continued to tell stories of small successes along the way to reinforce our sense of The Why.

In the next two chapters we will continue to explore how our special education focus areas helped guide our journey toward inclusion, with a focus on *improving instructional practices* and *increasing student voice*.

References

Bay Area Coalition for Equitable Schools. (2003). School Reform Initiative; tool set B: Unpacking adult mindsets. In *The Network for College Success postsecondary success toolkit.* https://ncs.uchicago.edu/sites/ncs.uchicago.edu/files/uploads/NCS_PSToolkit_2_26_18.pdf

Carter, E. W. (2019). Inclusion, friendships, and the power of peers. *Impact, 31*(2), 19–20. https://ici.umn.edu/products/impact/312/Peer-Power/#Peer-Power

Carter, E. W., Asmus, J., Moss, C. K., Biggs, E. E., Bolt, D. M., Born, T. L., Brock, M. E., Cattey, G. N., Chen, R., Cooney, M., Fesperman, E., Hochman, J. M., Huber, H. B., Lequia, J. L., Lyons, G., Moyseenko, K. A., Riesch, L. M., Shaley, R. A., Vincent, L. B., & Weir, K. (2016). Randomized evaluation of peer support arrangements to support the inclusion of high school students with severe disabilities. *Exceptional Children, 82*(2), 209–233. https://doi.org/10.1177/0014402915598780

Centers for Disease Control. (n.d.). *Communicating with and about people with disabilities.* https://www.cdc.gov/ncbddd/disabilityandhealth/materials/factsheets/fs-communicating-with-people.html

Eubanks, E., Parish, R., & Smith, D. (1997). Changing the discourse in schools. In P. Hall (Ed.), *Race, ethnicity, and multiculturalism: Policy and practice* (pp. 151–168). Routledge.

Giangreco, M. (1999). *Flying by the seat of your pants: More absurdities and realities of special education* (K. Ruelle, Illustrator). Peytral.

Im, M. H., Hughes, J. N., Cao, Q., & Kwok, O. (2016). Effects of extracurricular participation during middle school on academic motivation and achievement at grade 9. *American Educational Research Journal, 53*(5), 1343–1375. https://doi.org/10.3102/0002831216667479

Liebowitz, C. (2015, March 20). I am disabled: On identity-first versus people-first language. *The Body Is Not an Apology.* https://thebodyisnotanapology.com/magazine/i-am-disabled-on-identity-first-versus-people-first-language/

Snow, K. (2009). *To ensure inclusion, freedom, and respect for all, it's time to embrace people first language.* http://www.inclusioncollaborative.org/docs/Person-First-Language-Article_Kathie_Snow.pdf

CHAPTER 5

Improving Instructional Practices

One of our three focus areas for the ongoing work of our special education department is *improving instructional practices.* Every school and every district has great teachers. There are innovative and evidence-based instructional practices happening in schools every day. And every good teacher knows that there are still many facets of their instruction that could be improved to meet the needs of all students in their classes.

When we talk about *improving instructional practices*, we are talking about two areas of instruction. Both are critical to student success in inclusive classrooms.

1. Specialized instruction led by the special educator to help students reach their IEP goals

2. Daily instruction led by the general education teacher for all students in the class

And in inclusive classrooms the lines between these two areas begin to blur.

One of the underlying ideas in planning for lessons is UDL (Meyer et al., 2014). The concept of Universal Design originated with architecture and the design of the built environment. Consider the example of the door handle. The traditional round door handle works well for people with typical grasping ability. But for individuals with limited fine motor control in their hands, it may be difficult to wrap their fingers around the door knob, apply the correct amount of pressure, twist the handle to release the latch, and pull the door open. So designers came up with other ways to open doors—including handles that can be twisted or pushed by other body parts, like elbows, arms, or hips. People who previously had to rely on another person to open a door with a traditional round handle can now independently navigate their way through a building.

This kind of design does not change the functionality of the door. It does not make things more difficult for people who were already proficient at opening a traditional door knob. In fact, in some ways the new door handle designs make life easier for all people. For example, a parent who is carrying a child in one arm and a grocery bag in another arm can open a door with their elbow or knee. A teacher carrying an armful of papers to grade can open their classroom door with their arm or hip rather than having to find a place to neatly put down their load each time they come to a door on the way out of the building.

Other common examples of Universal Design in the built environment are ramps or curb cutouts and handles for sink faucets. Ramps and curb cutouts were designed for people who use wheelchairs, but they are commonly used by people with strollers, shopping carts, and rolling suitcases. Sink faucets with long handles allow people to turn on the water with their wrists, without touching the handles with their dirty hands. And it allows them to turn off the water without using their clean hands to touch the handles, which are potentially covered with millions of bacteria.

In all of these cases, the built environment is designed to be accessible to all people. Architects and designers are thinking about accessible design from the beginning, rather than designing a traditional building, door, or sink and then adding a way for a small group of people to access it differently. In the same way, teachers and school leaders should think about designing instruction to maximize accessibility from the start. This concept is called Universal Design for Learning, or UDL. While some students will definitely need specially designed instruction as part of their IEP, the starting point for planning should be how we make the classroom learning experience as accessible as possible to all students.

FRAMEWORKS THAT GUIDE OUR INSTRUCTIONAL PRACTICES

In our district, as in many districts across the country, instruction in the general education classroom is guided by The 5 Dimensions of Teaching and Learning™, a research-based framework created by the Center for Educational Leadership (2012) at the University of Washington. We have been using The 5 Dimensions as a districtwide framework for at least eight years now, and it has become the common language for teachers across the district.

With The 5 Dimensions as a guide, teachers are encouraged to think deeply about (1) Purpose, (2) Student Engagement, (3) Curriculum and Pedagogy, (4) Assessment for Learning, and (5) Classroom Environment and Culture. When teachers are reflecting on their practice within the context of PLCs, they use a series of challenging and insightful guiding questions from The 5 Dimensions.

We made sense of The 5 Dimensions in the context of UDL by thinking about structures and strategies for the All, the Some, and the Few. To be able to make an impact for the Few, we need to have high-quality instruction in place for the All. Many of these concepts are also expressed in our *special education focus areas* framework, particularly in the section dedicated to *improving instructional practices*.

Here are some of the key subtargets from our focus areas related to *improving instructional practices*. The next section will explore these subtargets in greater depth.

- Learning activities and environments are planned with a UDL lens.

- Learning targets are clearly articulated, developed from state standards, relevant, and measurable.

- Students understand what they are learning and why they are learning it, and how they will demonstrate what they have learned.

- Engagement strategies capitalize on students' strengths, maximize student talk, and ensure that all students are active participants in their learning.

- Each student has access to grade-level content, culturally responsive teaching, high-cognitive tasks, opportunities for meaning-making, and explicit instruction in their general education classroom learning community.

- Educators use common and consistent data to create clear through-lines in the present levels, goals, and progress notes, within each IEP and over time for each student.

- Educators collaborate to analyze data about student learning, using a variety of tools and approaches to inform instruction.

- The purpose of evaluation is to support each student to know themself as a learner and to strengthen the circles of support around that student—never to lower expectations or limit possibilities.

- "The 7 Components of Inclusive and Equitable Learning Communities" are evident in all classrooms.

LEARNING TARGETS

Targets from the focus areas:

Learning targets are clearly articulated, developed from state standards, relevant, and measurable.

Students understand what they are learning and why they are learning it, and how they will demonstrate what they have learned.

Identifying clear and precise learning targets for each unit and each lesson is the first step toward effectively engaging all learners. If a teacher can clearly articulate what they want students to learn, they can more effectively design activities with a range of entry points to help all students get there. They can also be more intentional about formative and summative assessment to guide instruction.

Principals and district leaders across Oregon have participated in learning walks organized by the Center for Educational Leadership. During our visits to classrooms, we are encouraged to ask students three simple questions:

1. What are you learning today?

2. Why is it important to learn?

3. How will you know when you've got it?

Students vary in their ability to answer these questions, but there are many classrooms where students are clearly prepared to answer these questions (and not just because the teacher knew a group of administrators was going to visit their classroom that day). A truly purposeful lesson will engage students in their learning by preparing them to recognize the specific skill or concept they are working on, where they stand in relation to the learning target, why it is relevant for them to learn the skill right now and for their future, and how they will be expected to demonstrate their mastery of the skill. It is important to note that very powerful inquiry-based instruction might begin with students exploring a question, rather than stating the learning target to the students at the beginning of the lesson. Teachers, however, need to be clear on the learning target from the start, and then make sure their students are clear on their exploration and learning.

In one fifth-grade classroom that we visited lately, the students were working on a poster to synthesize their ideas and represent their learning. One student brought his poster to the teacher and said, "I'm done." The teacher smiled, raised her eyebrow slightly, and said, "Are you really done?" The student paused, then looked around the room at his classmates and the directions on the board. Then he said, "Oh yeah. I need to check the success criteria." He headed back to his desk, pulled out the assignment sheet, reviewed the learning targets and success criteria, and made revisions to his project before turning it back in.

One middle school language arts and social studies teacher posts daily learning targets on the board with this series of sentence frames: *Today you will be able to . . . so you can . . . You will know you've got it when . . .* This student-friendly language helps the teacher in her planning and helps the students to organize their own learning. (She also had a drawing of a narwhal next to the learning targets, which probably had nothing to do with their daily learning, but her sixth graders love it.)

Once the teacher has clearly identified the learning targets that all students will be aiming toward during a unit and a specific daily lesson, it becomes much easier to think about multiple ways students can access and represent their learning. If we are clear about what we want students to know and be able to do, the classroom teacher and learning specialist can collaborate to identify multiple access points for many students, and the specific access points that may still be necessary for an individual student. Having clarity on what we want students to know and be able to do allows us to plan lessons through a Universal Design lens. By thinking in advance about how we can make the lesson accessible for all students, there is less need for accommodations and modifications after the fact.

For example in an English language arts class, the teacher assigns a three-page essay analyzing the motivations of three peripheral characters in *Romeo and Juliet* and gives the students the choice of writing about Friar Laurence, Tybalt, Mercutio, Prince Escalus, Juliet's father, and Juliet's nurse. If the learning targets are not clear, it may be difficult for the teacher and the learning specialist to know what to expect from a student with a disability that affects writing. Should we expect the same three-page essay as from other students? Should we shorten the assignment and have him write only one page? Should he write about only one character? Should we have him give an oral presentation?

If the teacher has articulated a clear learning target for the assignment, it becomes much easier to differentiate the task—for example, "I can analyze the motivations of a character and support my claims with evidence from the text." If this were the target, the teacher may be able to assess the student's analysis skills through any of the options considered above. However, if the learning target is "I can compare the motivations of multiple characters, using evidence to support my claims," the student could not demonstrate their analysis skills by writing about only one character. If the learning target is "I can use the conventions of standard written English, including effective word choice and sentence fluency, to make a claim and support it with evidence," then we could not have the student give an oral presentation.

A clear learning target opens the door to accommodations that provide meaningful entry points and allow students to access the same content as their peers.

If the student has more significant learning challenges, the learning target can help the team decide how to modify the content in a way that allows the student to continue to engage with their grade-level peers. Continuing with the *Romeo and Juliet* example from above, there is a range of possible modifications depending on the student's level of comprehension and expressive communication. The teacher may ask the student to write a sentence about each of the six characters and describe their relationship to Romeo or Juliet. Or the teacher may provide descriptors of each character and ask the student to match them to the character named. Or if comprehending the story of *Romeo and Juliet* is too difficult, the teacher may ask the student to identify the motivations of characters in a simpler format—perhaps a graphic novel or a simplified pictorial text. Clarity and precision in the original learning target allow the classroom teacher and learning specialist to distill the essential concepts and skills for a broad range of learners.

It is difficult to have truly inclusive learning communities without clarity and precision about what we want all students to learn, how they will demonstrate their learning, and how they will know that they are making progress toward their goals.

Because we start with the assumption that all students can learn, we never want to overscaffold or simplify the task beyond what is necessary for the student to engage with their classmates and continue to make meaningful progress toward their IEP goals. Again, the lens of Universal Design helps the teacher and learning specialist to provide access for all students.

You could argue that learning targets are not explicitly an inclusive practice. It is possible to have high-quality learning targets in a classroom community that remains segregated. This is the reality in many schools across the country. However, it is difficult to have truly inclusive learning communities without clarity and precision about what we want all students to learn, how they will demonstrate their learning, and how they will know that they are making progress toward their goals. For this reason, high-quality learning targets are an important component of inclusive classrooms.

ENGAGEMENT STRATEGIES

Target from the focus areas:

Engagement strategies capitalize on students' strengths, maximize student talk, and ensure that all students are active participants in their learning.

Once we have clearly identified the specific knowledge and skills we want students to learn, the next step is to think about how we will engage all students in meaning-making. One of the most important elements of this is student talk. A common mantra in our district is "The one who is doing the talking is doing the learning."

In most classrooms historically, teacher talk is the dominant form of discourse. The teacher lectures, and the students listen. The teacher asks questions, and the students respond. The teacher gives directions, and the students work quietly on their own tasks. Students who make noise or talk to their classmates are disciplined. The locus of control is squarely on the teacher.

As we learn more about the way the brain seeks out and assimilates new knowledge, we realize that the old teacher-centered model is often not the most effective. Students learn best when they are interested in a topic, have some control over how they encounter new knowledge and what to do with it, ask genuine questions, wrestle with real-world problems, talk to their peers about their formative ideas, contribute ideas to a group, and receive specific timely feedback.

This kind of learning environment is messier than a traditional classroom. Students are usually arranged in groups rather than rows. The teacher still has a critical role to play in helping students construct meaning. But it is more about facilitating the opportunities for students to engage with content and practice skills, rather than explicitly delivering content.

Student talk is a powerful entry point to deeper conceptual learning. For students with limited expressive communication skills, this can be particularly challenging. The role of the SLP becomes critical to collaborate with classroom teachers—providing entry points for all students to express their ideas to their classmates. If the expectation is that all students will be engaging with their learning through talking, we can begin to think about scaffolds and supports that allow students with communication challenges to participate. In Chapter 7 we will talk more about the role of AAC (augmentative and alternative communication) devices in promoting student talk.

> Students learn best when they are interested in a topic, have some control over how they encounter new knowledge and what to do with it, ask genuine questions, wrestle with real-world problems, talk to their peers about their formative ideas, contribute ideas to a group, and receive specific timely feedback.

In a traditional classroom, student talk is usually limited to the responses of a small number of students to teacher-led questions. The teacher asks a question, a few students raise their hands, the teacher calls on one of the eager students, and the class moves on. This kind of questioning rewards students who have relatively fast auditory processing—they hear the question, understand what the teacher wants to hear, retrieve background knowledge from their long-term memory, integrate their current learning, formulate a response, raise their hand, and verbalize their answer.

There may be 15 other students in the classroom who would have arrived at a similar answer and raised their hand, but their processing was just a little slower. There may be another 10 students who would have arrived at the same answer but would never raise their hand because they are unsure of their answer, lack confidence in their language skills, or do not have the social status to speak up in class.

And then there may be five students in the class who could have arrived at the same answer, but they did not understand the question or had gaps in their background knowledge that impeded their ability to formulate an answer.

Using classroom engagement strategies that promote student talk can help create a more accessible classroom environment for all students but particularly for students with disabilities. For example, a teacher could provide a sentence frame for the class to help all students organize their thoughts before responding to a question. This is a classic strategy for students learning English that also benefits students with cognitive-processing challenges.

The sentence frame could be written on the board for all to see. Or it could be on a handout or note card for a few students. If the teacher is having students respond using a personal whiteboard, they could tape the sentence frame to the top of the student's whiteboard. For a student who uses an AAC device the teacher could prepare key vocabulary cards and allow additional wait time so the student has an authentic way to share their ideas with peers.

Some teachers use consistent talk protocols in their classes to help students share their ideas with one another. For example, in a middle school mathematics class, student A reads the question aloud. Student B shares her answer and explains her thinking. Student A restates the argument he heard from student B and asks clarifying questions about her process. Student A then probes with additional questions to help student B determine if her reasoning would be true in all cases or just for this specific problem.

This is a complex process, but with a clear protocol and lots of structured practice and modeling, this kind of engagement strategy has the potential to deeply influence learning. If the one doing the talking is the one doing the learning, then both student A and student B are participating in powerful learning. In the more traditional model of teacher-directed questioning, both student A and student B may have remained silent the whole period while a handful of other students raised their hands and responded to the teacher.

While the students are engaged in this kind of talk protocol, the teacher can circulate through the room listening. Using a technique known as *selecting and sequencing*, the teacher chooses specific students to call on based on the ideas (and misconceptions) that she wants to make sure all students hear. She also chooses the order in which those ideas are presented in the class, intentionally calling on students in a specific sequence. This process of selecting and sequencing can highlight a range of ideas. The teacher can also elevate the status of students who may not raise their hand normally. In particular, if the teacher is not looking for completely formed and totally correct answers, she can draw bits of ideas from various students and weave them into a coherent concept for the class as a whole.

As a result, this method of selecting and sequencing is a powerfully inclusive practice. Students who have significant learning differences can still be recognized for making a contribution to the class.

ROUGH-DRAFT THINKING

One important concept when thinking about promoting engagement through student talk is to encourage "rough-draft thinking" (Jansen et al., 2016–2017).

Students have been taught to believe that there is a single right answer and a single pathway to that answer. In a traditional classroom teachers often communicate that they are expecting one pathway, and students who quickly see that pathway are rewarded with status and attention.

However, the best learning often happens when we allow students to wander around within a messy collection of facts and ideas. They explore and question. They bounce ideas off each other and challenge each other's assumptions and justifications. Each student may have fragments of clarity mixed in with misconceptions. If the teacher can draw out those misconceptions, creating a culture of rough-draft thinking, they can help students develop their half-formed ideas into a more coherent and deeper understanding.

Jansen et al. (2016–2017) point out the importance of promoting rough-draft thinking: "Some students are reluctant to participate in whole-class discussions. But if they do not participate, their peers will not learn from them" (p. 304). They assert that creating a culture of rough-draft talk in the classroom can "foster a culture supportive of intellectual risk-taking, . . . promote the belief that learning . . . involves revising understanding over time, . . . [and] raise students' statuses by expanding on what counts as a valuable contribution" (p. 305).

When a student asks a question or makes an assertion that reveals a misconception, it should be a moment of celebration for the class. Teachers can assume that if one student has a misconception others are probably experiencing the same confusion. By tackling the misconception head on with a spirit of genuine inquiry, the teacher helps students build critical analysis skills. This also reinforces the growth mindset idea that mistakes and misconceptions are necessary for deeper learning (Dweck, 2008).

VISUAL SCAFFOLDS

Another important engagement strategy is the use of instructional scaffolds to provide entry points for a variety of students. For example, students often create posters to demonstrate what they are learning. A simple poster may or may not be a valuable learning activity. The value comes in how the poster is used.

In a science or mathematics class the teacher may have students create posters as visual records to demonstrate their reasoning and justification for how they approach certain complex processes. For example, students may develop posters with multiple representations of the process for dividing fractions. If a student is struggling with remembering the process, they can look to the poster for a reminder. In addition, when the class is working toward developing conceptual understanding on other topics, the teacher can point to this poster and remind the class about how they arrived at their current understanding of dividing fractions. The poster is a scaffold that helps students enter into the task. It also reminds them of their own creativity and resiliency when facing new tasks.

In an English or language arts class, a teacher could have students make posters as they work their way through a class novel. Students can work in groups, generating a list of ideas, justifying their choices, and then drawing a visual draft before completing the final poster. This poster process serves as a formative assessment, allowing the teacher to know how well the students have understood the story up to this point. But more important, it provides scaffolds to support ongoing learning as the class moves into the second half of the book. By having posters on the wall with scenes, symbols, and quotes from the early part of the novel, the teacher and students can regularly refer to foreshadowing events and analyze the significance of events as they echo later in the story.

Of course, literature teachers have always asked students to analyze the effect of foreshadowing. Some students are very good at connecting foreshadowing with later events. Often, these students are confident readers, with a strong memory and well-developed recall skills. They can reach back through their memory of the book and even picture the place on the page where the scene took place. They can draw on those recollections to move easily into analysis.

But for students who struggle with recall skills, this task becomes much more challenging. If the purpose of the task (the learning target) is for students to demonstrate their analysis skills, then recalling details from earlier in the book becomes a barrier. By providing visual reminders about significant early events in the story (the posters created by students), the teacher allows each student to have an entry point to the task of analyzing the effect of foreshadowing.

As an engagement strategy, visual scaffolds promote access in an inclusive classroom. They lighten the cognitive load, allowing students to focus on the specific high-cognitive task (analysis) without being burdened or derailed by the lower-cognitive process (factual recall).

ALTERNATE QUESTIONING STRATEGIES

Another way to create entry points for a diverse range of students while increasing rigor is to vary the way we ask questions. For example, a common task in a mathematics lesson about subtraction may be something like $846 - 379 =$ _____. There is one clear answer to this question and a relatively limited number of pathways to get there. There is not a lot of room for meaningful student discourse. A student who is strong in mathematics will not have much to learn in this example from partnering with a student who struggles with mathematical concepts. Another way the teacher could create a problem like this would be to ask students to use all of the digits between 1 and 9 to create a correct mathematical sentence (Kaplinsky, 2019).

This is a much more rigorous task, but it can be scaffolded or supported in various ways. First, this kind of problem benefits from student discourse.

Because this problem requires more complex reasoning than simply applying an algorithm, the teacher can encourage students to talk with one another. Intentional student grouping and clear talk protocols can be very effective here. For example, a student who struggles with mathematical computation can still help select the numbers that the team starts with. The teacher or a paraeducator can help frame the conversation with guiding questions about the size of the numbers (Which number in a subtraction number sentence should be the largest: left, middle, or right?).

A second way to scaffold this activity (using all digits between 1 and 9 to create a correct mathematical sentence) would be for the teacher to provide some numbers in the number sentence already filled in. Like the difficulty levels of a sudoku puzzle, the specific arrangement of prefilled numbers can allow for a range of difficulties while still allowing a student to engage in the same task as their peers. For example, $8\_ - 5\_ = 2\_$ is an easier task than $\_3\_ - \_8\_ = \_1\_$. And $83\_ - 59\_ = 24\_$ is a much easier sentence to complete (essentially, it is $7 - 6 = 1$). The teacher could also provide a number line and blocks for students to cover up the numbers they have used.

This kind of activity increases rigor for all students, promotes meaningful mathematical discourse, allows for a range of access points, and values analysis and depth of thinking over speedy recall or rote adherence to algorithms. By designing instruction like this, teachers can create a classroom culture that promotes inclusion and improves learning outcomes for all students.

This kind of activity increases rigor for all students, promotes meaningful mathematical discourse, allows for a range of access points, and values analysis and depth of thinking over speedy recall or rote adherence to algorithms. By designing instruction like this, teachers can create a classroom culture that promotes inclusion and improves learning outcomes for all students.

ACCESS TO GRADE-LEVEL CONTENT

Target from the focus areas:

Each student has access to grade-level content, culturally responsive teaching, high-cognitive tasks, opportunities for meaning-making, and explicit instruction in their general education classroom learning community.

For powerful engagement strategies (e.g., talk protocols and selecting and sequencing) to be truly effective inclusive practices, they need to be in support of rich, complex, and culturally relevant curriculum. Students are not going to engage in rich dialogue, making claims and supporting them with evidence and analysis, if the content is dull, unambiguous, or irrelevant.

In previous versions of our special education focus areas, one of our targets was "Instructional materials, tasks, and tools are age appropriate, challenging, and culturally and academically relevant." Our special education department specifically articulated this statement because we recognized that teachers and students experience greater success in inclusive classrooms if the materials, tasks, and tools are rich, complex, and relevant. High-quality instructional materials inspire worthy tasks and greater student engagement. This is, of course, not a statement that is unique to the world of special education. It should be a target for all instructional materials in all courses.

MAKING SENSE OF CONSTRUCTIVISM AND DIRECT INSTRUCTION

Another of the targets in our special education focus areas is "In their general education classroom learning community, each child has access to grade-level content, high-cognitive tasks, opportunities for meaning-making, and explicit instruction." This statement brings together two traditions of teaching and learning: constructivism and direct instruction.

In our district we have a long-standing commitment to constructivist pedagogy. We believe that students learn best when they are able to make meaning, individually and in small groups, by wrestling with complex concepts. For example, in mathematics classes teachers do not simply show students the formula and have them practice it over and over. Instead, teachers pose questions and provide tasks that lead students to form conjectures and make sense of the underlying mathematical concepts. Eventually, they will learn the algorithms and practice them, but the emphasis is on meaning-making and conceptual understanding.

In special education we recognize that some students may experience barriers that interfere with their ability to engage in this constructivist pathway to knowledge. This doesn't mean that students with disabilities cannot develop deep conceptual understanding or that they should only be taught in a separate setting where the instruction is strictly direct and explicit. However, we recognize that some students will need much more explicit support to help them develop that deeper knowledge.

As a result, for a student to benefit from engagement in a constructivist mathematics lesson, they may need to experience explicit preteaching of vocabulary, concepts, or operations. For some students this preteaching serves to prepare them to participate in the kind of talk protocols we mentioned in the previous section.

Direct instruction has been the bedrock of special education. We value the role of task analysis, explicit modeling, and clear feedback for students. Often, this may be part of preparing students to participate in an inquiry-based lesson in the general education classroom. Other times, we apply direct instruction to some of the activities within the lesson. What is important is that we are open to adjusting our methodologies to what each individual student needs and that our use of these methodologies is in service of the student accessing general education as inclusively as possible. To frame this another way, "Don't be an *ist*! Adapt the strategies to what that student needs, while always working toward the general education setting."

Common and Consistent Data

Target from the focus areas:

Educators use common and consistent data to create clear throughlines in the present levels, goals, and progress notes, within each IEP and over time for each student.

Earlier in this chapter we talked about the three questions that school leaders ask students during learning walks:

1. What are you learning today?
2. Why is it important to learn?
3. How will you know when you've got it?

These are critical questions for teachers to be asking themselves as well. The first two questions are about identifying the purpose of a lesson or learning task. The third is about assessing whether students are making progress toward the learning targets.

Special educators have been doing this for years. IEP goals are written with specific, measurable outcomes. Learning specialists gather data about student progress toward those goals, then write periodic progress notes to update parents and students.

In our special education focus areas we emphasize the quality of the data: "Educators use common and consistent data to create clear throughlines in the present levels, goals, and progress notes, within each IEP and over time for each student." If we are going to make statements about student growth, and make future plans based on that growth, we need to ensure that the data are reliable and relevant.

This emphasis on quality assessment is particularly important for general education teachers in an inclusive setting. In a traditional (and outdated) model of education the teacher says, "I taught it. It's up to the student to learn it." Now teachers are realizing that students bring a vast range of background knowledge, academic skills, and language proficiency to their classroom. Teachers are not only responsible for teaching, they are also responsible for student learning. As teachers make this shift, it is essential for principals and district leaders to support them.

If teachers want to know what students are really learning, they need to have a toolbox of formative assessment techniques, ranging from informal measures like reading the student's tone of voice and body language to more formal measures like exit tickets, homework, and quizzes. There is a vast collection of resources about assessment for learning that are beyond the scope of this book. (Rick Stiggins and Jan Chappius would be a good place to start for more information about assessment for learning.)

For students to experience success in an inclusive setting, teachers need to know what students can do at the start and how they are improving over time.

The bottom line is that for students to experience success in an inclusive setting, teachers need to know what students can do at the start and how they are improving over time. By evaluating how students are responding to instruction, the teacher can refine their engagement strategies to help keep students on track.

ANALYZING DATA TO INFORM INSTRUCTION

Target from the focus areas:

Educators collaborate to analyze data about student learning, using a variety of tools and approaches to inform instruction.

Another target in our focus areas says, "Educators collaborate to analyze data about student learning, using a variety of tools and approaches to inform instruction." There are three key elements of this target:

1. Collaboration

2. Variety of tools

3. Informing instruction

Assessment provides the opportunity for meaningful collaboration between special educators and their general education colleagues. Special educators have access to specific assessment tools and have expertise in access strategies. General educators spend large amounts of time with students in an inclusive setting and have the opportunity to gather data frequently over multiple days. This shared role in gathering data can spill over into collaboratively analyzing the data and planning for future instruction.

In one of our middle school language arts classrooms a learning specialist was struggling with how she could gather the curriculum-based measurement data that she needed to report progress on IEP goals. In the past the learning specialist had worked with most of the students on her caseload in a separate Reading Lab period of the day. Now the learning specialist was coplanning and co-teaching with the language arts teacher to provide support to students in a more inclusive way. The learning specialist shared her concern with the language arts teacher, and they decided to give the quick-reading assessment to the whole class and review the scores together. When they analyzed the data together, they discovered that a number of students were having challenges with reading fluency and accuracy—not just the students served by IEPs. These two co-teachers then added some short fluency-building activities into the stations that the class did on Tuesdays and Thursdays. All the students were able to build more skills. Also, both teachers gained a deeper understanding of the entire class, and approaching this as a shared project deepened their collaboration for the future.

It is important to ensure that we are considering multiple measures of student learning. We should be very cautious of a single data point driving major decisions about a student's educational experience.

Beware that the necessity for multiple sources of data can sometimes be used as an argument against inclusion. If a student has been in a segregated self-contained setting, it is often difficult to find data that show that they can be safe or learn successfully in an inclusive setting. This comes back to the "burden of proof" argument. Our starting assumption is that students belong in an inclusive setting, and the burden of proof is on the data to show that a student needs a more restrictive environment, rather than the prevailing assumption that a student can't be included until they prove they can. This influences the way we think about collecting data.

For example, we had a parent request that a paraeducator shadow her seventh-grade daughter, Ripley, on a field trip to the Portland Art Museum. She was concerned that Ripley would run away into the busy downtown streets unless she had an adult holding her hand.

We could not produce evidence that showed that Ripley had safely navigated a field trip to downtown Portland without one-on-one adult support, because in her previous school district she was in a segregated classroom and had never been allowed the opportunity for a typical field trip experience. This is, of course, a circular argument based on the starting assumption that she lacks the skills to make safe choices in public. So we thought about what evidence we could gather that would approximate the context of the field trip. We asked the learning specialist and other school staff to gather data about her ability to make safe choices in unstructured settings around school: recess, lunchtime, passing times, pick-up and drop-off times, and so on.

Did Ripley wait on the sidewalk for the school bus without running away? Did she respond safely when given directions from an adult at recess? Was she able to safely and independently navigate the middle school hallways when moving from class to class? In this case the data showed that Ripley was able to do all of these things safely on a regular basis with relatively minimal prompting.

So we chose not to send an extra adult to provide one-on-one support for Ripley on the field trip. The classroom teacher arranged all students in small groups to keep track of one another on the trip. She selected conscientious students to partner with Ripley (and emphasized Ripley's responsibility to look after her friends too). The learning specialist also provided a social story about expected behavior on a field trip, including how to walk on a sidewalk and photos of street scenes in downtown Portland near the museum. During the trip the teacher checked in with Ripley and her group occasionally to monitor her state of social-emotional regulation.

In the end, Ripley was able to participate on the field trip in a way that was very similar to how her classmates participated. She was able to build social relationships with the other girls in her group, and she was able to develop a degree of confidence in her functional independence to navigate city streets like a typical 13-year-old. This was all possible because of a creative use of assessments to help the school team think about her safety and independence in a new way.

PURPOSE OF EVALUATION

Target from the focus areas:

The purpose of evaluation is to support each student to know themselves as a learner and to strengthen the circles of support around that student—never to lower expectations or limit possibilities.

Another important aspect of assessment in the world of special education is the evaluation process for determining special education eligibility. Much has been written about the tools and philosophies for determining eligibility (National Association of School Psychologists, 2019). In our district, we often have conversations about the difference between students who struggle in school and students who have a disability. There are many reasons why a student may experience challenges in school, including second language acquisition, acculturation, high mobility, lack of exposure to rich literacy, previous experiences of failure, fixed mindsets, absence of culturally relevant curriculum, ineffective instruction and engagement strategies, punitive discipline practices, socioeconomic factors, persistent hunger, lack of sleep, previous experience of trauma, and social-emotional instability. None of these factors should be considered "disabilities."

When we evaluate a student for a disability, we are careful to consider this broad array of other factors that may be affecting their learning. We are aware of the complex, and often intertwined, layers of a student's learning profile. The evaluation helps the team determine whether the student qualifies for special education.

However, as a district we want to think about evaluation in a more holistic way. According to our focus areas, "the purpose of evaluation is to support each student to know themself as a learner and to strengthen the circles of support around that student—never to lower expectations or limit possibilities."

This means we seek ways to include the student's voice in the evaluation process and in the interpretation of the data. A school psychologist might say to a student, "The tests show that you struggle with fluid reasoning. That means you may have a hard time keeping one idea in your head when you are working with another idea. And combining those two ideas can be hard too. What does that look like in class for you?" The student can identify specific occasions when they have experienced that struggle. And then the team can come up with skill-building strategies to help the student capitalize on strengths and navigate barriers.

By focusing on student voice, self-awareness, and circles of support, special education services can truly become individualized and empowering for the student, rather than a label or stigma that separates the student from their classmates and perpetuates cycles of failure.

References

Center for Educational Leadership. (2012). *The 5 Dimensions of Teaching and Learning.* University of Washington.

Dweck, C. S. (2008). *Mindset: The new psychology of success.* Ballantine Books.

Jansen, A., Cooper, B., Vascellaro, S., & Wandless, P. (2016–2017). Rough-draft talk in mathematics classrooms. *Mathematics Teaching in the Middle School, 22*(5), 304–307. https://doi.org/10.5951/mathteacmiddscho.22.5.0304

Kaplinsky, R. (2019, December 26). *Getting to the heart of what students know in math.* Edutopia. https://www.edutopia.org/article/getting-heart-what-students-know-math

Meyer, A., Rose, D. H., & Gordon, D. (2014). *Universal Design for Learning: Theory and practice.* CAST Professional.

National Association of School Psychologists. (2019). *SLD eligibility: Policy and practice recommendations.* https://www.nasponline.org/resources-and-publications/resources-and-podcasts/special-education/sld-eligibility-policy-and-practice-reccomendations

CHAPTER 6

The Components of Inclusive and Equitable Learning Communities

In addition to the elements of high-quality instruction and assessment described earlier in this book, there are certain components of school and classroom culture that can have a profound impact on a student's ability to engage in rich learning opportunities. In our district this has been a significant emphasis of our professional learning over the past few years. We developed this concept into a framework of high-leverage practices that we call "The 7 Components of Inclusive and Equitable Learning Communities." The 7 Components are a compilation of research-based best practices. They are drawn broadly from the work of Zaretta Hammond, the International Institute of Restorative Practices, CAST/UDL, CASEL (Collaborative for Academic, Social and Emotional Learning), Positive Behavior Interventions and Supports (PBIS), and the CEL.

The 7 Components are fundamental to creating classrooms where all students experience a sense of belonging and make a true contribution to the learning community. The 7 Components describe *what we should attend to* in creating classrooms and schools where all students succeed. School and district leaders who are committed to inclusive practices should engage their general education teams in exploring The 7 Components. It was important for us, as a constructivist district, to create our own framework. You may want to as well.

The 7 Components are as follows (see Figure 6.1):

1. Effective physical spaces

2. Teaching common expectations

FIGURE 6.1   The "7 Components" Circles

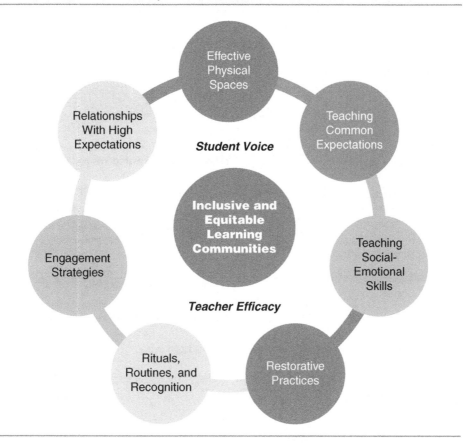

SOURCE: Used with Permission from West Linn-Wilsonville School District.

3. Teaching social-emotional skills

4. Engagement strategies

5. Rituals, routines, and recognition

6. Relationships with high expectations

7. Restorative practices

EFFECTIVE PHYSICAL SPACES

The starting point for any inclusive experience is that the classroom is set up to welcome all students and meet their needs. These needs include a physical space for every student in the class as well as structures to support learning and social-emotional and sensory regulation. As with all of The 7 Components, maintaining effective classroom spaces is about making the classroom a place where *all* students experience success (Table 6.1). These elements are particularly essential for students with more complex learning needs.

TABLE 6.1 "The 7 Components of Inclusive and Equitable Learning Communities": Effective Physical Spaces

EFFECTIVE PHYSICAL SPACES	
TARGETS	**GUIDING QUESTIONS**
• The physical arrangement of the room is welcoming and conducive to positive peer interactions and student learning.	• How does the physical arrangement of the classroom welcome students and promote positive peer interactions?
• School staff work proactively to eliminate barriers to access, using a lens of Universal Design.	• How do elements of Universal Design contribute to access for all students?
• Physical spaces help students maintain social-emotional and sensory regulation.	• How do students use physical space to maintain social-emotional and sensory regulation?
• When students walk into the classroom, they want to stay.	• How is student voice evident in the physical arrangement of the classroom?
	• How do materials and resources reflect diverse cultures and experiences?

SOURCE: Used with Permission from West Linn-Wilsonville School District.

PHYSICAL ARRANGEMENT

Target from The 7 Components:

The physical arrangement of the room is welcoming and conducive to positive peer interactions and student learning.

Many American public school systems were established in the early 20th century, when order and productivity were foundational values. Schools and classrooms were configured to maximize efficiency. Schools were built like factories, with long, straight hallways and bells to regulate production. In the classrooms desks were arranged in rows. Students were assigned seats in ways that served the teacher's needs—in alphabetical order to streamline taking roll or sometimes the best students sitting in the front of the class, with struggling students relegated to the back row.

The legacy of these practices lives on in schools across the country. The architecture of new school design has changed over the past 25 years, moving away from the factory design to include more flexible and collaborative work spaces. But many schools still retain the factory design as their basic structure. Of course, teachers and school leaders have very little control over the architecture of their buildings. However, we can control how we arrange our classrooms to be welcoming and interactive learning environments.

When teachers think about classroom design, they should begin by asking themselves two questions:

1. How does the physical arrangement of my classroom welcome students and promote positive peer interactions?
2. How does the arrangement of my classroom facilitate the engagement strategies I want to use for all students (with an emphasis on student talk and locus of control)?

There is no single answer to those questions. The answers will depend on the age of the students and the subject of the class, as well as the complex learning needs of specific students in the room. And, of course, the arrangement of the room can vary based on the lesson. Some tasks are best for individuals; others need pairs or small groups. Some tasks need large open spaces in the center of the room, while others may need students to have access to the whiteboards or bulletin boards on the walls. The key is to be reflective and intentional about the physical arrangement of the classroom.

ELIMINATING BARRIERS

Target from The 7 Components:

School staff work proactively to eliminate barriers to access, using a lens of Universal Design.

The passage of the ADA in 1990 radically changed the landscape of education in American schools for students with limited physical mobility. Students who use a wheelchair are guaranteed access to their classrooms. But it can still be a significant challenge to navigate a school building. And for other students with less visible disabilities, the barriers may be less obvious.

To live out the challenge of creating accessible learning spaces for all students, school leaders need to think with a UDL lens (Meyer et al., 2014). For example, many middle and high schools have desks that are attached to chairs. These standardized seats may have been efficient when the primary lens of classroom design was the factory model. But through a UDL lens, they can be quite restrictive. A student who uses a wheelchair cannot utilize one of these desks. So a teacher needs to find a different desk for that student, which often relegates that student to the back or a corner of the room. When the class changes desk configurations for a group activity, the student in a wheelchair may have limited options because they only have one desk that fits. The student in a wheelchair is present in the classroom but may not be truly included.

While the most visible example of this limitation is the student in a wheelchair, the attached chair-desk can also present barriers for other students. The desks tend to be built with an armrest on the right side, which makes it more difficult for left-handed students to use. In addition, these attached desks can be very uncomfortable for larger students. It can be difficult to sit comfortably when the chair is a fixed distance from the desk, and it can even be humiliating for a student who gets stuck in the desk.

Now it is common in our classrooms to see students sitting on yoga balls, perched on wiggle stools, or using standing desks. The variety of seating options supports academic engagement. Thinking with a Universal Design lens transforms the physical space to be more inclusive for all students. Or in other words, the elements that make the classroom more accessible for the few also make it better for the whole class.

This is the case for sensory awareness in the classroom as well. Supports that are necessary for a specific student to maintain sensory regulation may be beneficial for a broad range of students.

SPACES TO SUPPORT REGULATION

Target from The 7 Components:

Physical spaces help students maintain social-emotional and sensory regulation.

Traditionally, a student who is having a difficult time managing their behavior or emotions will be sent out of the class, to the counselor or principal or maybe to a behavior support classroom or sensory regulation room. These exit strategies may work for some students in some situations, but they all have one thing in common: the student is no longer in the classroom, exposed to high-quality instruction with their peers.

In some cases, if the student poses an imminent danger to themselves, other students, or adults in the classroom, it may be necessary to move them to another space. But in many cases it may be possible to avoid large-scale escalations by providing the student an opportunity to engage in self-regulation practices. An effective classroom includes physical spaces that help students maintain social-emotional and sensory regulation.

These regulation spaces may look different at different grade levels, but they can be beneficial for all students. We have seen examples of highly effective calming spaces in kindergarten, upper elementary, middle school, and high school classrooms.

Some common features of regulation spaces are as follows:

- *Visual cues to remind students what to do:* When students are in an escalated emotional state, they often do not respond well to verbal prompts.

- *Tactile objects or fidgets:* Having something to occupy the hands can help students to regulate their senses and emotions.

- *Comfortable seating or pillows:* A break space should be inviting, so it may be helpful to have a comfortable place to sit.

- *Soft lighting or calming visual effects:* Watching an egg timer, a lava lamp, or the sand in an hourglass can help students de-escalate.

- *Olfactory stimulation:* Pleasant smells can help some students relax. However, the sense of smell is incredibly powerful and can elicit deep emotional associations, so it is important to closely monitor how students respond to fragrances in the classroom. Also, some schools or districts may have policies that prohibit fragrances (especially open-flame candles and incense), so be sure that classroom practices are in line with your district's safety protocols.

- *Timer:* Many students lose track of time when they are escalated and then when they are recovering from dysregulation. A timer can help the student monitor their break and reenter the class when they have returned to a productive emotional state.

- *Art materials:* Drawing, coloring, or working with modeling clay can be deeply soothing for students at all grade levels.

- *Breathing exercises:* Focusing on deliberate breathing patterns can help students calm down. Some classrooms use strategies like figure-eight breathing to help students practice taking and holding deep breaths.

- *Energizing or calming physical activity:* Depending on the student's sensory needs, activities like yoga, stretching, or jumping jacks can be helpful. These activities can also be distracting to classmates, so teachers should be thoughtful about the location of the calming space in the classroom.

This list is not exhaustive. And it may even appear a bit contradictory. It is important for teachers to set up regulation spaces in the classroom to reflect the specific needs of the students in the room. If a student has a tendency to tear up paper when they are escalated, it may be better to have robust rubber fidgets in the break space rather than sheets of paper for coloring. If a student has a propensity to fall asleep in the break space, it may be better to remove the pillows and provide more active objects, like a balance board or stretch bands for heavy muscle work. If a student gets frustrated when they cannot complete a task, it may be best to have simpler coloring sheets, which they can complete in one brief calming break, rather than elaborately detailed coloring sheets, which may require hours of meticulous work to complete.

Another key to effective break spaces is to explicitly teach acceptable break behavior:

- Does the teacher want students to give a signal and receive permission before using the break space?

- How many students can use the calming space at the same time (we generally recommend one at a time so it does not become a social space)?

- Is there a visual timer so the student knows when their break is over?

- Are students expected to straighten up the break space before they return to their seat?

- How are students expected to reenter learning? Can they ask a friend what to do when they return to their desk?

Teaching expected break behaviors happens when students are in a calm emotional state. It is not advisable to try to teach a break strategy while a student is escalated.

One technique that can be effective for teaching break behaviors is video modeling. A teacher or learning specialist can film a student or an adult engaging in expected break behaviors. They can then show the video to the whole class when they introduce the break space. This normalizes the break space as an acceptable part of any student's classroom experience. If there is a specific student who needs more intensive practice with their regulation skills, it may be helpful to show them the video individually at the start of class or as their first step when they visit the break space.

At some point later in the class period, it may be helpful to debrief with the student after they have taken a calming break to help them take ownership of their choices. What was helpful to them? How did they feel before and after the break? What regulation strategies will they continue to practice throughout the day (even when they are not in the calming space)?

Calming spaces should be available in every classroom and adapted to the age level and context. For example, you might see a couch with a basket of fidgets in a high school classroom. In a kindergarten classroom it may be a corner with a bean bag, posters about deep breathing, a small whiteboard, and a timer. We have found that when teachers understand how a space within their classroom can be successfully used by students to regulate emotions and avoid escalations, they get excited about creating these spaces.

Thinking through the lens of All-Some-Few, these classroom calming spaces are available to all students. We know some students will use them and experience great benefits. We also know that a few students will need additional options for sensory or social-emotional regulation. So we need to consider other spaces in the building that could be effectively used to support regulation. Here again, it is important to think creatively and pay attention to individual student needs. Libraries are often calming spaces in schools, so for some students a prearranged time in the library can support their emotional regulation. Carrying heavy books or reams of paper can provide necessary sensory input. For others, having the opportunity for movement breaks may be key—so perhaps running laps in the gym or on the track between classes would be an effective use of existing spaces for those students' needs.

One alternative that several of our schools are exploring is the Wellness Room. Some of our partner school districts have seen great success with Wellness Rooms, and we have learned from their structures and strategies (see Chapter 9 for more about our partnerships with local districts). These are dedicated spaces for students to learn about and support their emotional regulation. Importantly, Wellness Rooms are generally for proactive prescheduled visits, not for students who are experiencing an intense behavioral escalation. Any student can sign up for an appointment in the Wellness Room (not just students with disabilities). The rooms contain a variety of stations that support sensory and emotional regulation in different ways (calming light displays, books in a tent, a soft meditation audio, guided stretching routines, etc.). Students also learn about brain and body chemistry and why an activity helps to reset and regulate their emotional state. We have observed Wellness Rooms used with great success as a way to de-stigmatize and normalize proactive mental health care at the elementary, middle, and high school levels.

WARM AND INVITING CLASSROOMS

Target from The 7 Components:

When students walk into the classroom, they want to stay.

We have all been in classrooms that are warm and inviting. The physical arrangement of the room and the messages on the walls communicate a sense of joy and belonging. We want to stay in these classrooms and meet the teacher and students. We are naturally inclined toward joining the classroom community.

And we have all experienced classrooms that feel sterile and uninviting. Maybe the desks are in long, straight rows and it is difficult to navigate to desks at the back of the room. The walls are blank, or the room feels messy, overcluttered, and chaotic. When we enter these rooms, we feel like our presence is undervalued. There is no personality to the room and no sense that a community of learners belongs there.

As leaders, this is a delicate subject. We do not want to convey an expectation that teachers go out and buy all kinds of fancy decorations and furniture for their classroom. When teachers are thinking about how they should manage their time, we want them to prioritize coplanning with colleagues, designing engaging tasks that have a variety of entry points for a range of learners, providing specific and meaningful feedback, and fostering relationships with students. Making the classroom look pretty is not their highest priority. It is not about winning "likes" on Pinterest. However, the physical space of a classroom conveys a teacher's beliefs about the value of each child in the room. What message do we want to send to our students?

Teachers come to the profession with a range of skills in this area. Some are naturally inclined to creating an atmosphere that is warm and nurturing. Others do not have an eye for design. This is not an excuse for leaders to allow some classrooms to be more inviting and others to be austere and cold.

Changing the arrangement of desks in a classroom can feel like a massive paradigm shift for teachers, especially in middle and high school. It may encourage them to reflect on the balance of student talk versus teacher talk. It may lead to redesigning learning tasks to incorporate more peer-facilitated learning. And it may shift the overall locus of control in the classroom. These are all changes that can have a positive impact on inclusive cultures as well as academic achievement. But they can also be very difficult for a teacher who is used to being the sage on a stage.

In our experience as administrators we have found teachers very willing to rearrange their classrooms and create visuals that clarify systems and promote community. But they sometimes need a nudge from someone who can help them think through the process. And they need permission to take risks and start with baby steps.

Visiting their colleagues' classrooms can be a great way to help teachers think about different ways to organize their own classroom. In this process, as with any learning walk, it is useful to have a framework or specific questions to guide the observations so they come away with something more substantive than "This classroom is pretty" or "Wow, she's so organized." We would use "The 7 Components of Inclusive and Equitable Learning Communities" so we have a common lens. This helps teachers connect the *physical spaces* they see in their colleagues' classrooms to the *specific learning outcomes* they want for their own students.

Another leadership move is to actually get into the classroom with the teacher and help move the desks around. We have known teachers who said that they wanted to change things up but didn't know what it would look like and didn't have the energy to scramble the desks around until they found the right configuration. When principals or assistant principals offer to come in and do the physical labor with a teacher, it goes a long way toward empowering the teacher and creating a sense of common commitment. Recruiting a learning specialist, occupational therapist, or physical therapist to help out with redesigning the classroom can also bring an important lens about physical access and sensory needs. And it may promote partnerships that will spill over into coplanning or co-teaching opportunities.

Teaching Common Expectations

As a society, we often assume that people know the right thing to do—and that some people just choose not to do it. While that may be true in a broad sense (we know right vs. wrong), we often forget that specific behavioral expectations are often very context dependent. The way we behave in the bleachers at a football game is different from the way we behave at a memorial service. The formal language we use in a job interview is different from the language we use when hanging out with friends.

The context determines the acceptable range of behaviors and language. And that context is socially constructed. There are unwritten rules that most people learn through observing their parents and peers. Some of our rules are explicitly taught, like appropriate behavior at the dining room table. And like anything else that is taught, some people need extra instruction and extra practice to learn these social expectations.

The same is true in the classroom. Students learn when to sit, when to line up, when to raise their hand, when to talk, and when to listen. Mostly, they learn these things through a combination of direct instruction and peer modeling. Many teachers—especially in upper elementary, middle, and high school—assume that students already know how to participate appropriately in class. But in reality many students have not yet mastered those skills. And in some cases they genuinely don't know the teacher's expectations. This is particularly common in middle and high school, where a student may spend their day traveling between classrooms where teachers have widely varying expectations for classroom behavior.

IDENTIFYING COMMON EXPECTATIONS

Target from The 7 Components:

Teachers have prepared in advance to identify schoolwide and classroom expectations for all students.

To effectively teach common expectations (Table 6.2) requires that we plan in advance to know what we are actually expecting students to do. Just like effective teaching in any subject area, teachers identify what skills they want students to

TABLE 6.2 "The 7 Components of Inclusive and Equitable Learning Communities": Teaching Common Expectations

TEACHING COMMON EXPECTATIONS	
TARGETS	GUIDING QUESTIONS
• Teachers have prepared in advance to identify schoolwide and classroom expectations for all students.	• What are the schoolwide processes for collaboratively identifying common classroom expectations, including student voice?
• Students know the common expectations through models/examples of positive classroom behavior.	• How are students introduced to high-quality examples of expected classroom behavior?
• Common expectations are taught at the beginning of the year and reviewed throughout the year.	• How often and in what context do teachers review common expectations throughout the year?

SOURCE: Used with Permission from West Linn-Wilsonville School District.

demonstrate and how we want to teach them those skills. Individual classroom teachers can do this on their own. However, schoolwide expectations can provide consistency.

Many students can adapt to different expectations in different classrooms and with different teachers. However, in trying to create inclusive schools, we know that there are students for whom a change in expectations can absolutely make school more difficult for them. Whether one is thinking through a trauma-informed lens, a culturally responsive teaching lens, or a positive behavior support lens, maintaining a few common and positively stated expectations is absolutely key.

For example, in some high school classes, the teacher may allow students to eat a snack if they are hungry. Their guideline is if you are too hungry to focus, eat something. If the food becomes a distraction that keeps you (or your classmates) from being able to focus, put the food away. But in another classroom down the hall students might get a detention if they try to sneak a snack during class. Without common schoolwide expectations, this could become confusing for kids and even divisive for staff.

Of course, we want to be intentional about how we approach the process of establishing schoolwide common expectations. Teachers will come into the conversation with widely varying perceptions of appropriate behavior, influenced by their own cultural, professional, and personal experiences and biases. For example, some teachers may perceive that it is disrespectful for students to wear hats in class. Others may not have a strong feeling about students wearing hats or may advocate for cultural differences that hats may represent to students.

A few years ago our middle school teachers tackled the question of cell phones collaboratively. There had been no common expectations about phones in the classroom, which was confusing for the students and frustrating for the teachers. More important, cell phone use had become a real distraction to learning for these very social middle school students. Teachers and administrators across our four middle schools agreed that we needed clear, consistent, common expectations to promote a positive learning environment. The staff created a common "off and away" expectation. Then they designed a common communication and teaching plan, positive ways to recognize students for following the expectation, and a clear response plan with parents and administrators if the expectation was not followed. This was a win for common expectations across classrooms and school buildings.

Leaders also need to be thoughtful about how they spend precious staff collaborative time. We witnessed a cautionary tale in a different district in the early 2000s. A committee of students and staff spent the first half of the school year drafting a schoolwide policy for the use of iPods. Then the full staff weighed in. During several hours of heated staff meetings over the last half of the school year, student iPod use dominated all other topics. Policies and procedures for responding to student use of technology became the primary topic of staff meetings, supplanting conversations about proficiency-based instruction and assessment, language-rich instruction, co-teaching structures, and other topics that the staff had hoped to dedicate their professional resources to learning about. Dedicating the bulk of staff collaborative time to negotiating school rules did not result in significant improvements in instruction and student achievement.

We bring this up as a cautionary tale about establishing common schoolwide expectations. School leaders need to identify core principles and beliefs about student learning behaviors that allow teachers to design clear student expectations. Leaders should consult with staff to identify tight/loose expectations. The core principles are tight, and we can expect that all teachers will hold these expectations for their students. Other principles may be held more loosely, allowing teachers to establish expectations that align with their personal style and the culture of their classroom. The key is to be clear about not just which principles are tight or loose but also what the *underlying beliefs* about students and community are that guide the selection of these core principles.

MODELS OF POSITIVE BEHAVIOR

Target from The 7 Components:

Students know common expectations through models/examples of positive classroom behavior.

When a student is demonstrating a behavior that is unexpected, disruptive, or unsafe, our first response is often to tell them not to do that behavior. While it is important to identify and stop inappropriate behaviors, it is more important for students to know what to do instead. Students learn from specific examples or models of positive behavior. If we demonstrate what we want to see students do in our classrooms, they are more likely to be able to replicate that behavior. Teachers can also seek ways to acknowledge, reinforce, and celebrate students' demonstration of expected behaviors. We will talk more about that when we discuss the next component (rituals, routines, and recognition).

One very effective tool for sharing examples of positive classroom behavior is video modeling (Merrill & Risch, 2014). A teacher can film themself performing the expected behavior (or possibly a group of students performing the behavior). Then, students can watch the video before engaging in a task that might prompt dysregulated or unexpected behaviors. If there is one particular student who is struggling with expected classroom behaviors, the teacher or learning specialist can film multiple takes of that student attempting the routine. Then they can edit out "errors" and splice together a final cut that shows the student successfully completing the routine in a way that approximates the classroom expectations. When the student watches the video, they see themself performing the behavior in a positive and productive way.

TEACH AND REVIEW EXPECTATIONS

Target from The 7 Components:

Common expectations are taught at the beginning of the year and reviewed throughout the year.

If a mathematics teacher wants her students to use exponents fluently throughout the school year, she teaches the concept at the beginning of the year and then gives students the opportunity to practice the skill embedded in tasks throughout the year. If she notices that they are struggling with a particular element of exponents (e.g., how to manipulate the coefficient of a variable with an exponent), she takes the opportunity to reteach in small groups or the whole class.

As with any skill that we want students to retain and master, it is important to review behavioral expectations throughout the year. For example, after completing a mathematics mini-lesson and releasing students to engage in individual or group work, the teacher may briefly remind students what to do if they get stuck or have trouble remembering the next step. In some classes that might be turning to a neighbor for guidance or checking a visual problem-solving reference chart. In other classes the student might be expected to review anchor charts on the wall, look back at their notes, or watch a brief refresher video on their laptop.

The key is that the teacher has established clear expectations for students. And then the teacher reminds the students of those expectations and gives them an opportunity to practice on a regular basis.

Even with this ongoing instruction in behavioral expectations, some students may struggle to regulate their behavior. For these students the teacher can give subtle reminders—brief verbal, visual, or gestural prompts. For example, if a student is staring off into space, the teacher may make eye contact and point to a poster on the wall (that the class has generated) with guidance for the next steps in the process. If a student is turning around in their desk and messing with another student's papers, the teacher may tap them on the shoulder and point to a specialized visual on their desk that helps the student refocus.

If the teacher recognizes that the student is learning the behavioral expectations and practicing the skill, they will be less likely to become frustrated and move toward punitive interactions. For students who are really struggling with behavior, it is important to gather accurate formative assessment data. The teacher or an assistant (or even the student themself) can monitor the times when the student is demonstrating the skill as expected. They can also keep track of approximations—when the student is close to the expected skill—and the times when their behavior is unexpected or inappropriate. Collecting these data throughout the year can help the student (and teacher) see the progress they have made, rather than being derailed by the more visible and more memorable behaviors that are disruptive to their learning and the learning of others.

See Chapter 8 for more a comprehensive discussion of significant behavioral challenges in an inclusive school community.

RITUALS, ROUTINES, AND RECOGNITION

The next section in "The 7 Components of Inclusive and Equitable Learning Communities" is about rituals, routines, and recognition (Table 6.3). All teachers have some routines and some patterns for recognizing student growth and accomplishments. The purpose of this component is to help teachers be more intentional about how they design rituals and routines and how they ensure that all students are recognized in authentic and inclusive ways.

RITUALS AND ROUTINES COMMUNICATE VALUES

Target from The 7 Components:

Routines and rituals are established to communicate the school/classroom values of community, inclusivity, and equity.

Rituals and routines can serve a variety of purposes in the classroom. There are opening and closing routines that are focused primarily on establishing a classroom culture that is predictable, welcoming, and inclusive. There are also routines that help students initiate tasks, manage their social-emotional state, and transition between activities. For example, some teachers will greet students at the classroom door. Others will end the day with a closing circle where each student shares a

TABLE 6.3 "The 7 Components of Inclusive and Equitable Learning Communities": Rituals, Routines, and Recognition

RITUALS, ROUTINES, AND RECOGNITION	
TARGETS	**GUIDING QUESTIONS**
• Routines and rituals are established to communicate the school/classroom values of community, inclusivity, and equity. • Routines and rituals contribute to a stable, predictable classroom environment. • Students are recognized for positive contributions to the school/classroom community.	• How and to what extent do the systems and routines of the classroom reflect the values of community, inclusivity, equity, and accountability for learning? • How and to what extent do the systems and routines of the classroom facilitate student ownership and independence? • What structures and systems are in place to recognize students for positive contributions to the school/classroom community? • How do rituals, routines, and recognition (in the classroom and schoolwide) provide opportunities for student leadership and voice?

SOURCE: Used with Permission from West Linn-Wilsonville School District.

compliment for a classmate or reflects on a goal of the day. Some teachers have clear expectations for the appropriate volume level of different activities in the classroom. Others have pathways or routines for gathering materials before starting individual or group work.

While routines have a range of purposes, they can also promote community, inclusivity, and equity. Many routines have the expectation that all students participate. They also provide access points for all students to engage with the learning community. In this way they also promote status for students who may have traditionally been isolated or alienated in the class.

ROUTINES AND PREDICTABILITY

Target from The 7 Components:

Routines and rituals contribute to a stable, predictable classroom environment.

Walking into an environment where we know what to expect is inherently more comfortable and regulating than walking into an unfamiliar place where we don't know what will come next. When students walk into a classroom where patterns and expectations change each day, it can be difficult for them to regulate their emotions and focus their intellectual energy.

Engaging in routines helps free up bandwidth in our brains to manage the more complex elements of learning in a social setting. Think about the opportunities for making decisions during an average morning and the liberating impact of routines: choosing what time to wake up, whether to do a morning workout, and what kind of workout to do; choosing when to shower, when to eat breakfast, and when to brush teeth; and choosing what to eat for breakfast, what to put in the morning coffee, and which route to walk the dog. For many people, these are well established routines. We have sliced a banana on our cereal the same way every morning for years.

We made a choice at some point in the past to establish certain habits, but now we just wake up and follow the routine. The power of the routine is that it does not require us to exert mental energy on making low-level decisions. We can save that mental space for preparing for our day: rehearsing for important conversations or thinking through potentially challenging situations. President Barack Obama famously followed a simple morning routine (eating the same breakfast, wearing the same suit) to minimize expending energy on low-level decisions. He said, "I'm trying to pare down decisions. I don't want to make decisions about what I'm eating or wearing. Because I have too many other decisions to make" (Lewis, 2012). The same is true for classroom routines. When students know the basic expectations for arrival, departure, and starting activities, they are more likely to settle in comfortably. They can dedicate their mental resources to intellectually rigorous tasks rather than wondering where to find a sharp pencil or where to turn in their homework.

We are often more familiar with routines in elementary classrooms. Traditionally, middle school and high school teachers hesitate to set up routines. Some may feel like routines are childish or that teenage students should already know how to be a student. But in well-managed middle school and high school classrooms, there are clear routines. Students know how to engage in group work with specific roles. They know how to listen and enhance the conversation during a Socratic Seminar. They know how to "clamshell" their laptop screens when the teacher needs to get their attention for a brief moment of reteaching. These routines are most effective when they are explicitly taught and reinforced for all students.

A middle school social studies teacher recently shared how she uses the "Get Ready-Do-Done" strategy to help her students prepare to engage in complex tasks (Jacobsen & Ward, 2016; Newton, 2019). After a brief mini-lesson (she sets a visual timer for eight minutes to hold herself accountable to brevity) and before releasing students to independent work time, the teacher takes a few minutes to explain the assignment.

Using the document camera, the teacher walks students through a process that will help them know what they are aiming for. She has a template with three large columns for Get Ready-Do-Done. She starts with the far right column ("Done"), drawing a visual or describing what the completed assignment will look like. For example, if the students are creating a chart listing arguments and evidence for various points of view on a historical controversy, she will draw a chart with bullet points and headings. She tells the students, "You will know you have the assignment complete when you have these parts done and your chart looks like this." She doesn't fill in the actual details (that's the work the students will do), but she may provide sentence stems to help make the task more accessible.

Then she moves to the far left column ("Get Ready"), asking the students to generate a list of resources that they have available to them, including textbooks, links on her virtual classroom page, articles they have read and notated, posters they have created in groups, and notes they have taken in class. She writes these resources in the left column. Depending on the needs of the students in her class, she could also include more basic steps for getting ready (find a pencil, turn your chair to face the table, get out a piece of paper, etc.).

Then she moves to the center column ("Do") and writes the steps that a student would do to actually complete the task: find relevant information in the sources, match the information with the headings on the chart, write details, label the source, identify the main idea, and so on.

She leaves the "Get Ready-Do-Done" chart on the board while the students work so they can refer back to it and keep themselves on track. She can stop the class at various points and point at the screen to remind them where they should be. For some students she can also make a copy of the chart and place it on their desk or in their planner so they can refer to it more directly.

At first, it may seem like this process takes a long time, cutting into the students' independent work time. But anyone who has taught a middle or high school class knows that releasing students to independent work is often a messy and disruptive process. Some students understand the task and can complete it with relatively little explanation. Some students think they know the task and just want to jump right in, but they end up moving quickly in the wrong direction. This leads to frustration for the teacher and discouragement for the student.

And then a number of students will sit there with no idea how to begin. Some of these students may have self-management goals on their IEP. Some of them may just struggle with the executive functioning skills associated with task initiation. The teacher tries to go around to these students one by one, repeating the directions (maybe mumbling something like "If you had just listened the first time . . ."), hoping to get them all on track before they get bored and start distracting their classmates.

In this typical scenario the teacher feels like they are putting out fires, and the bulk of their energy goes to getting students to start, rather than helping students to develop their ideas and giving feedback on their work. And even worse, students develop learned helplessness, a sense of dependency on the teacher (or paraeducator) to re-explain every assignment. Students learn that they do not actually need to listen to the teacher the first time, because someone will explain it to them one-on-one after everyone else gets started.

The middle school teacher in this example said that the Get Ready-Do-Done process probably ends up saving her (and her students) time. The actual explanation of the task takes slightly longer than explaining assignments did in the past. But now she sees that her students are able to initiate the task much more independently, freeing her up to engage with them on a higher level.

We first encountered this strategy when our occupational therapists, learning specialists, SLPs, and classroom teachers went to workshops led by Sara Ward. These specialists and our special education ICs have helped spread strategies like this to general education teachers through co-teaching and coplanning. These routines have become part of the fabric of the classroom rather than a special activity that is reserved for a specific student. The Get Ready-Do-Done process is another example of the All-Some-Few model. The teacher said that there are a few students in her room who absolutely need this kind of scaffolding to engage in complex tasks. But there are a significant number of students who also benefit from the increased clarity of expectations and the process.

An additional bonus in this kind of routine is that it requires the teacher to think through the task in advance to anticipate what tools the students will need and how they will engage with the content. This kind of forethought allows the teacher to be prepared for misconceptions or for any challenges that students may face as they work on the task.

Target from The 7 Components:

Students are recognized for positive contributions to the school or classroom community.

Recognition for positive or expected behavior has become a common feature in many schools as part of a schoolwide positive behavior system. There are plenty of reasons to be concerned about developing a token economy and the impact of extrinsic motivation on learner behavior. Rewards are not an effective way to teach complex social communication or decision-making skills (Ablon, 2018; Kohn, 2018).

However, recognizing and celebrating examples of positive classroom behavior can be powerful. Students who sometimes struggle with making expected behavioral choices often perceive that teachers are targeting them. "Why do you always bust me?" they ask, pointing out, often correctly, that other students with similar behaviors are not disciplined as frequently. When we are actively looking to recognize positive behavior, however, we are more likely to "*catch* kids doing good."

In a recent visit to a second-grade classroom we saw a beautiful example of this. The teacher had just presented a short mathematics mini-lesson, and the students were engaged in a pair-share protocol where they explained and justified their mathematical thinking. The teacher expertly complimented one particular pair of students for using their "mathematician voice" to quietly explain their thinking to each other. Immediately, other pairs who may have been a bit loud or off topic refocused on the structure and intent of the lesson. Then the teacher leaned in close to one student and gave him much more explicit recognition for how deeply he was explaining his thinking and using the appropriate mathematical vocabulary. Then, we noticed that he wasn't wearing any shoes! The teacher used her judgment to focus on what was important in that moment (engaging in the mathematics lesson) and positively acknowledged this students' contribution to the lesson. We are sure that later she addressed the shoe issue. But she knew that of all the elements happening in that moment, the positive acknowledgment of mathematics engagement was the most important.

Inviting students to recognize one another's contributions and accomplishments can be a powerful tool for building community in inclusive classrooms. For example, we were visiting a high school journalism class during the closing circle routine. The students were going around the class and "giving a rose"—a compliment or recognition of another student's work. BJ was a member of that class, but his participation in the learning and the creation of the student paper looked significantly different because of learning and communication differences. However, his peers provided authentic recognition for his contributions to the team. One student said, "I want to thank BJ for helping me pick the photos for the front page." The teacher noted to us later that the peer would hold up two photos and BJ would select the one he thought most appropriate by pointing to it. This authentic work and the public recognition elevated BJ's status in the class and reinforced the belief that everyone has something valuable to contribute.

ENGAGEMENT STRATEGIES FOR ALL STUDENTS

We discussed engagement strategies in more detail earlier in this chapter. In this context engagement strategies are not just about how students learn new content. They are also about how students connect to the classroom and feel a sense of belonging (Table 6.4).

CULTURALLY RELEVANT ENGAGEMENT STRATEGIES

Target from The 7 Components:

Engagement strategies connect to and build on students' academic background, life experiences, culture, and language to support rigorous and culturally relevant learning.

If teachers are intentional about designing their engagement strategies, they can be very powerful tools for inclusion. For example, using a broad range of culturally relevant materials will help students see themselves in the curriculum. Students who believe that their teacher and classmates recognize and appreciate their unique cultural experiences will be more likely to engage in

TABLE 6.4 "The 7 Components of Inclusive and Equitable Learning Communities": Engagement Strategies

ENGAGEMENT STRATEGIES	
TARGETS	GUIDING QUESTIONS
• Engagement strategies connect to and build on students' academic background, life experiences, culture, and language to support rigorous and culturally relevant learning. • Engagement strategies encourage equitable and purposeful student participation and ensure that all students have access to, and are expected to participate in, learning.	• Where is the locus of control over learning in the classroom? • What specific strategies and structures are in place to facilitate participation and meaning-making by all students? How are the options for engaging in learning differentiated? • How does the teacher ensure that all students have access to participation in the work of the group? How is participation distributed? • In what ways are issues of status and privilege addressed in engagement strategies?

SOURCE: Used with Permission from West Linn-Wilsonville School District.

the classroom. Two books that have been very influential in our understanding of culturally relevant teaching are Geneva Gay's (2000) *Culturally Responsive Teaching* and Zaretta Hammond's (2014) *Culturally Responsive Teaching and the Brain.*

In addition, one of the beneficial outcomes of an inclusive learning community is that students from the majority culture become more familiar with and connected to the diversity of our world. When all students are included in the classroom, "typical" children become more accustomed to students with different learning profiles, students who communicate differently, and students who have different modes of mobility. In the same way, when classroom materials and activities reflect the cultural and linguistic diversity of our students, the whole community learns and grows together.

EQUITABLE PARTICIPATION

Target from The 7 Components:

Engagement strategies encourage equitable and purposeful student participation and ensure that all students have access to, and are expected to participate in, learning.

Active participation in classroom activities should be an expectation for all students. In a traditional classroom, activities promote engagement from a small number of students. Often, those students are linguistically and ethnically homogeneous. Students from culturally and linguistically diverse backgrounds are often left at the periphery of the classroom, along with students with disabilities.

To promote equitable student participation, teachers need to actively design engagement strategies that value a range of student voices. Actively participating—and contributing ideas to the classroom community—leads to richer learning opportunities. As we have said before, the one doing the talking is the one doing the learning.

TEACHING SOCIAL-EMOTIONAL SKILLS

As brain research develops, we are learning more and more that social-emotional regulation is critical to learning. Rich learning experiences activate the prefrontal cortex, allowing students to draw connections between ideas and build neural pathways for long-term retrieval. When students experience social-emotional dysregulation, the brain reverts to a fight/flight/freeze reflex. This disengages the prefrontal cortex and inhibits meaningful learning opportunities (Hammond, 2014). To help students engage in highly rigorous learning, we need

TEACHING SOCIAL-EMOTIONAL SKILLS	
TARGETS	**GUIDING QUESTIONS**
• Teachers identify specific social-emotional skills to teach and have appropriate resources for instruction.	• How do the teacher and other school staff partner to provide instruction in social-emotional skills?
• Social-emotional skills (including self-awareness, self-management, and social/relational awareness) are taught in explicit and implicit ways.	• How does the teacher create opportunities to practice specific social-emotional skills within the context of classroom tasks?
• Students have opportunities to generalize skills across settings and with different peer groups.	• To what degree are students able to talk about their social-emotional needs and strengths in different contexts and identify specific strategies to match their current need?
• Students recognize their social-emotional strengths and areas for additional learning.	

SOURCE: Used with Permission from West Linn-Wilsonville School District.

to help them maintain social-emotional regulation. And therefore, we need to explicitly teach social-emotional skills (Table 6.6).

Another way to think of this is Bruce Perry's (2018) sequence of engagement: Regulate-Relate-Reason. First, we need to help students regulate their social-emotional or sensory state. Then we need to relate to them as individuals. Only at that point can we connect to their reasoning brain.

IDENTIFYING SOCIAL-EMOTIONAL SKILLS TO TEACH

Target from The 7 Components:

Teachers identify specific social-emotional skills to teach and have appropriate resources for instruction.

The first step for teachers and school leaders is to identify which social-emotional skills we want to teach and what resources we are going to use to teach them. This varies across grade levels. Some of the key areas to consider are (CASEL, 2017)

- self-awareness,

- self-management,

- social awareness,

- relationships skills, and

- responsible decision-making.

Specific lessons and activities help students develop the skills to identify and regulate feelings, build and maintain healthy relationships, use productive self-talk, and engage in effective problem solving. In our district, we use the Zones of Regulation at the elementary level and the Second Step curriculum in elementary and middle school. In high school we use School Connect and Sources of Strength. The specific curriculum is less important than the fact that students are learning to recognize their social-emotional state and use regulation techniques that work for them.

EXPLICIT AND IMPLICIT INSTRUCTION FOR SOCIAL-EMOTIONAL SKILLS

Target from The 7 Components:

Social-emotional skills are taught in explicit and implicit ways.

As with most other things in school, students will come to us with a range of proficiency in managing their social-emotional state. Some families will have taught students to recognize and regulate their emotions from an early age. Students who have experienced trauma may have developed pathways in the brain that lead to more frequent dysregulation.

Counselors and teachers in our district have been using the Hand Model of the brain to help students think about what they are experiencing and how to control it. Popularized by Dr. Dan Siegel, the Hand Model helps students understand how fear sensors in the "reptile brain" (amygdala) may trigger a fight, flight, or freeze response when they face unfamiliar or unexpected circumstances. When the brain is working most efficiently, the prefrontal cortex is active, and students can reason and relate effectively. But when the amygdala takes over, the prefrontal cortex becomes disengaged. Dr. Siegel (2010) calls this "flipping your lid."

Saying, "I flipped my lid" is not an excuse for bad behavior, however. Instead, it is a way for students to talk about what is happening in their brain using safe and accessible language. Helping students visualize what is happening in their brains when they are dysregulated, and giving them language to name it, helps to demystify what they are experiencing. This is empowering for students and allows them to develop a sense of control over their social-emotional regulation. It also helps teachers and classmates empathize with students who are struggling to control their behavior. Having a common language for students, teachers, and parents makes it easier to teach and practice effective social-emotional skills.

PRACTICING SOCIAL-EMOTIONAL SKILLS

Target from The 7 Components:

Students have opportunities to generalize skills across settings and with different peer groups.

We recognize that understanding what is going on in the brain is not enough. The whole point, after all, is that the reason centers of the brain are disengaged when the amygdala takes over. So once students have a framework and language to understand what is happening in their brains, the next step is to give them opportunities to practice their regulation skills.

Teachers can create opportunities to practice social-emotional regulation skills in a variety of ways. Some of the most common occasions for dysregulation are initiating high-rigor tasks (like writing), transitioning between activities (especially at the end of a high-interest activity), and unstructured times like recess and lunch. Before moving into one of these activities, the teacher can prepare the whole class by reviewing the Hand Model of the brain and prompting students to think about which social-emotional regulation strategy they will use if they feel themselves about to "flip their lid." Teachers can also lead the class in a brief regulation exercise, like deep breathing, stretching, or a movement break. While these activities may be targeted toward a few students with intense social-emotional needs, they are likely to benefit all students in the class.

In one third-grade classroom we observed, the teacher helped the students practice these skills at the end of a mathematics lesson. The students had worked in small groups or pairs on a challenging mathematical task. The teacher called the students to gather in a circle "around the perimeter of the room" (using mathematical vocabulary in the daily routine). Then she called on a few students to share about how they had worked with their partners, the challenges they faced in their work, and how they overcame those challenges. As she neared the end of the sharing time, there were many students with their hands raised. The teacher knew she did not have time for each student to tell the class about their work. So she said, "I'm going to call on one more friend to share with the class. So get ready to shrug and say, 'Oh, well' if you don't get called on." She called on a student to share. Then she modeled shrugging her shoulders and saying "Oh, well." The rest of the class followed along, and no one demonstrated signs of being upset or dysregulated.

This is a quick teacher-led activity to help students recognize a potentially upsetting situation in class (not getting called on when you have your hand raised) and practice a social-emotional regulation skill (shrugging your shoulders and saying "Oh, well."). It doesn't require any specific social-emotional learning curriculum or expertise. Any teacher can help build students' social-emotional skills through this kind of practice.

In addition, by teaching social-emotional strategies to the whole class, students become more empathetic to their classmates who are struggling with social-emotional regulation. When a student sees their peer in a state of escalation, they have some language to describe what's going on in their brain. This can help make the unexpected behavior seem a little less scary, resulting in the student who is dysregulated being less likely to be isolated or alienated from their peers.

SOCIAL-EMOTIONAL SELF-AWARENESS

Target from The 7 Components:

Students recognize their social-emotional strengths and areas for additional learning.

Similarly, when all students in the class have the opportunity to learn about social-emotional regulation, they begin to see patterns in themselves. In some cases we even have students gather data to monitor their own social-emotional state. They can see when they are most likely to be regulated—what times of the day or what classroom activities are most comfortable and successful for them. They can then reflect on what times of the day or what activities provoke feelings of social-emotional discomfort.

The purpose of this self-awareness is not about avoidance. We want students to be aware of the times or tasks that cause anxiety or disruptive patterns of thinking—but not so they can simply leave the room and avoid having to engage in challenging tasks or difficult interactions with peers. Instead, we want students to be able to recognize patterns so they can engage in intentional self-regulation activities before and during these challenging times.

For example, teachers in all of our primary school classrooms use the Zones of Regulation, a system of categories that helps students recognize their social-emotional state (Kuypers, 2011). Teachers emphasize that it is normal for students to move through a variety of social-emotional states throughout the day.

The Zones of Regulation are color coded to help students and teachers talk about them in simpler language.

- *Blue Zone:* very calm, sleepy, mellow, tired, sick, lonely
- *Green Zone:* alert, aware, engaged, happy, ready to learn
- *Yellow Zone:* silly, wiggly, excited, frustrated, worried, agitated
- *Red Zone:* angry, yelling, hitting, screaming, shouting

The message is not that students should always be in the Green Zone but that they should be aware of their zone and how to change into the desired zone for their current context. For example, when getting ready for bed, we may want to be in the Blue Zone. When playing tag at recess, we may want to be in the Yellow Zone. When cheering at a basketball game, we may want to be in the Red Zone. And when we are in class getting ready to learn, we usually want to be in the Green Zone.

This helps students accept that their emotions are natural and may be appropriate depending on the context. By acknowledging the range of emotions that we all feel, the Zones of Regulation can help students talk about their social-emotional state and how to practice getting into a desired state.

Teachers help students learn "Zone Changer" activities so they can get their bodies and minds into an appropriate state for learning. For example, if a student is in the Blue Zone, they may need to get up and take a vigorous walk down the hall to the drinking fountain. If a student is in the Yellow Zone, they may benefit from a pattern of deep breathing exercises to calm their mind and body. If a student is in the Red Zone, they may need to go down to the gym and throw a heavy ball against the wall or go into a room where they can shout really loud without disturbing other learners.

One of the key concepts in an inclusive school is building capacity in classroom teachers and paraeducators so students do not need to rely on a few specialists to help them access their education. The Zones of Regulation is a great example of this. Our learning specialists, school psychologists, occupational therapists, and SLPs have modeled lessons for teachers in Zones of Regulation, so the teacher can learn the language and then reinforce it throughout the day with their students. In Chapter 9 we talk more about the leadership moves to make these inclusive practices possible.

RESTORATIVE PRACTICES

School communities around the country have been developing restorative practices to shift the impact on the school community when a student has done something disruptive or hurtful. This is still an area where we have a lot to learn. We have seen promising results in schools that have been actively pursuing restorative practices (Table 6.6).

TABLE 6.6   "The 7 Components of Inclusive and Equitable Learning Communities": Restorative Practices

RESTORATIVE PRACTICES	
TARGETS	**GUIDING QUESTIONS**
• A proactive culture of community building allows restorative practices to be a natural extension of the classroom culture.	• What structures and routines are in place to create a positive and supportive classroom culture, where students and teachers naturally engage in constructive and restorative dialogue?
• Responses to inappropriate or disruptive behavior emphasize acknowledging responsibility, repairing harm, and restoring relationships, rather than emphasizing consequences.	• What structures are in place to help students identify the harm they have done to the school/class community?
• Schools use structures and strategies that promote restorative dialogue and build empathy (e.g., peacemaking circles, mediation, conferencing).	• What structures are in place to provide opportunities for repairing harm and restoring relationships?
	• How do students learn the skills to engage in restorative dialogue?

SOURCE: Used with Permission from West Linn-Wilsonville School District.

REPAIR VERSUS CONSEQUENCES

Target from The 7 Components:

Responses to inappropriate or disruptive behavior emphasize acknowledging responsibility, repairing harm, and restoring relationships, rather than emphasizing consequences.

It is ok for schools to have a system of discipline that includes consequences. Students do need to learn that their actions have an impact in the world and that there are often undesirable consequences to their choices. However, it is clear from generations of school experience that punitive consequences do not have a significant impact on behavior, particularly for students who demonstrate the most frequent disruptive behaviors.

The threat of consequences (or even the experience of consequences) does not serve as an effective deterrent. Nor do consequences help students learn and practice effective replacement behaviors. More often, traditional discipline systems serve to further alienate students from their teachers and peers. This increased sense of distance between the student and the learning community actually makes it more likely that they will engage in disruptive behaviors in the future and less likely that they will be able to engage deeply in academic work.

Restorative practices allow students to take responsibility for their actions while remaining a part of the classroom community, rather than becoming alienated and detached. Taking ownership of the restorative process gives the student a degree of control over their school experience that they may not have otherwise felt. As we discussed in the section on student engagement, shifting the locus of control to students is a key strategy to raise status and promote equitable outcomes, especially for students from traditionally disadvantaged groups.

Some people are concerned that restorative practices are "soft" and that kids are allowed to get away without consequences. However, when a student engages in a restorative process, they are required to confront how their behavior has affected their classroom community. This is not soft at all. Many students say they would prefer to spend a week in detention (a traditional punitive response) rather than be required to honestly wrestle with the way they have harmed their classmates.

PROACTIVE COMMUNITY BUILDING

Target from The 7 Components:

A proactive culture of community building allows restorative practices to be a natural extension of the classroom culture.

Engaging in restorative conversations is a socially challenging activity. It is easier for students to simply receive traditional discipline than to face up to people who they may have hurt. When faced with an opportunity to invest in a restorative conversation, a student may say, "Why do I have to talk to them about what I did? Can't I just pick up trash or spend lunch in the office?" But if we are looking to help students learn new skills and truly transform the culture of the school community, we need to support restorative conversations.

For students to successfully engage in a restorative conversation, there needs to be a community to restore to. As Ted Wachtel (2016), founder of the International Institute for Restorative Practices, says, "Where social capital—a network of relationships—is already well established, it is easier to respond effectively to wrongdoing and restore social order—as well as to create a healthy and positive organizational environment."

According to the International Institute for Restorative Practices, most of the work of creating a truly restorative community happens before a student causes disruption or harm. The institute estimates that 80% of the work is about establishing trusting relationships among students and building a sense of allegiance to a positive classroom community (Costello et al., 2009). Teachers who try to hold restorative circles before they have built a trusting classroom community may find that students are not ready to engage in truly open and productive conversations.

STRUCTURES FOR RESTORATIVE PRACTICES

Target from The 7 Components:

Schools use structures and strategies that promote restorative dialogue and build empathy (e.g., peacemaking circles, mediation, conferencing).

As with so many other aspects of an inclusive school community, restorative practices work more effectively when there is a proactive culture of community building within the context of a clear and familiar structure. In our district, teachers have been actively using circle protocols in daily or weekly routines. These protocols acknowledge the voice of each member of the community and distribute the locus of control throughout the classroom (Boyes-Watson & Pranis, 2015). When students are familiar with using a circle protocol for everyday classroom interactions, it becomes natural for them to engage in a circle for problem-solving or restoration after harm has been done to the community. The circle takes on the power of a ritual.

We have seen restorative circles in use across all grade levels. For example, a second-grade teacher regularly used a circle protocol to resolve disputes that arose during recess. Some students expressed feeling left out, and others took ownership of the way their behavior had caused their classmates to feel hurt. A high school teacher used a very simple "Feelings" circle to start class every Friday. Students passed around a talking stick and shared how they were feeling. At first, most students passed or said, "Fine." But as the year went on, students began to express more genuine emotions. One of the students told a group of administrators that she actually started looking forward to Feelings Friday because it helped her get to know her classmates in a more authentic way.

One of our high school students had a very visible episode where they shouted swear words at the teacher and stormed out of the classroom. The teacher and the other students were shaken by the disruption to the community. The counselor, the teacher, and the student's case manager worked together to lead a restorative circle that helped classmates express how the incident had affected them. This was critical to restoring a sense of community, which eventually allowed the student to return and engage with their classmates.

When a fifth-grade student died unexpectedly, teachers began class the next day with a circle protocol. Each teacher read a statement that informed the class about the student's death. Then, students had an opportunity to share their initial feelings. One by one around the circle, students could talk about what was on their mind, or they could pass. For many students this was a powerful opportunity to process their shock and grief. Teachers later said that these circles would not have been nearly as effective if students had not been familiar with the ritual of circles from daily or weekly practice.

HOW DO RESTORATIVE PRACTICES PROMOTE INCLUSION?

Restorative practices can be a powerful support for inclusion. Restorative practices are based on the underlying belief that each student's voice matters as a vital part of the classroom and school community. When students are practicing a circle protocol, for example, every student has the opportunity to speak. If a student communicates in a nontraditional way (e.g., with an augmentative communication device), they still can be part of the circle. Students learn to listen actively to each student's input, build on one another's ideas, or disagree respectfully. The circle protocol helps raise the status of students who may have been marginalized, including those with disabilities.

In a traditional system the students who are most often excluded from participation in general education classrooms are those with significant behavioral challenges. By focusing on repairing harm and restoring community, restorative practices allow students with disabilities that affect their behavior to reconnect with their peers, build empathy for those they have harmed, and generate strategies for managing their behavior in the future.

Restorative practices are not magic. There is still a lot of complicated work that teachers, leaders, and other adults need to do to support students with complex behaviors. But by giving each child a voice, raising the status of historically marginalized students, and creating opportunities for resolving disputes and repairing harm, restorative practices can be incredibly powerful in inclusive school communities.

Relationships With High Expectations

As we mentioned in the section on social-emotional regulation, for students to be able to engage in rigorous classroom learning, their brains need to be primed to activate the prefrontal cortex. Thinking about this in the context of Regulate-Relate-Reason is helpful. First, we need to help students *regulate* their social-emotional or sensory state. Then, we need to *relate* to them as individuals. Only at that point can we connect to their *reasoning* brain.

WARM DEMANDERS

Target from the 7 Components:

Teacher is a "warm demander," holding high standards while offering emotional and instructional scaffolds to help each student, every student access the classroom curriculum.

Of course, teachers and school leaders have known for years that relationships are important for promoting learning. Tony Wagner, founder of the Change Leadership Group at the Harvard Graduate School of Education, wrote an influential article in 2002 about what he called "the new 3 R's: rigor, relevance and relationships" (Wagner, 2002, 2006). Long before that, teachers and students had acknowledged the power of relationships to transform the learning culture in schools.

President George W. Bush captured the importance of high expectations when he cautioned us about "the soft bigotry of low expectations" in his speech to the NAACP in 2000 (Bush, 2000). The political outcome of that statement was the No Child Left Behind Act, which led to a massive increase in standardized testing regimes and other bureaucratic complexities for schools. But the sentiment behind the statement is valid. If we truly love our students, we must create systems that equip them to embrace the full range of college and career options.

In our district we express this same concept by thinking beyond achievement gaps to opportunity gaps and expectation gaps. If educators don't believe that a student (or a group of students) is capable or deserving of engaging in rigorous learning, then we will not create opportunities for that learning—resulting in the perpetuation of predictable achievement gaps. This is true for students from historically disadvantaged racial, ethnic and linguistic groups. It is also true for students with disabilities in segregated classrooms.

Hammond (2014) expresses this idea with her concept of a "warm demander." She describes four relational styles of teachers: The Technocrat, the Elitist, the Sentimentalist, and the Warm Demander. Hammond locates these four styles on a quadrant with one axis measuring the range from "passive leniency" to "demandingness" and the other axis spanning the range from "professional distance" to "personal warmth." The Warm Demander expresses genuine warmth and affection for their students while at the same time maintaining high expectations for each student's ability and potential (Table 6.7).

CULTURALLY RESPONSIVE PRACTICES

Target from The 7 Components:

Teacher uses culturally responsive teaching practices.

This book is about the leadership actions that support systemic change to create inclusive learning communities. The focus is primarily on students with disabilities, who have historically been segregated in self-contained classrooms. However, inclusion is also about ensuring equitable opportunities and outcomes for students of color, students who are learning English as an additional language, LGBTQ+ students, and other students who have historically been marginalized. Other books address this in more detail. In our district, we have been guided by Gay's (2000) *Culturally Responsive Teaching* and Hammond's (2014) *Culturally Responsive Teaching and the Brain*. In addition, school leaders and staff have been learning deeply about the profound impact of institutional racism through books like *White Fragility* by Robin DiAngelo (2018), *So You Want to Talk About Race* by Ijeoma Oluo (2018), and *How to Be an Antiracist* by Ibram X. Kendi (2019). This is critically important work that deserves so much more than these few sentences.

TABLE 6.7 "The 7 Components of Inclusive and Equitable Learning Communities": Relationships With High Expectations

RELATIONSHIPS WITH HIGH EXPECTATIONS	
TARGET	**GUIDING QUESTIONS**
• Teacher is a "warm demander," holding high standards while offering emotional and instructional scaffolds to help each student, every student access the classroom curriculum. • Teacher uses culturally responsive teaching practices. • Teacher shows respect and personal regard for each student, every student.	• How does the teacher create opportunities for productive struggle? • How does the teacher communicate high expectations for all students while providing emotional and academic support? • In what verbal and nonverbal ways does the teacher express warmth? • How do students respond to feedback and challenges? • How are students becoming more independent in their learning? • What structures in the environment and personal invitations from teachers engage each student, every student in rigorous study, coursework, cocurricular activities, and so on?

SOURCE: Used with Permission from West Linn-Wilsonville School District.

We encourage deeply engaging in the work of disrupting systems of racism that are beyond the scope of this book.

In this section of "The 7 Components of Inclusive and Equitable Learning Communities," we are focusing specifically on the importance of relationships with high expectations. True relationships are built on mutual respect. That includes acknowledging and seeking to understand the cultural factors that form the background of our students' lives.

Over the past 25 years educators have realized that we need to move beyond classroom celebrations of Kwanzaa or Dia de los Muertos. While these public acknowledgments of diversity are important, they also can feel like tokenism. If we put some felt Kwanzaa candles on the bulletin board or read a biography of Martin Luther King Jr. during Black History Month, we may feel like we have done our part for multiculturalism.

But creating a classroom that is genuinely culturally responsive requires a much deeper exploration of the assumptions that drive our instructional choices. This includes examining curriculum materials to ensure greater representation of different voices. It also includes thinking about classroom routines, communication structures, assessment practices, and discipline systems that may exacerbate historical biases.

Schools and districts that are truly committed to inclusion will need to confront these factors and engage in the challenging work of promoting equitable outcomes for *all* students—not just students identified with disabilities.

RESPECT AND PERSONAL REGARD

Target from The 7 Components:

Teacher shows respect and personal regard for each student, every student.

Students need to know that their teachers actually like them. It may sound silly to have to say that. But some students really believe that their teachers don't like them. They may feel targeted or marginalized because of their race, language, gender identity, or disability. Some students may demonstrate behaviors that make it hard for others to show warm regard. These are exactly the students who are most in need of our attention and affection. As one of our principals says, "The kids who most need our love are the ones who do things that make them hardest to love."

This is particularly important for students who have experienced trauma in their personal life. School needs to be a place of enduring welcome. Every student should feel that people at school are happy to see them, regardless of their history at home or in the classroom.

Teachers may need to go out of their way to show warmth and personal regard to some students. For some teachers it is helpful to have a systematic way to remember to demonstrate explicit kindness to each student every day. One example of this is to personally greet each student as they enter the classroom, like the viral video of the teacher who has a personalized high-five/handshake routine with each student. Other teachers keep a list of students to check in with over the course of the period or day, rotating through the class over the course of the week. The key is for teachers to be intentional about making connections with students in a way that feels authentic with their personal classroom style.

In addition, teachers should use an equity lens when thinking about relationship strategies. Teachers should make connections and show warm regard for all students. But some students may need more frequent and explicit connections with the teacher. This is particularly true for students who have experienced trauma, students who are struggling with academics or behavior, and students who have been marginalized or socially isolated.

One middle school teacher has identified a student named Jadon who needs some intensive relational focus. His behavior has been disruptive and sometimes even dangerous to himself and others. He feels disconnected from school and often expresses his frustration by swearing at adults and glaring menacingly at students. The teacher has arranged for the counselor, learning specialist, or assistant principal to step into her class for about 5 minutes each day to provide an opportunity for her to check in with Jadon during his independent-study period. They usually play a quick game. Or sometimes he shows her a silly YouTube video he has been watching. They talk about things he is interested in, and he has even started to ask about her family. Jadon still experiences behavioral challenges, but this teacher is beginning to build the kind of relationship that will help him feel more connected to school and invested in the people he interacts with every day.

Relationships are individual actions that take place on a personal level between students and teachers. However, it is also important for school leaders to be intentional about creating structures that promote relationship building on a school-wide level, to make sure that every student is noticed and no one slips through the cracks. This is particularly important in middle and high school, where students move from class to class and teachers may see 150 students in a day.

One leadership strategy is to create a visual web of the connections between adults and students in the school. For example, at a staff meeting the names of every student in the school are posted on the wall. Teachers walk by with highlighter pens to mark the names of students they have a strong relationship with. By the end of the activity, some students will have multiple highlights. Others may have none.

It may be useful to sort the student names (either before or after the initial marking) by grade level, race/ethnicity, English as a second language status, grade point average, number of discipline referrals, or category of disability. Teachers may see patterns emerge that identify which students have a network of strong relationships and which students are navigating school on their own.

The next step in this activity is for teachers to identify specific students who they will intentionally build a relationship with. In addition, leaders can help teachers develop relationship-building strategies that will lead to more equitable distribution of teacher attention—with teachers giving more time to students who need the most social-emotional, behavioral, or academic support.

References

Ablon, J. S. (2018). *The unintended impact of external motivators.* Think:Kids. http://www.thinkkids.org/the-unintended-impact-of-external-motivators/

Boyes-Watson, C., & Pranis, K. (2015). *Circle forward: Building a restorative school community.* Living Justice Press.

Bush, G. W. (2000). *Speech to the NAACP's 91st annual convention.* https://www.washingtonpost.com/wp-srv/onpolitics/elections/bushtext071000.htm

CASEL. (2017). *Core SEL competencies.* https://casel.org/core-competencies/

Costello, B., Wachtel, J., & Wachtel, T. (2009). *The restorative practices handbook.* International Institute for Restorative Practices.

DiAngelo, R. (2018). *White fragility: Why it's so hard for white people to talk about racism.* Beacon Press.

Gay, G. (2000). *Culturally responsive teaching: Theory, research, and practice.* Teachers College Press.

Hammond, Z. (2014). *Culturally responsive teaching and the brain.* Corwin.

Jacobsen, K., & Ward, S. (2016). *Strategies for improving executive function skills to plan, organize, and problem solve for school success.* http://www.glenbardgps.org/wp-content/uploads/2016/06/sarah-ward-executive-function-lecture-handout-December-6-2016-Glenbard-IL.pdf

Kendi, I. X. (2019). *How to be an antiracist.* One World.

Kohn, A. (2018). *Punished by rewards: The trouble with gold stars, incentive plans, A's, praise, and other bribes.* Houghton Mifflin. (Original work published 1993)

Kuypers, L. (2011). *The zones of regulation: A curriculum designed to foster self-regulation and emotional control.* Think Social. www.zonesofregulation.com

Lewis, M. (2012, September 11). Obama's way. *Vanity Fair.* https://www.vanityfair.com/news/2012/10/michael-lewis-profile-barack-obama

Merrill, A., & Risch, J. (2014). Implementation and effectiveness of using video self-modeling with students with ASD. *The Reporter, 19*(6). https://www.iidc.indiana.edu/pages/video-self-modeling

Meyer, A., Rose, D. H., & Gordon, D. (2014). *Universal Design for Learning: Theory and practice.* CAST Professional.

Newton, K. (2019, March 5). *"Get Ready, Do, Done" model: Support executive functioning for autistic students.* https://www.stairwaytostem.org/on-using-get-ready-do-done-a-model-to-support-executive-functioning-for-autistic-students/

Oluo, I. (2018). *So you want to talk about race.* Seal Press.

Perry, B. (2018). *Regulate, relate, reason.* https://www.bdperry.com/post/regulate-relate-reason

Siegel, D. (2010). *Mindsight: The new science of personal transformation.* Bantam Books.

Wachtel, T. (2016). *Defining restorative.* International Institute for Restorative Practices. https://www.iirp.edu/restorative-practices/defining-restorative/

Wagner, T. (2002). Secondary school change: Meeting challenge with the 3 R's of reinvention. *Education Week, 22*(13), 36–40.

Wagner, T. (2006, January 10). Rigor on trial. *Education Week.* https://www.edweek.org/ew/articles/2006/01/11/18wagner.h25.html

CHAPTER 7

Increasing Student Voice

The third area of focus for our inclusion transformation is *increasing student voice*. There are multiple components to this focus area, and each one is critical to achieving real educational change. First, we are deeply committed to including students' ideas, questions, and opinions in the big-picture planning of how we organize our schools for successful learning for all students. In addition, we prioritize ensuring that every student has an effective way to communicate their dreams, desires, and knowledge, as well as the social communication skills to engage in an authentic community.

Student behavior is one of the biggest questions related to inclusive practices. In Chapter 6 we talked about behavior within the context of "The 7 Components of Inclusive and Equitable Learning Communities." And Chapter 8 is devoted specifically to addressing behavior within an inclusive school system. The conditions we create, including common expectations, consistent routines, engagement strategies, and restorative practices, can all contribute to positive student behavior. In addition, we recognize that behavior is a form of communication. Therefore, it is equally important to listen to and understand student voices to help resolve behavioral challenges.

Finally, each student with an IEP should be involved in developing their own learning goals and determining the appropriate range of support to achieve those goals.

Growth Mindset Revisited

As we focus on student voice, we return to the idea of *growth mindset*, which we discussed in Chapter 3. A growth mindset is a critical orientation in this work. As educators, we know that our expectations for student growth are absolutely related to student achievement. We also know that our beliefs about our own skills directly affect our success with students. For example, if I believe "I don't have the expertise to work with this type of learner," I will likely struggle in teaching that student. Whereas, if my mindset is "I may not know yet, but I'm going to figure this out, and I'm absolutely the teacher this student needs right now," I am more likely to be successful with that student. Beyond our mindset as educators, cultivating the mindset each student holds for themselves is also critical to a successful change to inclusion.

The year before we started our inclusion journey, our district began deeply exploring Dr. Carol Dweck's (2008) research on growth mindset. At its heart, her work looks at the relationship between our beliefs and actions, how these develop or hinder a sense of self-efficacy, and how that affects student achievement. Embracing a growth mindset denotes a commitment to work and to struggle. The feedback loop of failure and success helps us develop more understanding of how we can move forward toward our goals. Dweck asks, "What are the consequences of thinking that your intelligence or personality is something you can develop (growth mindset), as opposed to something that is a fixed, deep-seated trait (fixed mindset)?" (p. 4). As a district, we wrestled with this question and its implications for our teaching.

One result was a commitment to explicitly teach the construct of growth mindset to all students. We aimed to empower students to understand the power of working toward goals and the role of productive struggle in their success. It is common to hear students at any school in our district use the language of growth and fixed mindset. You may see posters on classroom walls that illustrate the language of a fixed mindset ("This is too hard") versus a growth mindset ("This is going to take some time and effort"). Teachers actively encourage students to embrace mistakes in their academic efforts and recognize the learning that happens when they reflect on their process. It is common to hear students talk about their effort, about how they may not be good at this yet, and about what they learned from something they tried that may not have gone as planned. Teaching the concept of growth mindset to all students has become foundational to our work.

> As educators, each of us needs to approach our work with a growth mindset—challenging our beliefs, taking action, and reflecting on our own growth.

As educators, each of us needs to approach our work with a growth mindset as well. This involves challenging our beliefs, taking action, and reflecting on our own growth, which leads to efficacy in the work of teaching all children. Kristin Wiens, educator and inclusion advocate, crafted an outstanding visual that captures the construct of growth mindset in terms of inclusive practices (Figure 7.1).

We truly need a mindset shift in our educational system to make inclusion possible. If our starting stance is that all students belong and all students can learn, then our energy moves from perpetuating segregation to creating classrooms where this can actually happen.

We witnessed an example of this growth mindset process in action with a fifth-grade teacher a few years ago. This teacher was an experienced, competent, and compassionate educator. Yet he was facing a completely new challenge having a student with significant learning differences in his class. This student, Ethan, had a very limited oral vocabulary (less than 10 words), significant motor challenges, limited social interactions, and frequent seizure activity. The teacher had no frame of reference for how Ethan might engage in fifth-grade curriculum or be a part of his class. In our initial conversations the teacher said things like "I haven't been trained to work with students like this." To be fair, there was a lot of truth in that statement. His teacher licensure program would not have addressed students with complex needs, and he hadn't taught a student like Ethan in his previous years in the classroom.

We decided to support this teacher by giving him an opportunity to observe Ethan and begin to see him as a fifth grader, to see what he *could* do, to see how he *did*

FIGURE 7.1   Growth Mindset and Inclusion

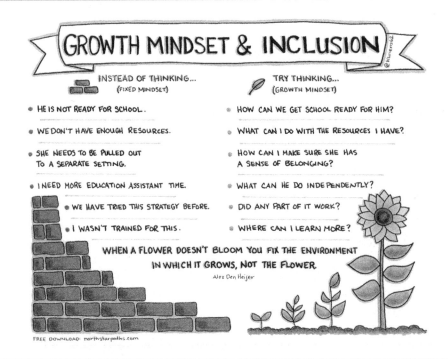

SOURCE: Used with Permission from Kristin Wiens.

connect with peers. We provided a full-day substitute for the teacher so that he could spend time observing Ethan, with no teaching responsibilities. This became a pivotal moment. The teacher came back with observations such as the following:

- "He can match items."
- "Ethan seems very interested when students are playing games."
- "He smiled when other students greeted him."
- "Ethan loves to touch different textures."

The teacher shared these observations with the learning specialist, and they began planning some tentative entry points into learning and community in the fifth-grade classroom:

- "When we are playing the math probability game, could Ethan sit with a team and match the number cards?"
- "What if Ethan helped take attendance in the morning? Students can check in with him, and he can match their name cards on an attendance board."
- "Instead of just having markers and paper out during the art period, could we make collage materials available for all students, and perhaps make sure some are very close for Ethan?"

These questions showed the dramatic shift in mindset that opened up possibilities for collaboration, focusing on what is possible and building on student strengths. A growth mindset is an absolute necessity for doing the work of creating inclusive schools.

Student Voice and Behavior

We were in a team meeting for Braden. We had the school psychologist, principal, learning specialist, special education IC, social worker, general education teacher, and Braden's mother sitting around a table. We were meeting because of serious concerns about Braden exhibiting unsafe behavior in multiple ways at school. We had gathered information from multiple sources for an FBA that would inform a behavior support plan (BSP). There were graphs set out on the table that included trend lines that indicated things were not getting better. The graphs tracked incidents of inappropriate language, unsafe hands (hitting others), and leaving class. The plan proposed teaching lagging skills, recognizing appropriate behavior, ignoring low-level misbehavior, and ensuring a consistent response to unsafe behavior. All indications were that the plan should be working, but it wasn't.

All of us around that table had used the statement "Behavior is communication." But somehow, we weren't really leaning into this belief with Braden. Eventually, the school psychologist asked, "What does Braden think?"

In many ways this is a more complicated question than it first appears. Most of us as parents—after our child has thrown our phone in the toilet or drawn on the wall in Sharpie—have asked, "What were you thinking?" And the most common answer in these situations is "I don't know." This is truly an authentic answer for many children. They may not yet have developed the emotional intelligence to understand the connection between their feelings and their actions. In the moment, their prefrontal cortex may not be operating at a level that allows them to rationally analyze their thought process.

Yet it is imperative that student voice is at the center of a BSP. We need to start with the premise that everyone is trying to meet a legitimate human need. All people are looking for love, acceptance, understanding, predictability, and novelty in their lives. Students in our schools are no exception, including students who may experience the most significant learning and communication differences.

We need to seek to understand how the student is experiencing the situation, and we need to find ways to feature student voice in this process. After conducting an observation where we look through a fairly behaviorist lens (What is the antecedent? What is the observable behavior? What are the consequences or the next things that happen?), we often bring those results to the student and ask for their perspective ("I noticed that when the teacher said it was time for writing, you made some inappropriate comments, and then you were asked to leave the room"). Students often have incredible insight about such a situation and may highlight something the observer didn't see ("I didn't care about the writing assignment. I was mad that I was expected to partner with John, and I know he doesn't like me").

In Chapter 6 we outlined "The 7 Components of Inclusive and Equitable Learning Communities" framework:

1. Effective physical spaces

2. Teaching common expectations

3. Rituals, routines, and recognition

4. Engagement strategies for all students

5. Teaching social-emotional skills

6. Restorative practices

7. Relationships with high expectations

After we had been using this framework with educators for more than two years, we finally realized that we needed to elicit student voice around these components in the process of problem-solving for behavior. In other words, if these are the components that we say are most important for teachers to focus on, we should ask how students are experiencing them in the classroom.

Coming back to our student Braden, our school psychologist followed up our team meeting with an interview/conversation with Braden to learn more about his perspective on The 7 Components. To all of the adults observing, it looked like the classroom teacher had a very positive relationship with Braden. She is a great teacher; she made many kind comments to him and went out of her way to feature his contribution in the classroom. Yet when Braden talked to the school psychologist about his school experiences, it became clear that he was convinced that the teacher did not like him. As adults, we understood that this was likely much more about the previous trauma that Braden had experienced than anything the teacher had done. However, the bottom line was Braden did not feel that he had a positive relationship with the teacher.

Listening to Braden's voice resulted in some important changes in the BSP. First of all, Braden was clear that he wanted to be successful in class. Based on this, the team changed the way they collected data. Previously, the primary data that they collected was "unsafe behaviors." Now they were counting the times when Braden engaged in class, completed work, and said respectful things to adults and peers. Even more important, the team came together to cover the class for 10 minutes three times a week so that the teacher and Braden could go outside and shoot baskets together. This time to invest in their relationship, which was not contingent on behavior, helped Braden build trust that his teacher did care about him. Building on that relationship, Braden began to respond to both the teacher's positive comments as well as her redirections.

When a student's behavior causes educators and families concern, it is often about how the student expresses themself in times of stress. As we listen and incorporate student voice into the planning and intervention process, we will experience more success in school settings, and we will support students in moving toward their own goals. We will come back to the subject of behavior in depth in Chapter 8.

Augmentative and Alternative Communication

Within our focus area of *increasing student voice*, one of our targets is "Each student has the tools and opportunities to communicate effectively about their learning, needs, interests, and preferences in school and in the community." For most students their primary mode of expressive communication is oral language. (As we discussed above, behavior is also a prominent mode of communication for all students, particularly students who have difficulties expressing their ideas and feelings through oral language.) However, a few students have developmental or cognitive barriers to producing typical speech. These students need some other mode of communication. For many of these students an AAC device is the right tool. In our district of 10,000 students we have about 45 students who communicate with an AAC device.

Alternative communication systems come in various forms, from low-tech picture boards to specialized high-tech devices with hundreds of icons organized in multiple layers of folders and screens. Most users select words and icons by pointing or touching the screen. However, some use eye-gaze systems, air-controlled straws, or head-tapping switches to make selections. Once the user has selected a word or created a sentence, the device reads the word aloud in a preselected computerized voice.

The most common AAC devices are touch-screen tablets (like iPads) with words and phrases organized in thematic groups. Users build motor patterns through repetition of familiar words. This is similar to the way smartphone users can swipe and tap their way to familiar apps without having to look closely at the screen. Another familiar form of habitual motor pattern is the way our fingers learn to navigate the letters on a keyboard.

For many people in the general public, the most familiar user of an AAC device was the theoretical physicist Stephen Hawking. The fact that Hawking is widely regarded as one of the most brilliant scientists of all time should remind us that lack of proficiency with oral communication does not indicate cognitive impairment. All people have valuable ideas to share with their community, and it is our moral obligation to find ways to help them communicate those ideas.

All people have valuable ideas to share with their community, and it is our moral obligation to find ways to help them communicate those ideas.

We encourage teachers, paraeducators, and families to think of an AAC device as a student's voice. The device should always be within arm's reach so the student can initiate communication. According to the helpful resource *Everyone Deserves a Voice: AAC Strategies for Success*, "If you can see the student, you should also be able to see their AAC" device (Zangari, 2017).

When a student is learning to use an AAC device, it is like learning another language. The only way to become proficient is to use the language over and over in many different contexts. We expect the student to make mistakes. Saying unexpected words through an AAC device is a playful way for the student to understand how the icons on the device make sounds that relate to ideas.

In addition, approximations are acceptable. A one- or two-word statement may be a good way for a student to start using the language. We don't require students to use grammatically complete sentences until they have become much more proficient with the device. Our first goal is clarity of communication, not precision of grammar.

How adults talk to a student who uses an AAC device makes a big difference. Here are some of the tips that we provide to teachers and paraeducators who work closely with students who use AAC devices:

- *Think about engagement.* What would the student want to talk to you about? We encourage staff to use the device during games and social interactions, in addition to academic tasks. This will encourage the student to use the device. It is particularly important for students to have their device with them during PE, lunch, and recess since these are times when natural informal communication happens.

- *Use a conversational tone and natural humor.* Talk to the student the same way you would talk to any student their age. A student who doesn't use verbal language should still be involved in conversations about things their classmates like to talk about.

- *Respect the student's processing time.* Allow wait time for a student to formulate a thought and find the icons to answer the question. Imagine if you needed to type or write a response to every question. It would take longer than speaking the answer. We all need time to organize our ideas into a form that can be communicated to the people around us.

- *Narrate what you are doing.* Saying "I'm drawing a square" while pressing the icons for *draw* and *square* helps students learn the connection between oral language, AAC use, and academic tasks. We recognize that adults will not know how to find every icon on the device. It is important to model the process of seeking new words and making approximations. Adults and students will learn to use the device together.

- *Ask questions that will prompt core word responses.* Students will rarely need to use specialized vocabulary (e.g., *photosynthesis*), so it is better to ask questions that prompt them to describe processes or ideas with everyday words. For example, the question "What happens during photosynthesis?" could prompt the student to respond with "green . . . plant . . . sun . . . air . . . food." This would reveal a deeper level of conceptual knowledge than asking a student "What is the name of the process that plants use to create food?" And the location of each of those words in their answer will be useful for them to learn for future communication.

- *Talk to the student, not about the student.* If a student is not able to produce verbal language, we often forget that they are still able to hear everything we say. It is important to ensure that we are always talking *to* students and eliciting their voice, rather than talking *about* students to the other adults in the room.

- *Involve peers.* Interacting with peers is highly motivating for most students. Using the device to communicate with peers can be a powerful way to develop language. Adults can teach peers to use the device to interact with the student. This also helps to demystify the device and normalize communication in all of its forms.

As with so many other aspects of our leadership for inclusive schools, we have learned that it is critical to build capacity across a range of adults to support students with AAC devices. Eight years ago, we started with a single specialist who had great expertise in AAC. But when we broke apart our self-contained classrooms and allowed students with the full range of learning needs to attend their neighborhood schools, we knew that one AAC expert would not be able to serve students at all 16 schools.

So we worked to decentralize the expertise. That AAC expert shifted her focus to building capacity in others. SLPs took the lead, with the support of occupational therapists. Some ICs, learning specialists, paraeducators, and classroom teachers also developed great proficiency with AAC devices. By demystifying the devices and making them a regular part of daily instruction, there is much more local ownership of the devices. Students cannot learn a new language if they only get to practice during a 20-minute session with the SLP twice a week. So teachers are planning for how to incorporate AAC devices into daily instruction.

Here are a few examples from across the district:

- In one first-grade classroom the teacher assigned the student with the device as the weather reporter for the first few weeks of school. The teacher, paraeducator, and parent would practice with the student to help her find the icons for sun, cloud, and rain (it's Oregon, so she got a lot of practice saying "rain"). After a few weeks the teacher realized that other students wanted to report on the weather. With permission from the student, the classmates used her device to say weather words at the morning meeting each day. This normalized the communication device and raised the status of a student who would have been in a self-contained classroom in most other districts.

- In one third-grade classroom the teacher used a student's device on the document camera to help classmates learn how to find icons. The student and her classmates took turns saying words on the device and laughing together. This modeled the natural way in which conversation can happen when peers have a basic understanding of the device, and it raised the status of the student who used AAC to communicate.

- At the social studies curriculum meetings one summer, middle school teachers were designing activities to promote collaborative learning. They had a series of photographs and other documents relating to a controversial moment in local history—how rising waters from Columbia River dams flooded the traditional Native American fishing sites around Celilo Falls. The first step for students would be to record what they notice and wonder at as they read the documents and look at the photographs. Each group of teachers had an AAC device on their table, and they took turns making observations and comments using the device. The teachers reported that this exercise helped them think more universally as they were designing lessons. The exercise reminded them that students who use devices can still engage in complex academic tasks, but we may need to adjust the kind of questions we ask and the mode of representation we expect.

- At all levels (K–12) students have been connecting AAC devices to laptops, which allows them to write essays and search the internet like their classmates.

In addition to building capacity for school staff to use AAC devices, we have partnered with parents to help them learn how to make AAC work for their child. Because parents have known their child since birth, they often develop shorthand communication systems. The parent knows the child's routines, so they can anticipate their needs—even when the child cannot express them explicitly. As a result some parents may not feel the urgency for their child to learn to use an AAC device.

As with learning any language, repetition and necessity build fluency. We can create opportunities for students to use the device at school, but they also need to use the device at home to accelerate their learning. One way we work with parents is through an AAC workshop that brings together the parent and the school staff who work closely with the student (general education teacher, learning specialist, SLP, paraeducators). School staff learn more about the student, and we give the family strategies to help them create opportunities for AAC language use at home. We found that developing some shared goals with the family about how the student will use the AAC device at home is critical. We don't want the family to feel overwhelmed. Instead, we want to help them establish some routines where parents and siblings can model communication with the device (e.g., during meals or bedtime routines). This promotes consistency between school and home and will support the generalizability that allows for richer language development.

STUDENTS AS LEADERS OF CHANGE

Movements for social change that do not empower the people at the heart of the work risk being ineffective, out of touch, or patronizing. In the education system there will always be aspects of the work that adults will need to lead. Yet we continue to learn the absolutely essential role that students can play as leaders of change in schools. This happens in formal and informal ways in our district on a daily basis. Every school principal will excitedly share stories of the powerful voices of students pushing for equity and inclusion in our schools, on issues of race, gender identity, bullying, and promoting positive mental health.

One structure that has been critical to launching student leadership focused on inclusive practices is the Youth Leadership Summit. This statewide event is organized by Special Olympics Oregon as part of the Unified Champion Schools program. The Youth Leadership Summit is organized by youth for youth, starting with the basic question "How can you make your school more inclusive?" Students from all of our middle schools and high schools attend the summit.

> We continue to learn the absolutely essential role that students can play as leaders of change in schools.

The first year, we primarily brought existing school leadership teams to the Youth Leadership Summit. This was a very important move to engage the ASB (Associated Student Body) officers and other elected student leaders in thinking about inclusion. But in that first year we also realized we were not practicing what we were preaching—none of these student leaders were served by special education. Through subsequent years the Youth Leadership Summit became an even more powerful experience as student leadership groups at our middle schools and high schools became more diverse and inclusive.

The Youth Leadership Summit is full of fun and energizing activities that help students build a deeper understanding of the importance of inclusive schools. The summit also provides opportunities for school teams to generate ideas and plan activities to make our school communities even more inclusive and welcoming. Many of the projects and ideas that emerged from the Youth Leadership Summit were outlined in Chapter 4, including Unified Sports, Respect campaigns, and Unified Clubs.

Another key way in which students have led change toward inclusive practices in our district is when they have directly shared their experiences with teachers. Ben, who had just completed high school, spoke to 150 of our teachers, specialists, and paraeducators at our annual Kickoff event. He had spent most of his school career in self-contained classrooms, grouped with other students who experience intellectual disabilities. After his sophomore year, we eliminated the Life Learning classrooms at our high schools. During his last two years of high school, his schedule resembled that of his peers without disabilities. He received a significant amount of academic and social support to be able to engage in grade-level courses, like Biology, English, and World History. It wasn't always easy, but he thrived in this inclusive environment. In segregated settings he had exhibited challenging behaviors. But in inclusive settings he followed peer models, and his behavior drastically improved.

When we asked Ben about this change from a self-contained classroom setting to an inclusive environment, he said, "When they let me out, I discovered I'm more of a different classes kind of guy. The work got harder, but I made more friends. I learned I could do more than I thought." We had not coached him for this presentation, and honestly, we weren't entirely sure what his perspective would be. Yet we knew it was important to have student voices leading our work. His phrase "When they let me out . . . " struck many people in the audience that day. It suggested the feeling of being trapped, imprisoned, or powerless. This was an evocative reminder of the way students can feel in a segregated self-contained classroom—even when we have the best of intentions as adults. His voice was more real for our teachers than all of the data and research articles we could have ever presented.

We bring students into our big-picture-planning, goal-setting, data review, and continuous-improvement processes. The primary structure for this is our Inclusive Schools Leadership Team, which we will discuss more in Chapter 9. Having students with and without disabilities providing input and becoming key communicators about inclusive practices is absolutely critical. Their presence keeps us focused on what our work is all about—the students! Having students present at these meetings also forces us to plan learning times that are engaging and fun. Adult learners need thoughtful, intentional, and engaging meeting facilitation too. Having students in the room forces us to think very intentionally about the structures and activities for our meetings.

Students bring their perspective in authentic ways. One year, we were working on a guidance document to help school teams plan peer support. The students on our Inclusive Schools Leadership Team shared what it is like to help other students and what it is like to be helped. They emphasized how important it is for a student to experience both roles. This deeply influenced the content and structure of our *Peer Support Handbook*.

Many students who have participated in our Inclusive Schools Leadership Team have gone on to pursue education majors in college. They have told us that the opportunity to engage in conversations about how to change systems influenced them and accelerated their commitment to making the world a better place.

STUDENTS AND THEIR IEPS

Based on our goal of fostering a growth mindset in all students, we started rethinking our process for developing and facilitating IEPs. Special education laws prescribe a detailed and complex process for the development of an IEP, including special factors for each team to consider, the required components of a goal, and how to document the frequency of a specific accommodation. Special education teachers take an entire college course on developing legally compliant IEPs. Too often this results in a compliance-focused IEP meeting, with a group of adults sitting around a table, a special education teacher reading through reams of paper about the student, and the parents chiming in from time to time. It can feel more like signing loan documents than a joyful conversation about a child.

Each of these points of compliance comes out of important hard-won rights for parents. For example, for many years students served by IEPs were excluded from statewide assessments. They were not expected to participate. Their progress was not included as a part of schoolwide accountability measures. And therefore, school leaders did not feel a sense of ownership or responsibility for their success. Now there is a full page of the IEP devoted to how the student will participate in statewide assessments. Ensuring that students with IEPs are part of the larger accountability system is an important part of ensuring that leaders pay attention to their needs as part of school improvement planning. Yet an unintended consequence of the detailed legal compliance required of the current IEP is that it can feel like an overly scripted, bureaucratic burden for teachers and parents. We often lose the idea that the IEP should be a positive process with the student at the center.

In our first year on this journey a principal shared frankly that she found the special education system to be broken—full of legal check boxes but not really changing learning trajectories for students. "Wouldn't it be amazing," we said, "if we could support a student in understanding their strengths and challenges as a learner, help them craft specific goals for improvement, and clearly commit to what we would do to support that student to achieve those goals? And wouldn't it be great if we did this in partnership with the student's parents and teachers? And wouldn't it be awesome if we helped the student track their progress and if we came back at least once a year to celebrate successes and adjust goals as needed?" She agreed that would be a terrific process. Well, that *is* the IEP process, or at least what it should be.

INVOLVE THE STUDENT IN THE IEP

The most high-leverage way to change the IEP process is to give it back to the student. This is *their* plan after all. A student leading their own IEP process, with appropriate support from their teachers and parents, is a game changer in the special education process.

Probably the most important reason to have students lead their own IEP development is that it leads to more effective learning for the student. We have found that students who help craft their learning plan are much more invested in achieving it. When we write goals *for* the student, rather than *with* the student, why are we surprised when the student doesn't reach that goal? As we discussed in Chapter 5, student engagement in knowing what they are learning and why they are learning it is a critical element of instructional practice. We are committed to teaching in such a way that learning targets are clear and students receive regular formative feedback so they can understand their next steps as learners. The student-led IEP process aligns with these beliefs.

Students who help craft their learning plan are much more invested in achieving it. When we write goals *for* the student, rather than *with* the student, why are we surprised when the student doesn't reach that goal?

When students are part of their IEP process, it demystifies and destigmatizes the support of special education. Students understand the IEP process as a way of knowing themselves as learners and use this as an opportunity to self-advocate. In a recent IEP meeting with a sixth grader, the student was talking about how she loves delving deep into the novels. But because of her dyslexia, it can be difficult for her to keep up with the pace of reading in her language arts class. Her awareness of her strengths as well as the impact of her learning differences enabled her to normalize her experience as a learner and advocate for her needs.

This leads to another important reason for the student-led IEP meeting—the power of the student's voice in ensuring that the IEP is implemented. At the IEP meeting for a seventh grader the student clearly shared his current strengths in mathematics as well as his goals for improvement. He explained that his processing time in mathematics is much slower than average but he can do well with the right supports. The student then turned to the mathematics teacher, looked him in the eye, and said, "Will you please make sure that I have a copy of all of the notes? And is it a problem if I have the extra time I need to complete classwork?" This teacher had probably supported hundreds of students with these sorts of accommodations over the years, but he never had a student look directly at him in a meeting and advocate so clearly. You can be certain that this made a huge impression on the teacher and he absolutely made sure that those accommodations were in place for that student.

Sometimes parents or staff wonder about how students feel about being involved in their own meetings. This is a valid question. When our IEPs have the right tone, focus, and flow, there is no reason why all students—even those as young as kindergarten—cannot be meaningful participants in their own meetings. A young student may present their strengths using a chart, book, poster, or slide show that they helped to create. They may talk about what they want to get better at, in terms of academic or social skills, and what is most helpful to their learning. Older students may provide more detailed input or more specific thinking about goals, objectives, and accommodations. The experience can always be amended depending on the interests, attention, and communication needs of the student. But we do believe that all students can and should be leading their learning and therefore leading their IEP meeting.

We began tracking student participation in the IEP process a few years ago by adding a question with a drop-down menu in our online IEP system. The case manager can quickly document the degree of student participation at each student's annual IEP meeting. This allows us to periodically review our progress toward our goal of 100% of students meaningfully participating in their IEPs (Figure 2.2). When we noticed fewer students than we hoped participating at the lower grades, we reached out to our learning specialists and asked what barriers they were experiencing. One of the barriers they identified was that many parents in elementary school did not want their children at the IEP meeting.

FIGURE 7.2 Student Participation in IEP Meetings

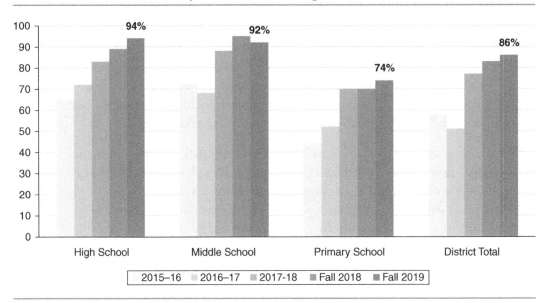

FIGURE 7.2 Student Participation in IEP Meetings

2015–16   2016–17   2017-18   Fall 2018   Fall 2019

NOTE: IEP, Individualized Education Program.

SOURCE: Used with Permission from West Linn-Wilsonville School District.

We asked the parents from our District and Parent Special Education Collaboration group to help us understand the parent's perspective. They told us that many parents had never been told the benefits of their child leading or participating in their IEP. We found a wonderful article—titled "Why Is This Cake on Fire?"—that explained the benefits of student participation in the IEP in parent-friendly terms, and we began sharing this with all parents of students who received special education services as part of their Parent Welcome packet (Van Dycke et al., 2006). By having case managers reach out to students and parents with intentional invitations, we have seen a steady upward trend in student participation in their IEP meetings across all grade levels.

PROVIDE IEP DRAFTS IN ADVANCE

Another important way to encourage authentic student engagement in the IEP meeting is providing parents with a draft of the IEP before the meeting. If they receive the draft ahead of time, parents have the opportunity to review the paperwork thoroughly. This allows them to come to the meeting with specific questions or areas to discuss. And more important, this eliminates the need to read through every aspect of the paperwork at the meeting. (Of course, there are times when a team or the parents may still need to go through each page of the IEP during the meeting. We always encourage our learning specialists to get to know the parents and what they need to feel fully part of the process.) As a result of sending the draft home in advance and streamlining the flow of the meeting, there is more "airtime" at the meeting for the team to celebrate the student's progress and for the student to share about their strengths, needs, and goals.

WHAT STUDENTS SAY ABOUT THE IEP

We thought it would be fitting to close this chapter on student voice with the words of two students. Marco, an elementary school student, shared with a group of teachers about participating in his IEP meeting. He described what it was like for him to lead the agenda, introduce everyone at the meeting, and share about his strengths and challenges. When he talked about helping to write his goals as part of the IEP team, he said, "If I didn't know my goals, how would I be able to reach them?" This statement struck us because it was so obvious and yet so often overlooked until we hear it spoken by a student who is living the IEP experience.

"If I didn't know my goals, how would I be able to reach them?"

Kenny, a senior, shared his insights about the IEP process:

> This fall, I spent a week creating a presentation for my IEP. I felt prepared, and it really felt like my meeting. In the past I didn't really like going to my IEPs because it was a bunch of adults talking about me. This year I was leading the meeting, and it was important to be part of it.

References

Dweck, C. S. (2008). *Mindset: The new psychology of success*. Ballantine Books.

Van Dycke, J. L., Martin, J. E., & Lovett, D. L. (2006). Why is this cake on fire? Inviting students into the IEP process. *TEACHING Exceptional Children*, *38*(3), 42–47. https://doi.org/10.1177/004005990603800306

Wiens, K. (2017, October 21–21). *Growth mindset and inclusion* [PowerPoint presentation]. PSA Super Conference 2017, Vancouver, BC, Canada. https://northstarpaths.com/graphics-free-downloads/

Zangari, C. (2017, June 5). *Everyone deserves a voice: AAC strategies for success*. PrAACticalAAC. https://praacticalaac.org/praactical/praactical-resources-aac-101-flipbook-handout/

CHAPTER 8

Supporting Behavior in Inclusive Schools

When you stay focused on the whole child, it can feel a bit awkward to write specifically about addressing behavioral needs. This is because we acknowledge how deeply interconnected the work is. When students feel they belong, when they have appropriate communication systems, when they are deeply engaged in their academic learning, when the staff operate with a trauma-informed lens, and when the skills of regulation and social-emotional learning are explicitly taught, most issues labeled as "behavior" are resolved within the context. *It is important to state that the vast majority of students with IEPs and the vast majority of students who experience significant disability do not engage in behaviors that present safety concerns.* Yet we do know that all students develop skills at a different pace. And mental health issues can contribute to situations where the needs of students may require a more intensive approach, particularly when the student's behavior is resulting in injuries to themselves, other students, or staff.

When educational leaders from other districts come to visit our schools to learn with us about inclusive practices, they often ask very real questions about students who have engaged in behavior that is truly unsafe. A classroom cannot be inclusive or equitable when students or teachers are concerned about their safety. It is important to understand this and to validate it. Safety is a basic human need, and it is always our priority. When you lead with inclusivity, restorative practices, and growth mindset as we do, it is critical to be crystal clear about the importance of safety. Unsafe behavior is unacceptable, and we take it seriously. And this should be said out loud and often. But when we take this behavior seriously, what should we then do?

When many of us were in K–12 education as students, the answer to unsafe behavior was straightforward: exclusionary discipline. Students were suspended for hitting and often expelled for fighting. But did that make schools safer—in particular, did it make those students less likely to engage in that behavior in the future? As a recent article in the National Education Association journal explains,

Kids who were suspended or expelled were more likely to drop out and disconnect from their education for three reasons: the true root of the problem was not addressed, their learning was interrupted, or the students did not feel valued or connected to their school community. Additionally, students of color are disproportionately targeted by the exclusionary practices. (Luster, 2018)

The practice of suspension is not effective in addressing the reason for the behavior or in helping the student develop the skills to solve the problem a different way the next time. And the implications related to disproportionality of race and exclusionary discipline make these practices unacceptable for schools that are committed to equity.

The other way schools have traditionally dealt with students who exhibited unsafe behavior was to use the special education placement process to gather all of those students into a segregated classroom. In Chapter 1 we clearly laid out the problems associated with separate classes in terms of peer modeling, self-concept, academic rigor, community belonging, and more. It may be hard for education leaders to imagine their schools without a self-contained behavior classroom, but we knew this was not the answer we were looking for as we sought to create inclusive and equitable schools.

One incredibly important benefit of a districtwide commitment to inclusive schools is that self-contained, behavioral-focused classrooms are not available as an option. This is critical for teams that are supporting a student who is significantly struggling in their social-emotional and behavioral skills. This is some of the most complex and emotionally taxing work in schools. Every educator reading this is certainly nodding emphatically at this statement! It is difficult and nuanced. If the IEP team think there is another option available (in the form of a segregated self-contained program), it may affect their ability to think creatively to establish structures and supports for the student within their own neighborhood school. Because the option of another place is not on the table in our district, we find that teams come together to create effective structures for students that result in successful outcomes—in much less restrictive settings.

ALL-SOME-FEW THINKING

We know that continuing to focus on the proactive work of implementing "The 7 Components of Inclusive and Equitable Learning Communities" (outlined in Chapter 6) will create the conditions for *most* students to be successful in our classrooms. At the same time, we must layer in the structures and supports that *some* students need to be successful. And there are very *few* students who will need a very comprehensive wraparound approach. The ideas behind The 7 Components are the same principles that we need to think about for those students who need more, but we may need to increase the intensity, frequency, or personalization of how students experience those components.

Rob Horner and George Sugai (2015) pioneered the model of a tiered approach to behavior support. Their work, originally known as Positive Behavior Interventions and Supports, or PBIS, is one of the most powerful frameworks for school improvement and safety. Their constructs of tiered supports, data-based decisions, and implementation science are also the foundation for much of today's emphasis on MTSS. Horner and Sugai remind us that we must simultaneously invest in whole-school practices while also developing effective and intensive interventions that some students will need more to be successful. This tiered thinking and proactive stance have become the standard approach in most schools, although implementation is certainly varied across schools and districts.

Having a tiered approach to behavior is strongly supported in the research on inclusive schools. The School-Wide Integrated Framework for Transformation (SWIFT) is a national technical assistance project promoting inclusive schools. SWIFT lays out a framework for successful inclusive practices—and inclusive behavior support is one of the key elements. Their Research-to-Practice Brief concludes that sustained focus on schoolwide PBIS is a major contributing factor to providing behavior support in inclusive settings (SWIFT Center, 2017).

In our district we made sense of the research-based practices of PBIS by connecting it with our long-standing vision theme of "Circles of Support." This All-Some-Few structure of our circle diagram is similar to the more familiar pyramid that is commonly used to represent PBIS and MTSS systems. The meaning of the circle is important to us—and it is not merely that we feel the need to put our own shape on things.

Circles are at the heart of restorative practices—a way to build community, where everyone is seen and everyone has a voice. Circles are a symbol of inclusion—who is in the circle is who belongs. Using the Circles of Support diagram helps us remember that all students belong in our circle, even as we acknowledge the importance of proactively preparing for the varied levels of need of our students.

All students need strong relationships with high expectations, and all teachers need to proactively create these relationships and expectations. Yet we must understand that some students also need more intentional relationship building and clearer expectations. A few students may need teachers to reach out even more explicitly and frequently. All-Some-Few thinking and structures help us create safe and inclusive environments, even for students with significantly lagging skills in communication or emotional regulation.

There are many components in our All-Some-Few work that are common to many schools, including check-in/check-out programs and data collection systems. Here we will highlight just three components of our work that are most relevant to the concerns about unsafe behavior.

FIGURE 8.1   All-Some-Few Circles

Circles of Support
- Invest in the **ALL**
- Involve all staff and students in owning and implementing the **ALL**
- Reinvest in the **ALL** circle when a student is communicating challenges
- Use the components of the **ALL** with some functional thinking when deciding whether to implement strategies at the **SOME** level
- As a team moves from **ALL** to **SOME** to **FEW**, levels of assessment and feedback need to intensify
- The student is always a student with unique gifts and an endless capacity to learn; they should never be labeled by the level of support

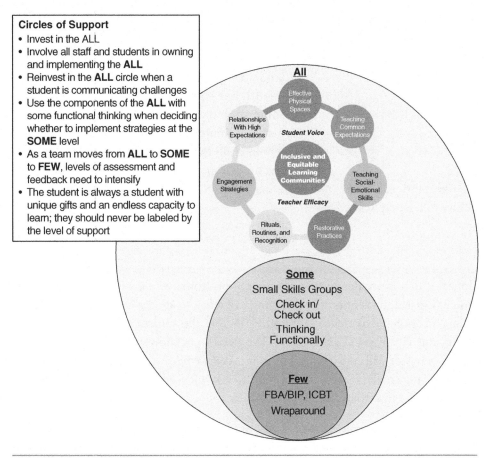

NOTE: FBA, Functional Behavioral Assessment; BIP, Behavior Intervention Plan; ICBT, Intensive Capacity-Building Team.

SOURCE: Used with Permission from West Linn-Wilsonville School District.

Team "Student"

Education is a team sport. We have curriculum teams, grade-level teams, and content teams. Each team has an important role in the work of schools. Most schools have existing teams that help students be more successful in terms of behavior (sometimes called Tier 3 Teams, Data Teams, or Wraparound Teams). Teams are a critical component of implementing tiered supports in a PBIS model (Algozzine et al., 2019). The IEP team, including the family and the student, also plays an important role by creating the conditions, crafting the goals, and outlining the support that the school needs to put in place for a student to become more successful behaviorally. In our move to inclusive practices we implemented many of these teams, and we agree that they play a very important role in implementation and data-based decision-making.

Yet when a student was showing us that they needed more support (moving into our "Few" circle), we noticed that things were most successful when a new team emerged: Team "Student." This team (Team Jack, Team Carly, Team Alastair, Team Dwayne . . . you get the idea) is a different kind of team. This team is fully focused on the student and engages the adults in seeing the situation from the student's point of view. This team meets frequently for short periods of time—weekly for some students, daily if needed, or perhaps for just 10 minutes at a time. This team keeps the whole-child thinking front and center. Three of the most important reasons for Team "Student" are the emotional nature of challenging behavior, the need for consistency, and the ability to adapt quickly.

> This team keeps the whole-child thinking front and center.

INTEGRATED EXPERIENCE

Behavior that is unsafe always evokes emotion from everyone involved. The Nonviolent Crisis Intervention training program refers to aggressive or unsafe behavior as an "integrated experience," reminding us that the student's behavior affects the adults and vice versa (Laska, 2016). We need to acknowledge that aggressive or unsafe behavior will evoke emotions in us. And we need to acknowledge that those emotions may make it increasingly hard to stay focused on the student's strengths and our belief that they can learn new skills.

Dwayne is a fourth-grade student who was developing his communication skills. As his family and the educators around him worked to help him develop those skills, he often expressed his frustration and discontent by hitting whoever was closest to him. A staff member was injured, and emotions were pretty raw at the school. The principal invited us to join the newly formed Team Dwayne meetings, scheduled for just 10 minutes every Monday, Wednesday, and Friday before school.

As the members of Team Dwayne arrived (the general education teacher, three paraeducators, the learning specialist, the special education IC, and the SLP), they immediately formed a standing circle. One member of the team led a short breathing exercise and invited each member to think of two words: one word about their day yesterday and one word that gives them strength. As each member shared those words, you could feel the power of providing space for the emotional part of this work. We have to acknowledge that supporting students who are displaying unsafe or aggressive behavior is inherently emotional, and we need to provide the space and care for the people doing the work. This took up about three minutes of the Team Dwayne meeting.

The next thing we observed with Team Dwayne really surprised us. The team members each went around the circle and shared one strength or thing they appreciated about Dwayne. This moment allowed us to remember Dwayne as a child, as a human being, as someone who is trying to navigate the world around him the best that he can. Taking this moment helped all of the adults on Team Dwayne keep their focus. We are here because we believe in Dwayne, we believe in education, and we believe that this situation can get better.

CONSISTENCY

You may have noticed that Team Dwayne had seven members. Because of the emotionality of the work for the adults, as well as to support student independence and generalizability of new skills, it is critical that there are several key adults supporting Dwayne throughout his day. However, the larger the team, the more challenging it is to have consistent understanding and implementation of the support plan. Is there particular language that is helpful or not helpful to Dwayne? Does everyone understand the nuances of body language when Dwayne is calm versus when he is showing signs of frustration?

So often there is a beautifully crafted BSP based on a thoroughly researched FBA with clear guidance about what behaviors to positively recognize, what new skills we are teaching, and how to safely react if an escalation begins. And yet some members of the team may have forgotten those key points or, worse, may never have seen those plans. Short Team "Student" meetings allow folks who actually work with the student to frequently and succinctly review the key points of the plan and calibrate their understanding.

The more intensive the behavior challenge, the more consistent we need to be in implementing the plan. At the Team Dwayne meeting, after checking our emotions and remembering Dwayne's strengths around the circle, the learning specialist handed out index cards that had bullet points of the two important skills that everyone should be teaching and reinforcing for Dwayne throughout his day. On the back of the card were the Zones of Regulation colors (blue, green, yellow, red) and a short phrase indicating exactly what staff should do if Dwayne is in a particular phase (Kuypers, 2011). A few staff asked clarifying questions, such as "What are the break space options?" or "What should I do if he doesn't want to leave the break space?"

The team finished with another quick cleansing breath and high fives of appreciation to each other. The entire Team Dwayne meeting lasted 10 minutes. People felt heard, the emotionality of the work was acknowledged, the humanity of the student was highlighted, and staff remembered the key areas to focus on for success and safety. This process was quick and sustainable, and it greatly increased the likelihood that Dwayne's plan will work.

ADAPTABILITY

Though it may seem paradoxical, adaptability is as important as consistency when supporting students with significant behavioral challenges. By this, we do not mean changing BSPs on a whim or inconsistent implementation of plans across team members. Rather, we use the term *adaptability* to refer to the way the team reflects frequently on student data, asks the right questions, and then is empowered to respond creatively.

One key question to ask is "When is the student most successful?" At a recent Team Carly meeting, we heard the IC ask that question about a middle school girl who was really struggling with self-regulation. The answer came from one of the paraeducators: "Well, if we could just allow her to dance through her day, she'd be doing great."

The team initially laughed. But then they considered this answer seriously and looked for more evidence that this was true. Sure enough, when the music came on, all safety concerns for Carly disappeared. The team asked Carly about it, and she was able to respond with her AAC device, "Music" "Love" "Dance." After a great discussion with the family and the PE/Wellness teacher, the team decided that opportunities to dance would be scheduled throughout her day. She would start each class period by leading warm-up dances for every PE/Wellness class. Then she would return to her regular classrooms to engage in her classwork. Knowing that she would have opportunities to dance to music throughout her day greatly relieved the frustration Carly was experiencing. And the incidents of aggressive behavior plummeted. The structure of Team Carly (particularly the presence of paraeducators who work with her daily) allowed the adults who support Carly to collaborate effectively and adapt the school structures to provide the support she needed.

You may be thinking, "How will we find the time to meet as Team 'Student' once a week or more?" Remember the context of All-Some-Few. When we are investing proactively in the structures and strategies for All and Some, there will be very Few students for whom safety-related behavior is a concern. For these students, investing in the Team "Student" structure is a proactive and more effective way to take seriously the safety concerns and really work to change things. And as we described above, these meetings are intended to be short, efficient, and focused on positive solutions.

The Intensive Capacity-Building Team

As we will discuss further in Chapter 9, we have chosen to organize our leadership structure with highly skilled ICs who have a range of specialized knowledge and skills, rather than dividing up our expertise by specialty area. That is, our ICs combine the roles of autism specialist, behavior specialist, assistive technology specialist, and instructional coach. They work with a small number of school teams (two to three schools each), so they develop meaningful working relationships with principals, teachers, parents, and students. When a student exhibits challenging behaviors, we don't need to bring in a behavior specialist, because the IC is already part of the team. And in most cases, this has worked really well.

We have noticed over the years that a very few students (typically one to four students in the district per year) had a pattern of escalations that were not being resolved or stabilized through our typical behavior support process (frequent Team "Student" meetings, FBA, BSP, IEP team meetings, etc.). To address this, we developed a new support structure that we call the Intensive Capacity-Building Team (ICBT).

The ICBT is a group of two to four specialists who come alongside a school team when there is a significant safety need that the school team hasn't been able to address at the classroom or building level. The ICBT is made up of some combination of ICs, school psychologists, and other district-level specialists (most often a social worker).

We recognize that bringing in a team of specialists from outside the school could reinforce the feeling among the school team that they are unable to address the student's needs on their own. And, even worse, the need for an external team of experts might spread the belief that the student's needs are so complex that they need to be somewhere else (in some specialized program outside their neighborhood school). As the name suggests, the purpose of the ICBT is to build capacity in the school team. To ensure that the ICBT does not take over responsibility from the school team and reinforce unhelpful beliefs about students, we created a guidance document to clearly state the purpose and process of the ICBT. We review that document with the ICBT members and school teams before and after each ICBT response.

Here are the guiding principles for the ICBT:

- *School teams have the capacity* and the desire to meet the unique and diverse needs of all learners; sometimes school teams need temporary support to help extend their capacity in response to new or complex student needs.

- *Capacity building is an investment* in the effectiveness and future sustainability of a school team.

- *Relationships are powerful*—school teams know their students well, and ongoing support for social-emotional learning happens best in a context with familiar adults.

- As part of our professional learning, *we all benefit from additional perspectives*—growth mindset.

- *Adult staff have their own emotional responses* when working with students who present with complex behaviors.

- Complex student behaviors affect other students and staff in the classroom and the school—*we are all committed to a safe learning community* for all students and staff.

The work of the ICBT requires two to four staff members to drop everything they are doing and embed themselves in a school for three to four days. It is a significant investment of time and emotional energy. It would not be sustainable to bring together an ICBT every time a student is exhibiting frustrating or challenging behavior. The ICBT is for the very highest level of concerns (students who might be considered for an outside placement in an intensive therapeutic school). Therefore, we have a threshold for how we initiate an ICBT response. This includes a conversation between the principal and our student services administrators about the following:

- The student's strengths and how those strengths can lay a foundation for positive steps

- The frequency, duration, and context of the problem behavior—including any triggers or antecedents the school team has identified

- Intervention strategies, accommodations, and modifications that are already in place—and data the school team has gathered related to those strategies

- What the team process has looked like and how that process has involved all team members (general education teachers, office staff, student, family)

- What capacity we want to build—in the school team and in the individual student's self-management and social-emotional regulation skills

Based on these conversations, we are often able to point the principal and teachers to resources that they currently have within their team (e.g., their school psychologist, IC, occupational therapist, or social worker). However, on a few occasions we find that it is necessary to call together the ICBT. In the first year of this new team we had four ICBT responses. In the next year we had two ICBT responses, in the fall and in winter (school was closed in spring due to the coronavirus outbreak). We have called together the ICBT at the elementary, middle, and high school levels, but most of the responses have been at the elementary level.

When the ICBT arrive at a school, they don't just jump in and "fix the problem." Instead, they begin by observing the student, interviewing the staff, and reviewing data to gather a more complete picture of the student's strengths and lagging skills. The team uses "The 7 Components of Inclusive and Equitable Learning Communities" to observe the context, as well as the more traditional antecedent-behavior-consequences observations of the student. The ICBT provides check-ins and social-emotional support for the adults in the building, because we know that the team would not be called in if the school staff were not exhausted and frustrated—and possibly also feeling defeated. Then they get to work helping to build capacity—which can be done, for example, in the following ways:

- Collaborative facilitation to help teams learn to gather and analyze data

- Specific support and modeling with skill building for staff (crisis intervention training), collaborative problem-solving, trauma-informed practices)

- Support with restorative practices (e.g., leading/supporting classroom circles)

- Support for the school leadership team, including communication with staff and parents

- Creating documents, visual supports, and observation/data-gathering tools for the school team to use with specific students

- Creating or improving relationships and communication with outside mental health/wraparound teams

Calling in the ICBT does not mean giving up any control for the school-based leadership team. In fact, the purpose of the ICBT is the complete opposite—empowering school-based staff to develop the skills and tools to support a student in a behavioral crisis. For that reason the presence of the ICBT is intentionally visible in the school. We want the school staff to know that their concerns are being heard and the school team is developing the skills to support the student in the long run.

> The purpose of the ICBT is to empower school-based staff to develop the skills and tools to support a student in a behavioral crisis.

The ICBT never looks the same twice. There is no script or formula. Instead, it is designed to be iterative and responsive to the needs of the student and the school team. So far, by focusing on building capacity rather than simply solving problems, the ICBT has led to long-term, sustainable growth for students and school teams.

THINKING INCLUSIVELY ABOUT OUTSIDE PLACEMENT

There have been very few situations where, even with all of the strategies, structures, and beliefs that we have described here, we have not been able to resolve the safety issue regarding student behavior. In these cases we have had to look at the possibility of a different setting, like a day treatment program for a significant mental health crisis. In a district of about 10,000 students, we average about 5 students in an outside placement at any given time. We are grateful that these more intensive options are available for students and families when they need them.

However, even with outside placements, we strive to think inclusively. We continue to keep the family connected with their neighborhood school. We have that school's learning specialist or principal continue to communicate with the student, go to meetings at the outside placement, and send pictures of encouragement. The message is that the student and family still belong at their neighborhood school and we are ready for them to return as soon as they can.

It is incredibly important that we are explicit and intentional about continuing to build connection and belonging throughout the difficult process of making a team decision to change placement. Students and their families can experience feelings of shame or rejection in these times ("I'm not good enough for that school," "They don't like my child"). So we need to continue to reach out and build bridges.

Tyler entered kindergarten with great curiosity about the world around him and the ability to read at the fourth-grade level. His intellectual strengths were, however, paired with profound delays in his ability to regulate his emotions and impulses. The team ensured that he was matched with a great teacher who could challenge him academically and who had terrific classroom management skills. "The 7 Components of Inclusive and Equitable Learning Communities" were clearly evident in the teacher's classroom. Yet Tyler's behavior continued to become more aggressive and unsafe, first toward staff, and then toward peers.

The team developed a check-in/check-out system, worked through FBAs, and implemented strong BSPs. But the data did not show improvement. The family engaged in meeting after meeting with the team and worked to provide consistency between home and school, bringing their ideas, which the school team incorporated. The team tried to find ways to listen to Tyler's voice to better understand *the why* behind his actions. We made new observations and collected more precise data. But we could not find a way to shift his behavior.

It came to the point where we needed to make a change for the safety of other students. The family and the school district worked to get a deeper evaluation from a clinical psychologist, and ultimately intensive day treatment services were recommended.

This was a heartbreaking situation for the family. They lived near the school. They felt guilt and shame that they couldn't find a way to change this behavior pattern in their son. They felt hurt that the school team hadn't found a better way to meet his needs. But because the process had been so collaborative and thorough, they knew that the move to day treatment was best for their son at that time.

Tyler remained in day treatment for two years.

During those two years, the IC from Tyler's neighborhood school maintained a connection with Tyler and his family. He did the expected things, like showing up at IEP meetings at the day treatment center. But he also did unexpected things, like continuing to call the family to check in. He made sure that they were still invited to buy books at the school's book fair. He made sure that when all students got a T-shirt with the school slogan on it, Tyler got one too. He maintained relationship and connection.

As Tyler's emotional regulation skills grew and his mental health crisis began to wane, the IC and the family looked for small opportunities for Tyler to begin to return to his neighborhood school, even though he was still attending day treatment full-time. One of the first steps was to set up some small play gatherings on the playground when school was not in session. They kept these short and positive, and Tyler began to build on that success. Tyler and his family joined a group that worked on the school garden over the summer, and then we arranged for Tyler to be part of an afterschool enrichment class.

When the team was ready for Tyler's placement to change back to the public school setting, the process was much more successful because the relationships and sense of belonging had been carefully nurtured all along the way. That meeting ended in hugs all around and Tyler saying, "I'm ready. I know how to be safe. I have tools to use. I don't have to be perfect, I just need to be safe. And this is my school." There were definitely tears all around.

References

Algozzine, B., Barrett, S., Eber, L., George, H., Horner, R., Lewis, T., Putnam, B., Swain-Bradway, J., McIntosh, K., & Sugai, G. (2019). *School-wide PBIS Tiered Fidelity Inventory*. OSEP Technical Assistance Center on Positive Behavioral Interventions and Supports.

Horner, R. H., & Sugai, G. (2015). School-wide PBIS: An example of applied behavior analysis implemented at a scale of social importance. *Behavior Analysis in Practice, 8*(1), 80–85. https://doi.org/10.1007/s40617-015-0045-4

Kuypers, L. (2011). *The Zones of Regulation*. www.zonesofregulation.com

Laska, M. (2016). *Team intervention strategies: How to help yourself and others stay safe*. Crisis Prevention Institute. https://www.crisisprevention.com/Blog/January-2016/Team-Intervention-Strategies

Luster, S. (2018, July 19). How exclusionary discipline creates disconnected students. *neaToday*. http://neatoday.org/2018/07/19/how-exclusionary-discipline-creates-disconnected-students/

SWIFT Center. (2017, July). *Sustaining SWPBIS for inclusive behavior instruction* (Research-to-Practice Brief). https://files.eric.ed.gov/fulltext/ED576681.pdf

CHAPTER 9

Leadership Moves to Make It Happen

On a learning walk with a group of principals and district leaders visiting from Tennessee, one of our principals summarized the change process by saying, "Change is hard—until it's easy." When talking about a child who demonstrated complex and challenging behaviors, one of our principals said, "You're going to learn something from this child that you can learn no other way."

Over the years we have heard many teachers and leaders express similar sentiments. We look for opportunities to share them as a way to help others find their Why too. As leaders, we need to create space and time for principals, teachers, paraeducators, school secretaries, custodians, and the rest of our school staff to discover their Why. And we need to create structures and systems to navigate the practical details of the work. This chapter focuses on some of the leadership moves that have been essential to making—and sustaining—our shift to inclusive practices.

COMMUNICATION AND RELATIONSHIPS

One of the guiding principles throughout our district is that relationships matter. At all levels of the organization, personal connections are meaningful. We value peer-to-peer relationships among students. We seek to foster relationships with high expectations between teachers and students. We want to cultivate trusting relationships with parents and community partners. Fundamental to all of these relationships is clear and trustworthy communication.

When we think about the leadership actions and decisions that form the foundation of our inclusive practices, we are constantly reminded of the importance of building relationships through clear communication. A big key to building relationships is simply to be present—making time to be with people and making sure people know they are valued because we choose to spend our time with them. Also necessary to these relationships are the intentional structures of communication.

A few years ago we heard that some teachers were feeling overwhelmed by the complexity of including all students in their classes. At two schools in particular there were rumblings of frustration in the early spring. So we made time to go to those schools and have a Coffee Talk with the staff. We came to listen with purpose. We knew that the teachers needed to feel like we truly heard and understood their concerns. We provided supports in response to their specific concerns. We stayed in the conversation through the hard times, returning to check in with the teachers from time to time through the rest of the school year.

The next fall we decided to expand the Coffee Talk structure to include all 16 schools. We visited 1–2 schools a week, bringing coffee and breakfast treats to the staff. The gatherings were intentionally informal and voluntary. At some schools we had five or six teachers and paraprofessionals join us. At other schools we had a standing-room-only crowd.

We did not come to the Coffee Talks with an explicit agenda or presentation. Instead, we were there to listen. We asked folks to share about the inclusive practices in their schools—what was going well and where they had questions, concerns, or suggestions. We learned a lot from taking the time to listen. In most cases the concern was about supporting students with complex behavioral needs. The feedback we heard from teachers helped us

> We learned a lot from taking the time to listen.

design and refine the Inclusive and Equitable Classrooms workshops, which we will describe later in this chapter. The Coffee Talks also helped us generate the idea of the ICBT, which we described in Chapter 8.

On balance, we believe that the Coffee Talks were a helpful leadership strategy. However, they required a significant investment of time, and at some schools the Coffee Talk conversations also stirred up discord and seemed to amplify the feelings of frustration. The following year we chose not to repeat the Coffee Talk format. Instead, we visited staff meetings more often and held more frequent meetings with our Certified and Classified association leaders. We are considering revamping the Coffee Talk structure to use in the future. Regardless of the format, we remain committed to engaging in conversations, listening to understand, and maintaining trusting relationships.

Another important form of communication is weekly, monthly, and quarterly newsletters. Most organizations have newsletters, but most people don't read them. So we are constantly vigilant to ensure that we maintain a purposeful focus in the content and style of our newsletters. If we take the time to write something—and if we expect people to take the time to read it—it should provide inspiration to help people connect with their Why and provide practical examples to help them move forward with The How and The What.

Our most frequent written communication is a weekly newsletter that we call the *Monday Message* (although we sometimes call it the *Monday-ish Message* if it comes out a few days late). This newsletter is for our special education staff, counselors, and principals. We highlight success stories related to our three focus areas: *creating inclusive cultures*, *improving instructional practices*, and *increasing student voice*. We also provide specific procedural guidance and reminders of upcoming professional learning opportunities.

Each month, we send the *Learning Together* newsletter to all our district staff. In addition to classroom teachers, administrators, and paraeducators, this two-page newsletter reaches staff whose work is less focused on the classroom (e.g., payroll specialists, nutrition services, custodians, library assistants, and school secretaries). The subtitle of the *Learning Together* newsletter is "General Education and Special Education Teachers Working Together to Support All Students." The articles focus on specific examples of inclusive practices in schools across the district. We highlight successes like coplanning/co-teaching, UDL, tools for promoting access and student voice, and Unified Sports. By sharing these stories, we hope that all staff will be inspired by the great work being done by their colleagues—helping to build both The Why and The How of inclusive practices. We often hear feedback from support staff that they appreciate the inspiring glimpses into our inclusive classrooms.

Three or four times a year, we also publish the *Parent Connection* newsletter for parents of students served by special education. This is another opportunity to promote inclusive practices and build a collaborative community of stakeholders. We also advertise ways for parents to get involved—like the AAC we described in Chapter 7 and the District-Parent Special Education Collaboration Group, which we will describe later in this chapter.

THE ROLE OF THE CENTRAL OFFICE

The process of creating truly inclusive schools is really not the work of the Special Education department. The most obvious shifts in structure, eliminating segregated self-contained classrooms, will affect the Special Education department more than the other departments in the district. However, making a school community truly inclusive requires collaborative leadership from executive staff and administrators who are not specifically assigned to supporting special education.

Shifting structures and practices to make them more inclusive cannot be a unilateral decision by the Special Education department.

We often joke that collaboration and co-teaching cannot be a unilateral decision. A learning specialist cannot tell a classroom teacher that they are going to co-teach without the active consent of the classroom teacher. In the same way, shifting the structures and practices of a school or district to make them more inclusive cannot be a unilateral decision by the Special Education department. This section will describe some of the central office supports that are necessary for creating truly inclusive schools.

VISION FROM THE CENTRAL OFFICE

It is common for school districts to adopt a motto or vision statement that claims to support all students. Here are a few that came up from a quick search of district mottos:

- Every Student, Every Day

- Educating All Students to Ensure the Future of Democracy

- Each and Every Child Prepared for a World Yet to Be Imagined

- A Great Place for All Kids

Our district goal #1 says, "Grow student achievement through the use of high-leverage instructional and engagement strategies to raise rigor, disrupt systems of racism, and generate equitable outcomes for all students while eliminating opportunity and achievement gaps." There are many words to interpret and unpack in this goal. Our district leaders and teachers often start meetings by thinking about key words and concepts in this goal: *grow, high leverage, rigor, systems of racism, equitable, eliminating, opportunity gaps, achievement gaps.* When we develop a common understanding of what these words mean and how we are working to address this goal, we have a better chance of meeting the goal. Of course, the most important word in the goal is *all*. If we grow student achievement and raise rigor but we only aim to do this for some students, what is the value of the goal?

Having a goal that points us toward truly meeting the needs of *all* students—with a rigorous curriculum and high expectations for student performance—is a great starting point for creating truly inclusive school communities. A goal needs to be more than just the words on a district website. Central office leaders need to embrace the goal and strategically plan to move the goal forward.

HIRING PRACTICES

An important role for the central office in strategically moving toward more inclusive school communities is setting the expectation for equitable hiring practices. There has been much written about the imbalance of racial and ethnic representation in the education workforce. Teachers and administrators in America are predominantly white, even while white students are no longer the majority in many schools across the country. Addressing the need for (and the impact of) hiring and retaining a diverse staff of teachers is incredibly important to all goals of equity and inclusion; discussion of that is beyond the scope of this book. We are focused here primarily on inclusive practices related to students identified with disabilities. However, many of the inclusive practices we describe in this book will also support greater diversity of racial, ethnic, linguistic, and gender identity and experience.

When hiring teachers, we are, of course, looking for people who are experts in their content area, with the pedagogical skills to inspire rich learning experiences for students. And we want to hire teachers who love kids. We also need to hire teachers who believe in the capacity of each child, every child to learn, to belong, and to contribute to the classroom and school community.

In our district we have a thorough hiring process for all licensed staff. Principals start by reviewing applications and conducting brief screening phone calls. Then a selection of candidates comes to an interview with a team of teachers and other key staff. The top two or three candidates then move on to a follow-up interview with the principal and one or two assistant superintendents. Finally, we bring the top candidate forward to a final interview with the superintendent.

For the past 40+ years the superintendent has met with every teacher before the final hiring decision was made. This is a significant investment of time for a district with 10,000 students and over 600 teachers. It is part of what the previous superintendent, Dea Cox, called the "People Strategy." Education researcher Richard Sagor (2000) has described the People Strategy in terms of prioritizing, hiring, and retaining the best educators as a key to all effective school improvement processes.

Our current superintendent has continued this practice, making a personal connection with every new teacher who joins the district. In the final interview she asks the candidate to reflect on their beliefs about and commitment to equity and inclusion. She pushes them to articulate why a student who would previously have been relegated to a self-contained classroom should be taught alongside their peers in general education settings. If the superintendent is not convinced that the new teacher is committed to truly serving all students, we do not hire them. This is true not only for special education teachers. She also asks these questions of kindergarten teachers, middle school Spanish teachers, high school physics teachers, librarians, and music teachers.

> If the superintendent is not convinced that the new teacher is committed to truly serving all students, we do not hire them. Every teacher knows that they are expected to be a leader for equity and inclusion.

Every new teacher entering the district knows that they are expected to be a leader for equity and inclusion. Every teacher is expected to take ownership of all students, creating a classroom community where all students truly belong. This expectation comes directly from the superintendent and is supported by the other district leaders and building principals. This coherence of purpose and vision has helped us move forward together toward more inclusive learning communities.

LEADERSHIP FOR PROFESSIONAL DEVELOPMENT

In addition to hiring new teachers who are committed to inclusive practices, another key role of the central office is support for professional development that promotes inclusive instruction. To that end, we design our professional development to be intentionally inclusive. For example, whenever we bring together classroom teachers for professional learning, we make sure learning specialists are always part of the learning. When our middle school mathematics teachers are learning about engagement strategies to promote high-level conversations in mathematics, the learning specialists are sitting right beside them, helping them think about how to create access points for students with significant communication challenges.

> Whenever we bring together classroom teachers for professional learning, we make sure learning specialists are always part of the learning.

Each summer, our Teaching and Learning department sponsors Curriculum Camps for grade-level teams from across the district to come together to create new units and lessons. Learning specialists participate with their teams, helping to generate lessons that engage the full range of learners. Through these partnerships, general education teachers have developed a deeper understanding of the concepts of UDL. For example, in Chapter 7 we described an activity at the Social Studies Curriculum Camp, where teachers learned to design lessons that allow students to engage in high-level concepts while using AAC devices.

Our central office staff plays an important role in keeping these Curriculum Camps inclusive. A few years ago, learning specialists reported that they felt like they were on the outside of the process. The classroom teachers were welcoming, and the learning specialists enjoyed the task of creating units and lessons. But they felt like their expertise was not being maximized by the current format. The Assistant Superintendent for Teaching and Learning heard this feedback. Before Curriculum Camp the following summer, she brought together a team of learning specialists to help plan the event. They decided that a key role for learning specialists would be helping to build capacity in teachers to plan through a UDL lens.

The role of the central office was crucial here. Not only were special education staff invited to the Curriculum Camps, they were given the opportunity to take a leadership role in planning the camps. Central office leadership plays a key role in promoting other forms of inclusive professional development as well.

Students in our district have no school during the week of Thanksgiving. Instead, the first two days of the week are professional development days. This has been a great opportunity for teachers from across the district to get together for intensive professional learning. The past few years, all of the elementary teachers in the district have gathered to focus on a specific content area (reading, writing, mathematics, science). These sessions are planned and facilitated by our ICs. Each elementary school has an IC, a teacher on special assignment who functions like an assistant principal, focused specifically on instructional leadership. In addition to these building-level ICs, we have four special education ICs who support the nine elementary schools.

Throughout the fall, school-based ICs and special education ICs meet together to plan the lessons and activities for the Thanksgiving week professional development. Then they cofacilitate the professional development sessions, modeling the structures of coplanning and co-teaching for the teachers. What the teachers experienced was a day learning about best practices for teaching writing for all students, with concepts of how to extend the learning and scaffold the learning built in. The old ways of having professional development for classroom teachers on writing instruction in one workshop and for special education teachers on access tools or explicit instruction strategies in another workshop are gone for us. Inclusive schools start with inclusive professional development.

FACILITIES AND OPERATIONS

Our Facilities and Operations staff have been heroes in the work of inclusion. We no longer contain students with significant disabilities in separate spaces in our schools. All students now have access to the full range of instructional and cocurricular opportunities. That means all students need to have physical access to the entire school building and the athletic facilities. Of course, our buildings and fields are ADA compliant, but we have learned that true access sometimes requires more thoughtful consideration of the design of our physical spaces.

A few years ago our physical therapists met with our Director of Operations and our Facilities Manager to review the accessibility features of all 16 of our schools. They looked at pictures of the entry, office, classrooms, hallways, common areas, playgrounds, and athletic fields. They even traveled together to visit some schools.

They found some locations where specific students in that school would be unable to participate with their peers because of physical barriers to access. The Facilities team acted quickly to install remote opening devices at the front door of several schools to ensure that students in wheelchairs would be able to navigate their school. They also widened narrow pathways, installed adaptive swings, and laid down rubber mats over the bark chips on some playgrounds to enhance accessibility. While we are still working to make our playgrounds more accessible, the Facilities and Operations team have been very helpful in the process of creating and implementing our vision for inclusive and accessible schools.

One of the highlights of the partnership with our Facilities department was their work to enhance the accessibility of one of our high school stadiums. Brinna, a high school student who uses a wheelchair, wanted to cheer along with her classmates at football games. The stadium has been ADA accessible since it was built in the mid-1990s, but the locations for wheelchair seating are not ideal for inclusive participation. Brinna could either be on the track in front of the bleachers or on the upper concourse behind the bleachers. If she were on the track, she would not be able to see over the players on the sidelines. If she were on the upper concourse, she would be right behind the student section. Students traditionally stand throughout the game, so she would not be able to see over her classmates. She could, of course, sit on the upper concourse behind the parent section, where fans generally sit all through the game. But do high school students really want to sit with their parents during a football game?

Brinna brought this concern to her case manager and physical therapist. They encouraged her to raise the question with the athletic director as well. The athletic director gathered a team of stakeholders to consider the problem—including the case manager, physical therapist, facilities director, maintenance supervisor, and student services administrator. Most important, Brinna was part of this meeting too. We listened to her express frustration with her inability to cheer alongside her classmates. We asked her to describe the barriers she was facing. Then we asked her to show us what she was actually experiencing. We took a short trip out to the stadium so we could all see what it looked like to be sitting in a wheelchair behind a crowd of standing fans.

This conversation happened on a Thursday after school. The Facilities crew got to work the next day. By Friday night they had built a platform in the bleachers that allowed Brinna to sit with her classmates, watch the game, and experience the frenzy of the student section like a typical high school student. In the picture Brinna shared with us we could see her sitting next to two of her best friends. And in the corner of the frame we could see that another student in a wheelchair was sitting on the platform as well.

This kind of action happened because the adults listened to student self-advocacy. And because the athletic director, facilities director, and maintenance supervisor had had previous opportunities to reflect on the importance of creating an inclusive school community. This could not have happened if the only people working toward inclusion were the special education staff.

BUSINESS OFFICE

As we have become more inclusive in our instructional practices, the staffing picture has become more complex. We are still required by the IDEA to meet Maintenance of Effort standards. That is, we continue to spend a consistent amount of money to support students with disabilities. However, that spending looks a little different now that we no longer have self-contained classrooms. We have added staff in some areas, moved some staff to different buildings, and continue to build capacity throughout the system.

For example, we quickly discovered that the amount of occupational and physical therapy staffing we used to need in a centralized model was not nearly enough as we shifted to support every student in their home school. As we will discuss later in this chapter, the role of paraeducators has shifted dramatically as well. Our staffing is more flexible and nimble than in the past. We believe that is beneficial for students, but we recognize that managing the payroll can be more complex for the business office. Having strong working relationships with the finance director, grant specialist, and payroll specialist has helped us when students' circumstances have necessitated additional staffing or additional hours of student support.

HUMAN RESOURCES

As we mentioned above, our hiring practices promote inclusion: the interview process focuses on each teacher's commitment to serving all students. In addition, we have found it critical to involve the Human Resources (HR) department in developing our districtwide commitment to inclusive practices. Occasionally, teachers, paraeducators, or union leaders bring forward questions about inclusive practices. These concerns may be real or perceived issues about safety (for students and staff) or about the impact of student behavior on the learning of other students. In both cases these are important topics for our leaders to take seriously. We do not want students to be unsafe. And we do not want learning to be disrupted. When teachers, paraeducators, and union leaders ask about opportunities for professional learning to help them support students in inclusive settings, it is important for the HR staff to understand our processes. And on the rare occasion when someone asks the HR director if there is another place where the student could be safer, it is critical for the HR director to have deeply reflected on The Why of inclusion.

We have also partnered with HR leaders to create the *Paraeducator Handbook*. In addition, the HR director has been a member of the Inclusive Schools Leadership Team (which we will describe later in this chapter). We know that a great part of our ability to move forward comes from the leadership and support of our HR Resources team.

SALARY STRUCTURES, JOB DESCRIPTIONS, AND UNION CONTRACTS TO SUPPORT INCLUSIVE PRACTICES

Over the past few years leaders from districts around the country have come to visit our schools to learn together with us about inclusive practices. One of the things they have shared with us is the range of structural barriers that result from salary schedules, job descriptions, and union contracts. There are a few conditions related to these factors that we have found helpful in promoting inclusive practices.

It is common in some districts to have different pay structures for teachers, specialists, and paraprofessionals. For example, special education teachers may receive a stipend for case management duties. As advocates for the amazing work that special educators do, we have supported the idea of these sorts of stipends in the past. Yet differential pay can become a barrier to the collaborative and co-owned work necessary in inclusive schools.

In our previous model, where we supported students with complex needs in segregated settings, one could argue that the work was different—very specialized and maybe even more difficult. Some districts may justify paying higher salaries to staff who work with these students. Some teachers and leaders informally call this *combat pay*—a disparaging term that hints at underlying beliefs about the value and potential of students with complex needs.

When we move to supporting all students in their neighborhood schools and in general education classes as much as possible, the professional dynamics change. General education teachers take on a larger part of the responsibility for teaching students with complex needs. If salary structures still reward specialists more than general education teachers, there may be some legitimate questions about compensation.

For example, in the old model a general education classroom teacher may look at a self-contained behavior program teacher and say, "I can see that your students have more difficult behaviors than mine. You experience physical and emotional challenges in the classroom every day that I don't experience. I can see why you should get paid more for your work." But now the classroom teacher is taking greater ownership for every student: coplanning with special education teachers, teaching social-emotional skills, implementing BSPs, providing a range of accommodations, modifying the curriculum, engaging with AAC devices, attending long meetings with a roomful of specialists, and emotionally investing in each student's success. It would be reasonable for that teacher to look at the behavior specialist and say, "I am an equal partner in this work. I am equally committed to this student's success. I am providing many of the services for this student and spending a lot more time planning for this student than I used to. Why should you get paid more for this work?"

To be able to successfully educate all students in inclusive settings, we need to build *collective efficacy* (Donohoo, 2016). We are trying to build capacity in teachers so they have the skills to support all students. At the same time, we are trying to build teachers' *belief* that they truly have the capacity to do this complex work well. For years we had communicated to classroom teachers that there is a unique set of skills that they do not possess. When students had really complex needs, we used to say, "We will send them to this other program where we have specialists who can support them better." Implied in that statement was an unspoken belief: "You don't have the skills to meet this student's needs." Now we are telling classroom teachers, "We believe you are the right person to teach all students, and we can bring additional support to your classroom." If we pay those support specialists more than the classroom teacher, there is an underlying message that the teacher is still not capable. This can create unnecessary divisions and dissention between teachers and specialists who are already working extremely hard.

There is a similar dynamic among paraeducators or instructional assistants. When we began this journey, we had three different divisions of paraeducators: general education, special education resource, and special education program. The job descriptions were different. General education and resource paraeducator job descriptions were primarily about supporting students with academic tasks like reading, writing, mathematics, and organization. The special education program paraeducator job description included activities like behavior support, communication, feeding, and changing diapers. Program paraeducators worked 6 hours, so they were eligible to receive benefits. General education and resource paraeducators worked 5.5 hours, so they did not receive benefits.

When we eliminated self-contained classrooms and returned all students to their neighborhood schools, we realized that we would need to restructure how we assign paraeducator duties. A school that did not previously host a specialized program may now have three or four students with complex personal care needs, including safe eating or bathroom protocols. When we assigned general education or resource paraeducators to those tasks, we occasionally received pushback, particularly if they were partnered with a program paraeducator. People said, "That person is getting paid more than me; why should I have to do the same work?"

We resolved this issue in two ways. First, we increased paraeducator hours so that all paraeducators are six-hour employees and therefore are eligible for the same level of benefits. This was a significant additional investment of district resources. However, we believe that this marginal increase in salary and benefits has led to a substantial improvement in the quality of our student support. By equalizing the working hours for paraeducators, we have vastly increased the number of staff members who are available to work with students with more complex needs. Now that those students are attending general education classes in their neighborhood schools instead of being clustered in self-contained programs in centralized locations, we need more adults available to be in different locations. Providing consistent working hours for paraeducators has helped us provide a continuum of supports for all students in their neighborhood schools.

We would like to increase our paraeducator hours even further so they have more opportunities for daily collaboration and professional development. Right now, paraeducators work "bell-to-bell," so they do not have time during their regular daily work day to connect with learning specialists and classroom teachers. We have added one hour per week of additional time that principals and case managers can organize for collaboration and professional learning for paraeducators, and we would like to expand that to at least 30 minutes per day.

Second, we revised the paraeducator job description to eliminate the distinction between general education, resource, and program-level paraeducators. Now the job description for all paraeducators includes supporting students in academics, social-emotional learning, behavior, communication, and personal care. When paraeducators are hired, regardless of the fund they are paid from, their job description says that they may be supporting any student, including those with the most complex needs.

Of course, we need to continue building capacity in these critical staff members so they can do the work that is outlined on this revised job description. We will describe professional learning for paraeducators later in this chapter.

Some districts have very specific language in their contracts about caseload ratios for special education teachers. In conversations with principals and central office administrators from these districts, we have learned that this contract language has presented barriers to their progress toward greater inclusion. For example, in one district in a nearby state, teachers in a self-contained behavior classroom had a contracted limit of 7 students on their caseload. Resource teachers had a caseload limit of 30.

We have learned that it is very difficult to have one teacher be the case manager for every student with significant disabilities when those students are based primarily in general education classes. The case manager needs to collaborate intensely with so many different teachers that they are tempted to remove the students more than necessary or cluster them in a few classrooms rather than have students spread evenly across general education classrooms.

Our solution has been to redistribute caseloads so our case managers work with students based on grade level rather than complexity of needs or disability category. Teachers who previously had a larger caseload of students with mild learning disabilities now have a slightly smaller caseload that includes students with more complex needs. Teachers who previously had a small caseload of students with significant disabilities now have a larger caseload that includes more students with mild learning disabilities. For example, at one of our primary schools, the teacher who previously taught a self-contained ASD support class for grades K–5 (which we called the Communication Resource Center) would now have a caseload of all students in grades K–2 or 3–5, regardless of their disability category. We recognize that contractual limitations on how we define and assign caseloads would have been a significant barrier to implementing this kind of flexible case management system.

Addressing these contractual barriers can be challenging. Once language is embedded in a union contract, it is extremely difficult to remove. Union leaders are doing their jobs to support the needs of their constituents, protecting teachers' rights and working to ensure favorable compensation and working conditions. At heart, of course, the union leaders are educators who got into the work because of their passion for students. There is no inherent reason why a teachers' association or classified school employees' association would be opposed to inclusive practices. Most of their members are very much in support of inclusion. However, unions tend to take a conservative approach when it comes to changing contract language related to working conditions. So it is essential for district leaders to engage union leaders to explore The Why of inclusive practices. The more union leaders (and the larger body of union members) understand and embrace a vision of inclusive school communities, the more likely they will come to the table willing to engage in productive dialogue to revise contract language to support inclusive practices.

STRUCTURES FOR PROFESSIONAL LEARNING THAT SUPPORT INCLUSIVE PRACTICES

Leaders and teachers from across the country have contacted us to learn more about the professional learning structures that make inclusion possible. Some have asked us about specific professional development for "how to do inclusion." We don't have a simple answer to that question (in some ways, this book is the answer). There is no single training or professional development workshop for inclusion. Instead, inclusive thinking needs to be built into every aspect of professional learning within the school and district.

> There is no single training or professional development workshop for inclusion. Instead, inclusive thinking needs to be built into every aspect of professional learning within the school and district.

We occasionally lead professional learning activities about The Why of inclusion or about specific access tools (Unique Learning System, AAC devices, Co:Writer). However, in general, we focus our professional learning on high-leverage instructional strategies that promote access and engagement opportunities for a full range of learners: coplanning and co-teaching, engagement strategies that increase student voice, learning targets that allow for a range of entry points and demonstrations of learning, and so on. By focusing on these instructional practices for all students, we are able to partner closely with the Teaching and Learning department to make our professional development as inclusive as possible for teachers.

At the school level, learning specialists are often members of the grade-level or subject-area PLCs. This helps the learning specialist develop a deeper understanding of the grade-level curriculum. And it promotes co-teaching and coplanning by strengthening the collaborative relationships between the classroom teacher and the learning specialist.

The majority of the professional development for inclusion happens in conjunction with general education teachers, as described above. However, there are three specific structures for professional learning that have helped our district move toward becoming a more inclusive learning community, which we will describe in more detail here:

1. The Kickoff

2. Inclusive and Equitable Classrooms workshop series

3. Paraeducator Workshops (and other opportunities for paraeducator professional development)

THE KICKOFF

We believe in setting the tone for the year and starting off with a big event. The day before teachers report for their preservice activities in their schools in August, we gather all of the Student Services staff for an event we call the Kickoff. It has taken different forms over the years, but in general there are a few main components of the event:

1. Build a common commitment to The Why of inclusive practices.

2. Renew and strengthen the relationships between staff members.

3. Build specific skills related to the work.

4. Introduce new guidance, policies, and procedures.

5. Energize the Student Services staff with a sense of joy and purpose.

Build a common commitment to The Why of inclusive practices. Sometimes we have students as guest speakers at the Kickoff to share about their experiences in inclusive classrooms. In Chapter 7 we told the stories of Ben and Marco. Ben told teachers at the Kickoff about how his world opened up "when they let me out" of the self-contained Life Learning classroom. Marco talked about leading his IEP meeting and wondered, "If I didn't know my goals, how would I be able to reach them?" These statements, directly from the mouths of students, struck a powerful chord with a roomful of educators, helping to reinforce our commitment to The Why of inclusive practices.

In addition to having student speakers, we have also watched inspirational videos. One year, we watched Dan Habib's TED talk about disrupting segregation in schools. He tells the story of his son Samuel and the impact inclusive schools had on him. He also tells about the impact that Samuel had on his classmates, which is an equally compelling reason to advocate for inclusion (TED[X], 2014). Another video we have watched at the Kickoff is *Intelligent Lives*, a documentary about three young adults with intellectual disabilities (Habib, 2018). There is so much promise and possibility in their lives, and it raises all kinds of questions about the assumptions we make about intelligence and individual capabilities. We also showed *Intelligent Lives* to our school board and all the principals and department leaders throughout the district. Several principals have screened the documentary for their full staff. In addition, we have partnered with a local theater for a free screening to share the message of inclusion with the broader community.

Renew and strengthen the relationships between staff members. These people need to rely on each other through complex and challenging situations throughout the year. A solid base of trust, built on common experiences, will help them work well together. We plan community-building activities that will help school teams get to know one another better and help new staff feel a part of their teams.

Build specific skills related to the work. At the Kickoff we often have teachers lead one-hour workshops about specific instructional tools and strategies to support inclusive classrooms. We provide a planning template and paid time for workshop leaders to prepare. Workshop topics in recent years have included co-teaching, progress monitoring, using communication devices, designing BSPs, and creating sensory spaces in the classroom. Teachers attend two workshop sessions, so the workshop leaders also get a chance to learn from their peers.

Introduce new guidance, policies, and procedures. This is the least inspirational part of the Kickoff. But it can be a valuable time to make sure we are all on the same page about procedural compliance. For example, we have spent time at the Kickoff talking about changes to the state IEP form and eligibility requirements for Autism and Developmental Delay. We tend to keep this portion short because procedural compliance is not the most high-leverage way to affect student learning.

Energize the Student Services staff with a sense of joy and purpose. This is often closely connected to building a common commitment to The Why of inclusive practices (inspirational videos, testimonies from students). We also like to have people share celebrations about their work. For example, during an end-of-the-year survey, we asked our staff to share something they were proud of. We got numerous responses telling of the great things they had done that year in their work with students and colleagues. For the Kickoff we printed each response on a full sheet of colored paper and tiled a wall with them. Throughout the day of the Kickoff, we encouraged teachers to spend time at the wall, soaking in the great work that they and their colleagues had done the previous year. We also had blank pages available for folks to add new things they were proud of to the wall.

The Kickoff started as an event for licensed staff (learning specialists, SLPs, occupational therapists, physical therapists, school psychologists, nurses, etc.). Some years we have asked learning specialists and principals to invite general education teachers to join us—particularly when we were focusing on co-teaching and coplanning strategies. In recent years we have also invited paraeducators to join us at the Kickoff. This has been a key strategy to help paraeducators build a deeper sense of The Why of inclusive practices, as well as to help them become more connected to their school teams.

INCLUSIVE AND EQUITABLE CLASSROOMS WORKSHOP SERIES

One of the most powerful structures we have created for professional learning about inclusive practices is our Inclusive and Equitable Classrooms workshop series, which we started three years ago.

As we continued to support all students in their neighborhood schools, we recognized that there were complex needs—particularly supporting students with challenging behaviors. (See Chapter 8 for more detail about our structures to support students who demonstrate challenging or aggressive behaviors.) Teachers across the district were working to understand and implement "The 7 Components of Inclusive and Equitable Learning Communities." As we discussed in Chapter 6, this is not a prescriptive system. Instead, The 7 Components are structured with a series of targets and guiding questions that help teachers and school staff think about promoting student engagement and positive behavior through the following:

1. Effective physical spaces

2. Teaching common expectations

3. Rituals, routines, and recognition

4. Engagement strategies for all students

5. Teaching social-emotional skills

6. Restorative practices

7. Relationships with high expectations

To help teachers develop proficiency in supporting all students in the general education classroom, we hosted a series of five monthly workshops on "Inclusive and Equitable Classrooms: Supporting Positive Behavior for All." In the first year, nearly 80 people attended from all 16 schools, including classroom teachers, counselors, principals, ICs, learning specialists, school psychologists, and SLPs. The first workshop began with an overview of all the seven components, including using video examples. Then the attendees engaged in activities to explore each component in depth.

During the first year we structured the first three workshops to focus on introducing The 7 Components and thinking about strategies for the All. Then, the fourth workshop session focused on the Some, and the final session highlighted strategies for the Few. Feedback from the attendees was overwhelmingly positive, but we learned that it would be more effective to weave All-Some-Few strategies into each monthly workshop, allowing teachers to view each component through the lens of All-Some-Few. So the following year, we restructured the workshops to focus on one or two components each month.

The planning and facilitation of the workshops were shared among a team of general education teachers and special education ICs. This served several purposes. First, it allowed us to draw on the full range of strategies and practices that are in place at all grade levels across our district. General education teachers could talk about what they do in their classes each day. It was particularly powerful when they showed videos from their classrooms. Then the special education ICs could bring in expertise about access strategies and tools for students with more complex learning needs (the Some and the Few). It also allowed us to model the kind of coteaching partnerships that we are encouraging our teachers and learning specialists to explore. Most important, this general education/special education partnership clearly communicated that "The 7 Components of Inclusive and Equitable Learning Communities"—and the goal of creating truly inclusive schools—is not the work of the Special Education department alone but the work of all district staff.

We also made a point of explicitly modeling strategies and practices during the workshops—and then pausing to highlight the strategies and talk through our reasons for choosing those practices. For example, we emphasized relationships by assigning a facilitator to greet every attendee at the door and help them find their table (especially folks who arrived after the session started). We had preassigned table leaders to help the teachers work through graphic organizers and talk protocols—ensuring that they stayed on task and that every participant had an opportunity to contribute their voice to the learning conversations. We had fidgets on the tables and a comfortable "chill space" at the back of the room to help the attendees maintain sensory regulation. We also projected a timer on the screen alongside the discussion prompts so that the table facilitators and participants could gauge their time and overall workshop facilitators could keep the pace brisk and efficient.

Another key element of the workshops is that we wanted to acknowledge the vast breadth of knowledge and experience in the room. We had 80 teachers, principals, and other specialists in the workshops. They were there because they wanted to learn new ways to support students in inclusive settings. And they also came with great experience and a wealth of strategies that they use every day in their classrooms. We capitalized on that expertise by gathering strategies, practices, and tools from the teachers in their table groups. Then, we consolidated these ideas into lists, which we distributed back to the teachers to try in their classrooms. For example, the workshop participants generated lists of classroom routines (opening, closing, transitions, and classwork routines) and lists of strategies for building teacher-student relationships.

The attendees ranged from kindergarten through high school, so we made a point of including examples and strategies that could work across a range of student ages. High school teachers sometimes have the perception that effective classroom design, engagement strategies, and classroom routines are only for younger students. But some of our best examples came from our middle school and high school teachers.

At the end of the five-month workshop series, the teachers told us they were eager to learn more. So we put together a three-part follow-up series that dug deeper into specific strategies, including the impact of trauma on the brain, escalation cycles, and thinking functionally about behavior. This smaller series was also cofacilitated by general education and special education staff and helped us generate resources to share more broadly with our teacher teams.

The following year we repeated the workshop series, while continuing to make adjustments based on feedback from participants and facilitators. By the third year (the most recent school year) we found that over 150 teachers and specialists had participated in the workshops. The principals and district leaders decided that the next step would be to bring the workshops to the school level. Each school now had a handful of teachers who had participated in the full workshop series, so they could serve as facilitators for their school-level workshops. The principals partnered with these teachers and their special education ICs to design activities for the whole school staff to engage with The 7 Components during their regularly scheduled staff meetings and professional development days.

Moving the workshop series to the school level meant that we (as district administrators) were no longer directly planning and leading this explicit professional development structure. It had been a lot of work, but it was also so much fun. We missed leading the workshops, but it was the right decision. By decentralizing the professional learning, we were building capacity in teacher leaders across the district and making the workshops more accessible to a broader range of staff members. Or, in other words, we were making it more inclusive.

PARAEDUCATOR WORKSHOPS

The Inclusive and Equitable Classrooms workshop series that we just described was a powerful learning opportunity for classroom teachers and specialists throughout the district. We have also been working to support professional learning for paraeducators.

Paraeducators play a critical role in our work of supporting all students in inclusive settings. The primary role for paraeducators is to support students in learning academic skills. In addition, they support students in communication, behavior, organization, social-emotional regulation, mobility, transition, and skills for daily living. While some students may need significant support from paraeducators, we are always working toward developing independence and phasing out support (in accordance with the principles of LRE and inclusive cultures). Because of the importance of paraeducators in promoting inclusive learning communities, we have implemented a range of professional learning opportunities for them.

The most visible professional development for paraeducators is a monthly Paraeducator Workshop. We design these workshops to address timely and relevant parts of the paraeducator's work. Topics have included the following:

- Literacy
- Mathematics
- Promoting Independence
- Facilitating Peer Interactions
- Behavior Support

In addition, these workshops are tailored to specific grade levels. While many of the concepts of providing supports in inclusive classrooms are the same across grade levels (promoting independence, *increasing student voice*, facilitating peer relationships, etc.), we found that paraeducators valued hearing specific examples and stories about students at the grade band they work with (elementary, middle school, or high school).

Initially, these workshops were specifically targeted at paraeducators who work with students served by special education. As we became more inclusive, we realized that all paraeducators (not just the ones funded through IDEA) need to be equipped to serve all students. So we have opened up our paraeducator workshops to all. We even occasionally have a library assistant, preschool paraeducator, or school secretary join us at the workshops.

In addition to these workshops, we have a variety of other professional learning opportunities for paraeducators. In August we host a New Paraeducator Orientation to help folks learn more about inclusive practices. We talk about some of the foundational ideas of inclusion and the paraeducator's role in making it happen. A few years ago we collaborated with the HR department to put together a *Paraeducator Handbook*, which is a collection of materials to help staff think about ways to support students in inclusive settings. We introduce this in the New Paraeducator Orientation and also use it at the monthly paraeducator workshops.

As we discussed in the section about salary structures earlier in this chapter, we also provide an additional hour of collaboration and professional learning time for paraeducators each week. Some schools choose to use that to include paraeducators in special education team meetings. Some have their paraeducators attend full-school staff meetings. Others use it for specific professional development activities led by learning specialists or the special education IC.

Some schools have also used that time for paraeducators to watch helpful videos. In particular, our district has subscribed to the *Parasharp* and *Trauma Informed* series from 321 Insight. These videos provide short (5–12 minutes) descriptions of key concepts for supporting students in inclusive settings. They are a great entry point for paraeducators, and they have been the foundation for powerful discussions among our staff. We have also found the videos to be beneficial for teachers and parents.

Two other resources that we have found to be very valuable in supporting the professional learning of our paraeducators are the documentary film *Intelligent Lives* by Habib (2018) and *The Paraprofessional's Handbook for Effective Support in Inclusive Classrooms* by Julie Causton-Theoharis (2009).

STRUCTURES FOR LEADERSHIP AND STAKEHOLDER INPUT

Transforming an organization is a dynamic process that requires ongoing input from a variety of stakeholders. This serves the dual purpose of ensuring that the change is moving in the right direction and creating a coalition of supporters who are invested in The Why and committed to positive outcomes.

We have created several levels of stakeholder groups to address both of these purposes: Inclusive Schools Leadership Team, Core Team, Principal Levels Groups, and District-Parent Special Education Collaboration Group.

INCLUSIVE SCHOOLS LEADERSHIP TEAM

The Inclusive Schools Leadership Team brings together special education and general education staff once a month to set goals, review data, celebrate growth, generate guidance, and calibrate our processes. The team originated as the Special Education Leadership Team with representatives for each of the different roles within the Special Education department: learning specialists, SLPs, school psychologists, occupational and physical therapists, paraeducators, and so on. We changed the name as we expanded the membership—adding general education teachers, counselors, administrators, central office staff, and students. The current name (Inclusive Schools Leadership Team) reflects the broader makeup of the team and the broader mandate for the work.

At the beginning of each year this group establishes goals and then provides direction for teachers and district staff to work toward those goals. In recent years those goals have included the following:

1. All schools will improve their school culture in terms of equity, belonging, and inclusivity.

2. One hundred percent of students served by special education will participate in their IEP this year.

3. All Student Services staff will engage in one co-teaching experience this year.

4. One hundred percent of students will engage in effective learning partnerships with peers this year.

5. One hundred percent of teachers will use learning targets that clearly identify what students will learn and how they will demonstrate their learning, and provide entry points for access and/or modification.

As we discussed in Chapter 4, we set goals with a target of "All" or "100%" because we would not be satisfied with some students being denied the opportunity to participate in their IEP or some teachers choosing not to use effective learning targets.

These goals have then led the work of the group, including helping to craft guidance for promoting student participation in IEPs and helping to create a *Peer Support Handbook* to enhance peer learning partnerships across all grade levels.

Members of the Inclusive Schools Leadership Team are key communicators, helping share the vision of inclusion with colleagues in their schools. They also help bring forward important concerns. One of the most important concerns that we have heard through this group is student and staff safety. When the leaders of our teacher union raised these concerns, we invited them to join the Inclusive Schools Leadership Team. If we were to begin the process of creating inclusive school communities again (going back eight years), we would have invited union leaders to join the leadership team from the start.

Another key feature of this group is that we rotate the membership. By having each participant serve for two years, our goal is to eventually have every special education staff member serve in this leadership capacity. Many of the team members are vocal and active supporters of inclusive practices. But we also want to include staff members who have not yet taken up an active leadership role or who have not yet formulated a personal commitment to The Why of inclusion. Participating in the Inclusive Schools Leadership Team helps move more people toward a greater sense of purpose and alignment with the vision of the district.

For the past five years we have had several high school students participate on the team as well. Having students on the Inclusive Schools Leadership Team has been beneficial in a number of ways:

- *Voice/input:* As we explored in Chapter 7, one of our special education focus areas is *increasing student voice*. We place a very high value on student input in the design of their educational plan and in their day-to-day classes. When we are thinking about the big picture of special education services and inclusive practices in our district, we are equally committed to engaging student voice.

- *Modulating our language:* We recognize that language is powerful. Our beliefs shape our language, and our language shapes our beliefs. When students are present in the room, we are more conscious of the tone and connotations of the language we use. We are more likely to model a growth mindset and speak in ways that are affirming and hopeful.

- *Engagement strategies:* When we are designing activities for the meetings, we are not only thinking about how to keep the teachers and other professional educators engaged for a three-hour meeting on a Friday afternoon, we are also thinking about how the students will have a role. We often ask ourselves how each activity or task will engage students and keep them interested. We consider what role students will have and what unique input or perspective they will be able to provide to the team.

- *Accessibility supports:* When we recruit students for the Inclusive Schools Leadership Team, we are looking for students with and without disabilities. Student members experience a variety of barriers from intellectual disability to orthopedic impairment to visual impairment. As we plan the agenda and design activities for the meetings, we need to think about accessibility supports. For example, when we looked at research related to the role and impact of paraeducators, we provided the team with multiple documents: a full article from a research journal, a summary article from *Educational Leadership* magazine, and a one-page document we created with bullet points, highlights, and visuals. Team members could self-select which document to read so they could contribute to the synthesis of the whole team. For the student with a visual impairment, we emailed a copy of the PowerPoint and documents before the meeting so she could follow along and enlarge the text on her iPad. As district administrators, this is a good opportunity for us to practice the Universal Design and access strategies that we are asking our teachers to use in their classrooms every day.

CORE TEAM (SPECIAL EDUCATION ICS)

Our Core Team is the group of special education ICs who lead the work on a daily basis in schools (along with our Student Services administrators). This team meets each week. We used to meet on Tuesdays but recently shifted the meeting to Friday afternoons. While most people cringe at the idea of a Friday afternoon meeting, we have found that this is a great time to meet with our Core Team. After a week of intense work with students, teachers, and parents, our ICs have found it very productive (and sometimes cathartic) to wrap up the week together.

Core Team meetings are less formalized than the other meetings and PLCs that we lead. We have a shared online document that special education ICs and administrators can fill with agenda items throughout the week. Facilitation of the meeting is rotated each week to build capacity in the ICs as leaders.

Some of the key goals of the Core Team are as follows:

- Celebrations of inclusive learning communities
- Consistency of vision—calibration

- Problems of practice
- Planning common professional development for school special education teams
- Reviewing materials/tools for supporting inclusive instruction
- Other logistics and planning

As we have mentioned before, we start all meetings with an opportunity to share celebrations of what is going well. We know how complex and challenging our work can be, so we place a high value on articulating stories about progress and growth. We are not Pollyanna-ish. We are not burying our heads in the sand and ignoring the hard realities of our work. But we know that dispositions toward the work can be affected by the stories we tell. Sharing celebrations can give us the inspiration and motivation to keep going when it gets tough.

Celebrations can also help us to build and reinforce our common vision for inclusive school communities. Another way we calibrate our vision and purpose is through reading articles or watching videos about The Why of inclusive practices. This helps the members of the Core Team to reinforce our common vision, and it also helps in sharing resources for ICs to use with the school teams and parents they work with each day.

After celebrating the great work that is going on in all of our schools and the amazing progress we have seen in students, we dig into problems of practice. Sometimes these are questions about unique issues of procedural compliance (How do we make sure we are protecting the student and family's rights while addressing their individualized needs in an inclusive setting?). Sometimes an IC brings forward a challenge related to a student whose complex learning and behavior needs have the school team perplexed. Other times, the IC knows how to proceed with the student but is looking for guidance on how to communicate with the teacher or parents. By puzzling through these scenarios as a team, we can learn together and come up with better solutions than if we try to resolve things on our own. After all, in this incredibly complex work we believe that *the magic is in the team*.

Another part of the work of the Core Team is planning to lead professional development in schools. The ICs have developed common lessons and activities to use at school special education team meetings. Some of the topics of this professional development have been learning targets, differentiation and universal design, access tools (e.g., Co:Writer or Learning Ally), social-emotional regulation, escalation cycles, and behavior support. The ICs plan for these professional learning activities and then debrief with one another about what worked and what would need to be improved for the next time. In this way we are building their capacity as leaders to model reflective instructional practice.

In addition to celebrations, calibration, problems of practice, and planning professional development, the Core Team engages in other logistical and practical activities. For example, when we are considering a new access tool or curriculum resource, we often have an IC conduct a pilot project and share their findings with the team. We also spend time at Core Team meetings planning for other events, including transition meetings to prepare for students moving between schools.

Of all the leadership structures and supports to create inclusive learning communities, the Core Team has probably been the most valuable. We have hired and retained incredible ICs, and we have used the structure of the Core Team meetings to build their capacity to lead their school teams toward more inclusive practices.

PRINCIPAL LEVELS GROUPS

Most school districts have a structure where building principals meet together frequently for their own professional development and to collaboratively work through the business of leading schools. These groups can be a powerful avenue for promoting inclusive learning communities.

Principals need to deeply understand and embrace The Why of this work, as well as the changes in staff roles and instructional expectations. Building principals are the instructional leaders, the climate and culture leaders, and the procedural leaders of their schools. They are critical to this work and can be the strongest advocates of inclusive practices.

One example in our district was the development of "The 7 Components of Inclusive and Equitable Learning Communities." We coplanned with the assistant superintendents who oversee the Principal Levels Groups to bring an initial draft to the principals for their input and response. The principals had time to make sense of what The 7 Components looked like in their schools, and their questions and ideas were incorporated into additional drafts. They helped create it, so they are deeply committed to its implementation.

In Levels meetings and in learning walks with our principal teams, we are always listening for what else the principals may need from the central office (tools, communication, or support) and the next challenges that need to be addressed. We also hear celebrations from principals, including specific stories about how their schools have become more inclusive.

DISTRICT-PARENT SPECIAL EDUCATION COLLABORATION GROUP

We have worked hard to cultivate partnerships with parents throughout our transformation to inclusive practices. We have had active parents who are deeply committed to their child experiencing their education in an inclusive setting. And we have had parents who are longing for their child to spend their day in a nurturing self-contained classroom. We have had parents who form strong, trusting partnerships with their teachers and principals. And we have had parents who operate from a position of fear and distrust of educational institutions.

Building and maintaining relationships with stakeholder groups is critical to the success of any effort to reinvent the long-standing structures of a school district. It is particularly important to involve parents in the process. Of course, we want parents' primary connection to be with their child's teacher. We want parents of students served by special education to engage with their school in the same ways all parents do—by participating in parent-teacher organization meetings, supporting school fund-raisers, volunteering in classrooms, attending student performances and athletic events, and so on. Some parents may also want to engage with the district special education department in a more formal way. One way we have done this is through our District-Parent Special Education Collaboration Group. During the quarterly meetings we share updates about inclusive practices and ask for parent input and feedback.

This group does not have a formal membership process. We know of districts in our area that have a parent collaboration group with specific representatives elected or nominated from each school. In our case we decided to let participation in the group to be more flexible and open-ended. Over the past eight years, there have been a handful of parents who have come to nearly every meeting. And there are some parents who have come once or twice. Some schools have multiple parents attending. Other schools have never had a parent attend. We are considering ways to encourage attendance by parents from every school.

We invite all parents of students served by special education to participate in the District-Parent Special Education Collaboration Group. We advertise in the quarterly parent newsletter, and we send an email invitation to all parents of students served by special education. We also specifically invite some parents who we know to be vocal advocates in their schools. During contentious IEP meetings it is not unusual for us to extend an invitation to the parent collaboration group. We might say something like this: "We can see that you have some really passionate opinions about special education and you are really passionate about success for all students. We would love to have you join our parent collaboration group to make sure your voice is heard." Most of the time when we offer this invitation, the parents end up attending the next meeting—and they often become regular attenders. Building relationships and providing an opportunity for voice can be particularly important for these parents to know that we are on the same team, focusing on what will be best for their child's growth and development—even if we do not yet agree on the particulars of how we will make that happen.

Building relationships and providing an opportunity for voice can be particularly important for parents to know that we are on the same team.

One thing we have learned is that it is essential to engage with all parents, particularly those who raise critical concerns and those whose children have the most complex needs. It is easy to build a "coalition of the willing" with parents who are actively vocal about their desire for inclusive classrooms for their children. We certainly need these parents to help keep us on course and provide inspirational stories.

But we also need parents who are not yet convinced that an inclusive setting will serve their child's needs. These parents ask questions and raise issues that push us to seek out new learning and refine our practices.

Inviting these parents has proved beneficial in several ways:

1. *Diversity of viewpoints:* It is important for leaders to hear a diversity of opinions. Inviting parents who may see things differently helps us make sure we have clearly defined our purpose. And it can help us refine our practices in the future.

2. *Parent/peer influence:* All of the parents who regularly attend the collaboration group have powerful stories about the barriers their children have faced and the ways in which our schools have worked to create a sense of belonging for them. Meeting these parents and hearing their stories can have an impact on the parents who are currently disagreeing with the district about how best to serve their child.

3. *Reframing the conversation:* Working together to move the system forward helps parents and district leaders look in the same direction rather than focusing on disagreements about individual elements of an IEP.

4. *Building relationships:* The time we spend together learning and sharing our experiences helps build a common understanding. These relationships can pay off in future contentious situations. We know that we will not always agree with parents about the specific details of how to serve their child's needs in the LRE. But we know that a foundation of common experiences can build goodwill to help us navigate those disagreements.

We have also had at least two parents whose students do not attend our schools join the collaboration group. In one case it was a parent whose child had been in a private school for elementary and middle school, and she wanted to learn more about the culture and beliefs of the district to help her see how we would be able to support her child in high school. She spent a year on our collaboration group and then decided to enroll in our district for ninth grade. Another parent from a different school district came to our collaboration group to learn about inclusive practices so she could go back to her home district and advocate for her child's needs.

The group helped push us toward some very practical steps that we believe have had a powerful impact on our journey. For example, the parents on our collaboration group first introduced us to the All Born (in) Conference, which has allowed us to meet educators and parents from around the region who are committed to inclusive practices. We will describe this conference in more detail later in this chapter.

The parent group also strongly supported our involvement in the Think College program at a local university and encouraged us to pursue more comprehensive college options for students with intellectual and developmental disabilities (see Chapter 10 for more about these exciting opportunities).

To help facilitate parent engagement, the parent collaboration group encouraged us to create a welcome packet for parents who are new to special education in our district. This packet includes a welcome letter, lists of people to contact (case manager, SLP, counselor, etc.), and information about inclusion, student participation in the IEP, and ways for parents to get involved. The parent group also encouraged us to find ways to communicate more clearly about Procedural Safeguards. They pointed out that most parents may not even know what we mean by "Procedural Safeguards." So we created a one-page "Parent Rights at a Glance" to help students and parents make sense of the protections they are entitled to under IDEA.

The parent collaboration group has also helped us review student outcome data. Another project was creating a survey for parents of all students served by special education. The purpose of this survey is to help us better understand how parents experience special education services.

The members of the District-Parent Special Education Collaboration Group are also key communicators in their communities. We look to them for feedback and to help us take the pulse of parents in our district. We also encourage and equip them to be a voice for inclusion. They are present in their communities, talking with friends and neighbors about their child's school experiences. They can share their own stories and make connections to the specific steps that the district is taking to make our schools more inclusive for all students. Members of the collaboration group have also shared their stories with the school board to help our citizen leaders understand the power and promise of inclusive practices. This has been particularly important as the board has heard concerns from other community members about students who exhibit disruptive behaviors in class.

PARTNERSHIPS WITH OTHER DISTRICTS AND OUTSIDE ORGANIZATIONS

The culture of our district is inherently collaborative. We believe that the magic is in the team. We recognize that complex, systemwide transformation requires us to form partnerships with other districts and community organizations. This has helped us broaden our learning and focus our purpose.

Partnering with other organizations also helps us because it requires us to tell our story. The process of telling others about our vision and actions has led us to clarify our beliefs and focus our leadership moves. Michael Fullan calls this "talking the walk" (Fullan & Quinn, 2016).

Some of the most important partnerships we have formed over the years are with other local districts, All Born (in), FACT (Family and Community Together), Tualatin Valley Fire & Rescue, and local medical and mental health providers.

OTHER LOCAL DISTRICTS THAT ARE COMMITTED TO INCLUSION

For the past four years our district has had a reciprocal relationship with two other districts in the Portland metro area that are committed to inclusive practices. These districts are of different sizes and have different demographics from ours. Throughout the year we gather for learning walks to visit classrooms in one another's schools. This has helped us see how other school and district leaders are thinking creatively about supporting students in inclusive settings. In particular, we have learned a lot from the creative ways these districts have addressed social-emotional needs in their schools.

These partnerships have also helped us continue to *talk the walk*—reinforcing our beliefs and allowing us to celebrate the great work of our school teams and the great successes that our students are experiencing. And it has been essential for us to have thought partners—people outside our district who help us reflect on our practices and continue to challenge us to get better.

PARENT ADVOCACY GROUPS

It is important to seek out and partner with local parent advocacy groups. Special education is built on the premise of the parent-district partnership, and we need to live into that vision. Two groups with whom we have worked closely are All Born (in) and FACT.

All Born (in), an organization founded by the Northwest Down Syndrome Association, promotes inclusion in school and community settings. Their primary event is an annual cross-disability conference on inclusion. The conference is unusual because its audience includes parents, educators, and individuals with intellectual and developmental disabilities. It is a wonderful opportunity to learn about inclusive practices in an inclusive setting.

Our district has been a sponsor of the conference for the past four years. We have presented sessions and brought a team of parents, special education teachers, general education teachers, principals, paraprofessionals, and central office staff (including our curriculum director and superintendent). Each year, we learn new ideas and connect with new partners in the work.

Participating with All Born (in) was the outgrowth of a conversation in our District-Parent Special Education Collaboration Group (see above).

Another organization that has been critical in our journey toward more inclusive schools is FACT. This is a parent group whose mission is to support families of students who experience disability. It is certified by the Oregon Department of Education and the Office of Special Education Programs as Oregon's Parent Training and Information Center.

We have taken a different approach to our relationships with parents and advocates. We want parents to be as knowledgeable as possible about special education processes and their rights. We want parents to seek support when they have questions or concerns. And we want parents to see the district as partners rather than adversaries in planning for their child's educational needs.

We want parents to see the district as partners rather than adversaries in planning for their child's educational needs.

We partner with FACT to host parent information nights and to provide guidance materials for parents about the IEP process. When a parent is expressing a high level of frustration with school or district policies, we encourage them to contact FACT to help them feel like they have an advocate and that they can come to the table on equal ground.

Often parents feel like they are outnumbered by the school team in the IEP meeting. Teachers, school psychologists, speech pathologists, and other district staff are experts in their fields. They generally have years of experience and have worked with many students with complex needs. Parents, on the other hand, may feel like they are new to the process, uncertain about legal and procedural requirements, and overwhelmed by the task of advocating for their child's needs.

We want to communicate to parents that their input is tremendously valuable. Classroom teachers are the experts in the grade-level standards and general education curriculum. Special educators are the experts in creating pathways for students with disabilities to access that curriculum. We regularly remind parents that they are the experts on their own child's developmental history and unique needs.

Partnering with FACT has helped us communicate this message to parents. And it has helped equip parents with the skills and tools they need to be confident in their expertise about their child. For example, FACT offers support for parents and students to create a person-centered plan. This is a process that brings together important people in the child's life—family, friends, personal support workers, employers, and other members of the community—to generate a comprehensive plan.

A person-centered plan starts with the student's strengths, interests, and aspirations. The team then generates a list of long-term goals for academics, employment, and independent living. What will life look like for this student when they are 25 or 30 years old?

This process usually culminates with a one-page document that highlights strengths and interests and provides lists for "what works for me" and "how to help me when I'm having difficulty." The student or parent can share this document with teachers, personal support workers, bus drivers, employers, and other members of the community. This document is also tremendously helpful for the IEP team when planning for postsecondary transitions.

By partnering with an organization like FACT, we are empowering parents, giving students a stronger voice, and making the IEP process more robust and authentic.

FIRST RESPONDERS

In the past few years our district has hosted quarterly round-table discussions with local first responders and community agencies. These breakfast meetings have helped us think through security at sporting events, threat assessment protocols, and procedures for reunifying students with their parents after a school evacuation. (We had to evacuate a middle school due to a gas leak the same week that we met for this round-table discussion.) These meetings have also helped foster relationships that have led to ongoing productive conversations to support student safety and access.

For example, after conversations sparked by a round-table discussion, we met with the local fire marshal to help us think through safe evacuation procedures for students with limited mobility. In the previous special education model, the district and the fire department needed to think about specialized evacuation procedures only for the few school buildings that housed self-contained classrooms for students with significant developmental disabilities or orthopedic impairments. Now that all students are served in their neighborhood schools, we realized that we need to examine safety procedures for all of our schools. We found out that the fire department did not know that we had students with complex needs attending all 16 schools in the district (because it had not occurred to us to tell them).

Our fire marshal helped us think through how we would lead students safely out of each building, particularly students in wheelchairs who are on the second floor of the school when the elevator stops working in a fire. Through this collaboration with our local fire department, we decided to use safety money from our capital bond to purchase evacuation chairs for all of our multilevel schools.

The Facilities department partnered with our physical therapists to determine the best location for the chairs. Then the physical therapists coordinated with the principals to train school staff to use the evacuation chairs, practicing each time we have a fire drill.

Schools have the opportunity to make a tremendous impact on the lives of students. However, we recognize that there are some student needs that require the support of professionals outside the school. We could write a whole book about the need for partnerships between schools and medical/mental health providers. In this section we want to highlight two elements of our work to connect with outside providers.

Over the years we have heard from counselors, school psychologists, principals, and teachers that communication with medical and mental health providers is often difficult and sometimes even counterproductive. For example, Michaela was having some difficulty in school. She had some great strengths, particularly in reading and writing and in attention to detail in mathematics. However, she struggled with applying mathematical concepts and justifying her reasoning. The school team had recognized these strengths and challenges, and they engaged in a Child Study process to identify interventions to help her develop her application and justification skills.

As the school team started the Child Study process, Michaela's parents brought a report from a doctor that diagnosed her with generalized anxiety disorder and obsessive-compulsive disorder. The doctor's report included a prescription for an IEP with a list of 20+ accommodations.

It was possible that Michaela did indeed need specially designed instruction through an IEP to allow her to access the grade-level curriculum with her classmates. But the school team was not convinced that was necessary. They were hoping to start with a less restrictive level of support through Child Study interventions. The report from the doctor, particularly the recommendation for special education services, raised the stakes and had the potential to short-circuit the thorough, inquiry-based process of classroom-based intervention and support.

This kind of doctor's recommendation that goes beyond what the school team believes is necessary for a student (or even openly contradicts the data that teachers see in school) happens so often that we decided to seek a proactive solution. We invited pediatricians, psychiatrists, private SLPs, and other community medical and mental health providers to join us for a collaborative luncheon. We shared about the differences between special education eligibility processes and medical diagnoses (IDEA vs. *Diagnostic and Statistical Manual of Mental Disorders*, fifth edition). We highlighted the importance of the relationship between schools and outside providers. We gave examples about what is and is not helpful. We asked about how we can support students' treatment goals during the school day. And we asked for feedback from providers about the ways in which we can continue to engage in ongoing, productive conversations.

In addition to hosting the annual luncheon to learn together, we also worked to maintain open lines of communication with medical and mental health providers through our school social workers. We have increased the number of social workers in our schools. As with most districts, our budget constraints mean that we don't have as many social workers in our district as we would like. We are hoping to expand this number as we move forward, but we are excited about the work that these people have been able to do for students and school teams.

One of the major tasks for our social workers is to serve as a liaison between families and providers. We know that families have the best interests of their children at heart. Unfortunately, for some students who need additional medical or mental health supports, parents may have a difficult time navigating the system. Our social workers have expertise working with various state and county agencies, including our local Medicaid affiliates and child protective services agencies and our county's Behavioral Health department. This allows them to come alongside families to help them apply for services and connect with providers. Parents have reported that without this "warm handoff" they would have given up before completing the complex process of securing services for their children.

Closing Thoughts About Leadership Moves

This chapter is full of suggestions and guidance about the leadership actions that can help guide a district toward greater inclusion. You may have recognized some of the structures you have already put in place to become more inclusive. Some readers may find this list overwhelming. You may be asking yourself, "How can I do this all at once? It may take months or even years to get all of the people and departments pointing in the same direction."

Our response is once again to remember the words of Richard Milner (2010), "Start where you are, but don't stay there." *You can't do it all at once.* But you can begin to take steps and set processes in motion that will have an impact across your organization. *And you can't do it all alone.* Build a core team of partners who will be allies in the work. It starts with belief—understanding your Why and helping the people around you find their Why.

Once you have established a foundation of belief (your Why), make a "skinny" plan that outlines the basic framework for your action steps (Fullan, 2010). And then jump into the work using the philosophy of Ready-Fire-Aim. *Never pass up an opportunity to invite others into the conversation about inclusion.* As momentum builds, more people will become part of the movement. New challenges and complexities will arise. And new allies will emerge to support the work.

> Never pass up an opportunity to invite others into the conversation about inclusion.

The final chapter in this book addresses some of the next steps that we anticipate in our district. We have eliminated segregated self-contained classrooms in kindergarten through 12th grade, and all students attend their neighborhood schools. Now we are working to make our preschools and adult transition services more inclusive. We are also thinking creatively about specialized transportation and how to partner with teacher education programs and the mental health system.

References

Causton-Theoharis, J. (2009). *The paraprofessional's handbook for effective support in inclusive classrooms.* Brookes.

Donohoo, J. (2016). *Collective efficacy: How educators' beliefs impact student learning.* Corwin.

Fullan, M. (2010). *Motion leadership: The skinny on becoming change savvy.* Corwin.

Fullan, M., & Quinn, J. (2016). *Coherence: The right drivers in action for schools, districts, and systems.* Ontario Principals' Council; Corwin.

Habib, D. (Producer & Director). (2018). *Intelligent lives* [Film]. www .Intelligentlives.org

Milner, R. (2010). *Start where you are but don't stay there: Understanding diversity, opportunity gaps and teaching in today's classroom.* Harvard Education Press.

Sagor, R. (2000). *Guiding school improvement with action research.* Association for Supervision and Curriculum Development.

TED^X. (2014, April 22). *Disabling segregation: Dan Habib at TEDxAmoskeagMillyard* [Video]. YouTube. https://www.youtube.com/watch? v=izkN5vLbnw8

CHAPTER 10

What's Next?

So much has changed in our district over the past eight years, philosophically and structurally. But most important, so much has changed in the outcomes and possibilities for our children with and without disabilities. We intentionally and frequently take stock, reflect, and celebrate our growth. Our fundamental beliefs about who belongs in our classrooms have changed. Our structures and resources are now set up to support each individual learner's needs at their neighborhood school. Yet with each celebration it becomes clearer how much work there is still to be done. Making sure that every student experiences belonging, feels safe, and is learning at high levels—that is a lifetime journey that will likely never have a finish line.

There are some specific areas of inclusive practices that we are moving our attention toward now. Streamlining school transportation, desegregating early-childhood education, increasing access to college, rethinking teacher education programs, and partnering with the mental health system are some of the important emerging areas of focus for our work.

TRANSPORTATION

Like many aspects of special education, specialized transportation has become institutionalized. For 40+ years it has been part of the infrastructure of schools. It is so much a part of our culture that "the short bus" is a commonly understood (and disparaging) euphemism for students with developmental disabilities.

Transportation is one of the most segregated aspects of our school system. Many school leaders have not questioned why it is so segregated or even considered that it could be structured differently. If every student attends their neighborhood school, we have an opportunity to think differently. What if wheelchair accessibility was present on all buses? What if students who need a smaller bus for sensory reasons could still ride with a few friends from their neighborhood? In other words,

> If every student attends their neighborhood school, we have an opportunity to think differently.

what if school transportation was made up of different vehicles (large and small) and different routes (longer and shorter) and these were created planfully with students' individual needs in mind but without the stigma and segregation of the current system?

Thinking differently about transportation presents specific challenges for school leaders who are seeking to create more inclusive school communities. Some districts own their own buses and hire their own drivers. Other districts contract with a transportation service. Either way, there are institutionalized barriers to inclusive transportation services. The number of wheelchair-accessible buses in the fleet can have a real impact on the ability to desegregate transportation, especially in smaller districts. We acknowledge the reality of these variables, yet we believe that continuing to question the status quo and looking for opportunities to be more inclusive is the right thing to do.

One structural reality we encountered was that the dispatcher who plots the routes, coordinates the buses, and assigns drivers for the main buses is a different person from the dispatcher who coordinates the specialized buses in our district. As we were trying to get more students with disabilities integrated onto the regular school buses, the organizational structure of the bus company was not set up to handle the change.

Another unexpected barrier we encountered was that our bus company has a large inventory of specialized (small) buses. As we have significantly reduced the number of students who ride smaller buses, the bus company has surplus buses that may not be in service every day. One solution we are experimenting with is to incorporate the smaller buses into the regular bus routes. This requires some reframing for students and families to shift the cultural expectations of what it means to ride a bus. If some neighborhoods have a smaller number of students, they could be served by a smaller school bus. Parents and students may perceive a stigma associated with riding that bus. But what if we helped students and parents think about the smaller bus like they think about smaller class sizes? Instead of 50 students on the morning bus route, their child is on a bus with 15 friends from the neighborhood. There are fewer students to pick up, so their child spends less time on the bus. The bus driver can get to know the students better. There is less opportunity for students to be invisible on the bus or to cause disruption and bully others. The overall bus experience could be enhanced for everyone, not just the student who previously rode a segregated bus.

ARDEN'S STORY

Arden, one of our incoming kindergarten students who uses a wheelchair, provided us an opportunity to explore the possibility of desegregating our transportation structures. For several years we had been reducing the number of students who rode specialized transportation. We had created guidance for IEP teams to rigorously consider the necessity of specialized transportation based on levels of independence, safety concerns, mobility concerns, or sensory concerns. Case managers, parents, bus drivers, and peers had developed creative solutions to help many students access the regular bus through accommodations and skills training. But students who use a wheelchair for mobility were still limited to using a specialized bus with a motorized lift.

When we were preparing for Arden's transition to kindergarten, his mother asked if he could ride the bus with his older brother. Arden had been watching his brother and other friends from the neighborhood ride a regular bus for several years. He was so excited about going to kindergarten and wanted to ride to school with his big brother.

As we talked about the idea, we were immediately confronted with the absurd inefficiency (and inequity) in the fact that two different buses would be coming to Arden's neighborhood: one regular long bus to pick up his brother and friends and one small lift bus to pick up Arden in his wheelchair, alone.

We contacted the bus company and our district Operations department to see what it would take to reconfigure bus routes in the neighborhood. The bus company needed to reconcile some of their internal structures. Historically, regular buses were routed by the general transportation dispatcher. Lift buses were routed by the specialized transportation dispatcher. With a nudge from our district operations director to the bus company manager, the dispatchers were willing to work together to find a creative solution.

The bus company arranged for a lift bus to serve the regular route through Arden's neighborhood. We partnered with the bus company to write a brief letter to communicate with the parents whose children would be riding this bus. We did not specifically name Arden, but we did acknowledge that one student on the bus would be accessing the ride through the wheelchair lift. We highlighted the fact that their neighborhood bus would allow for a smaller group of students to ride together with their siblings and friends. With fewer kids to pick up, the students would get to school a little sooner. They would not need to be standing out at the bus stop quite as early in the morning. We thought the parents would particularly like this idea given that it rains nine months of the year in Oregon. We included contact information in the letter in case families wanted to reach us to raise questions or express concerns. In the end we only heard from one family, who shared that they were thrilled that their children would get to ride on the bus with Arden and his brother.

GISELA'S STORY

When we met with Gisela's family to begin planning her transition to kindergarten, we knew transportation would be an important discussion. Gisela's older brother already rode the large school bus that stopped right in front of the family's apartment complex. The IEP team wanted to use this existing transportation for Gisela too. But she was still learning self-regulation strategies and boundaries, and the team had serious concerns about Gisela being able to stay safely in her seat on the bus. The team initially thought that a smaller bus with a safety vest that provided a secure seat belt would be the safest option. Then the IC who was leading the team asked, "Why couldn't we put the safety vest on the large bus that her brother rides? Then she could ride safely to school with natural support from her brother and all of the peer role models."

Our first conversations with the bus company about this modification involved many perplexed faces and raised eyebrows. We had never done anything like this before. There were some real logistical issues, such as who would buckle Gisela into her safety vest. The bus company's policies prevented the driver from buckling her seat because he had many other children to supervise during this time.

Some flexibility and creative thinking shortly brought up a workable solution. Gisela and her mom were given priority to board the bus first at the bus stop. While Gisela's mom was buckling Gisela in, the other students proceeded to board the bus and find their seats. Her mom was able to buckle the seat so quickly that the bus was not delayed in keeping to its assigned route and stops. When the bus arrived at school, a paraeducator boarded the bus and unbuckled Gisela's seat while the rest of the students filed off the bus. In the afternoon the same process happened in reverse.

As the year went on, Gisela learned the skill to sit safely in her seat, and eventually the IEP team removed the safety vest accommodation. We attribute this partly to the fact that she was surrounded by peers who were modeling appropriate bus behavior every day. And because she was already on a bus route with her brother and others in her neighborhood, she was able to seamlessly move into a less restrictive transportation plan.

The impact this had on Gisela, her family, and the community was profound. In our old model Gisela would have ridden a separate bus, a different bus from her brother. Gisela would not have had the role models for safe bus riding. Gisela's family would have had to juggle two different bus pickups for Gisela and her first-grade brother. Gisela would have been seen as separate or other by her peers because she wouldn't have been part of the regular morning gathering where all the children waited to catch the bus. And once she had separate transportation on her IEP, she might never have moved to a less restrictive bus.

GUIDANCE FOR SPECIALIZED TRANSPORTATION DECISIONS

As with all aspects of inclusive practices, we recognize that one size does not fit all. We are not saying that all students must ride the same bus to school or that no one will ever need a specialized ride. We are simply challenging ourselves to question the underlying structures that assume that students with significant cognitive or mobility differences *need* to ride a separate bus.

We began with these guiding principles:

- Traveling to and from school is an important part of a student's overall school experience.
- The concept of least restrictive environment applies to transportation settings as well as to the rest of the child's school day.
- The opportunity to be around peers without disability is an important part of social development.
- The goal is always to move students toward greater independence and inclusion in all parts of their school experience.

There are four key areas of concern that might necessitate a specialized bus: level of independence, safety concerns, mobility concerns, and sensory concerns. In all cases, our default assumption is that students can ride their neighborhood bus unless we have strong evidence to the contrary.

The evidence for this can be a little complicated to come by. That is, if a student has always ridden a specialized bus, there may not be any evidence of their ability to successfully navigate a bus full of their classmates. So the school team needs to look at other forms of evidence that would support the student's emerging skills in navigating a complex physical and social environment. How does the student handle the hallways? How do they manage the cafeteria? Do they respond well to redirection? Do they follow clear directions when presented visually?

Another key consideration is the difference between ideal bus behavior and typical bus behavior. If we wait for a student with disabilities to be able to demonstrate bus-ready skills with 100% success (or even 80% success), are we setting a higher standard than what we expect of other students on the bus? We don't encourage or condone disruptive or inappropriate behavior by any student on a bus. But we recognize that it does happen. And it is only in extreme cases that a student not served by special education would be removed from riding a bus because of behavior. Why would we force a student with a disability to ride a segregated bus for demonstrating behavior that is within the typical range of student bus behavior?

PARENT TRANSPORTATION CONCERNS

As with self-contained classrooms, some parents may advocate strongly for their child to ride a segregated bus. Some parents are concerned about (real or perceived) bullying on buses. Others are concerned that the cognitive and emotional load of navigating a bus to school might use up mental resources and leave the student less able to engage successfully in their classes once they arrive at school.

And some parents have not yet seen their child successfully navigate the world independently, and they want to maintain structures and protections that they believe will keep their child safe.

These are valid concerns, and it is important to take them seriously when parents raise them. It is also important to question the assumptions underlying these concerns, use accurate student-specific data when analyzing the concerns, and address any real barriers that may exist (e.g., bullying). We are always looking to promote independence in students. Riding a regular bus is a great way for students to build confidence in their ability to navigate the physical and social worlds independently.

Of course, some students will need help building their skills to ride a bus. In some cases there are unwritten social rules that dictate where students can sit. Case managers can coach students to recognize these social patterns and select a seat near supportive peers. Students can also be assigned a specific seat to reduce the potential anxiety of selecting their own seat. For other students, peers may be recruited to help with the transition onto the bus, reminders about appropriate bus behavior, and cues about when to get off the bus.

For some students, practicing on an empty bus may be helpful. After the buses complete the morning drop-off, the driver could stay at the school for a few minutes to greet their new passenger, help them find their assigned seat, and begin to establish a relationship.

Another technique that could be helpful is video modeling. A case manager or another student could create a first-person video of what it looks like to board the bus, greet the driver, find a seat, interact with other students, and sit safely during the ride. The student could watch the video each day before the bus ride, to help establish a successful routine.

Of course, bus drivers are critical allies in this process as well. We have amazing bus drivers who are positive and deeply committed to doing what is best for kids! Our building leaders don't take this for granted, however. They hold occasional meetings with bus drivers to check in about how they are connecting with the students. Our leaders have brought donuts and coffee and invited them to stay for a meeting after dropping students off in the morning. To respect confidentiality, we didn't talk about specific students. Instead, we talked about the guiding principles (safety, respect, relationships, community, equity, and inclusion). And we shared strategies that other drivers had found effective to build relationships and keep students safe on their buses.

When case managers are working to transition a student from a specialized bus to a general bus, it is essential to involve the bus drivers. Even if the student is equipped with strategies and the peers are prepared to support the student, the driver needs to know how they can support as well. This is particularly important because the driver sets the tone for how all students will be treated on their bus.

Without clear communication from the case manager or principal, the driver may have assumptions or preconceptions about the student that affect the way they engage and support the student on the bus.

We know that we are lucky to have great partners in leadership in our bus company who support the goals of inclusive practices. We understand that not all needs for specialized transportation are addressed as easily as what happened with Gisela or Arden. There may indeed be some students who have particular needs that require different methods of transportation. Yet as we learn to expect inclusion and to question segregation, we can creatively find more ways to eliminate transportation practices that separate students because of disability.

INCLUSIVE EARLY-CHILDHOOD EDUCATION

This book describes the leadership decisions and actions that have led to creating inclusive learning communities for students in kindergarten through 12th grade. That will continue to be the primary focus of our work. However, we have recognized that students are experiencing less inclusive systems and structures on either end of their K–12 experience—in preschool and college. That means one of our next great areas of opportunity is how we create inclusive learning communities for students before they begin kindergarten.

Structures for providing ECSE (Early Childhood Special Education) vary from state to state, but in many cases the agency responsible for ECSE is not the local school district. Funding streams for ECSE are also different from those for K–12. Preschool is not compulsory, so many students attend private, community-based preschools or do not experience preschool at all.

In Oregon, ECSE services are provided by the local Education Service District (ESD), a large public agency that encompasses multiple school districts, sometimes across multiple counties. In our case the ESD serves all districts in our county. Most of the districts in our county contract with the ESD for Early Childhood Evaluations, in addition to the actual special education services. For the past six years our district has conducted our own Early Childhood Evaluations. Once a child is found eligible for services, they will receive services from the ESD.

The preschool landscape in our district includes three general categories. The ESD supports eligible students in any of these three settings through consultation or direct service:

1. Private, community-based preschools
2. Public preschools run by the school district (parents pay tuition)
3. Self-contained preschool classrooms for students with significant disabilities (run by the ESD)

We have eliminated self-contained classrooms for school-age students, but some younger children were still experiencing segregation before coming to kindergarten. In some cases the ESD rented space from the school district, resulting in a district-run preschool classroom right next door to an ESD-run self-contained preschool classroom. We knew that we wanted to change this.

Creating an inclusive preschool experience for young children with and without disabilities requires flexibility, collaboration, and vision. Fortunately, we found like-minded partners at the ESD who are helping us find ways to make it happen. Over the course of nearly two years of conversations and work sessions, we developed a plan that we are aiming to launch for the next school year. The key strategy is a co-teaching partnership between a district-funded preschool teacher and an ESD-funded ECSE teacher. As with our K–12 classrooms, we will first create inclusive communities and then bring adult support to the children, rather than segregating children for the efficiency and convenience of adults.

We are excited about the possibilities and new learning opportunities this will bring—for children with disabilities, for children without disabilities, and for the adults who work with them.

ADULT TRANSITION SERVICES AND INCLUSIVE COLLEGE OPPORTUNITIES

Another opportunity for growth and innovation is how we make our Adult Transition Services more inclusive. For students who have been in our K–12 schools the shift to our 18–21 years Transition program may feel strangely noninclusive. They have been included in general education classes in their neighborhood schools for their entire school experience. But after high school graduation, there are no more general education peers to be included with.

Most of the students in our district graduate with a standard diploma (including most of the students served by special education). Then they move on to a range of postsecondary options, such as four-year university, two-year community college, trade schools, apprenticeships, military service, and full-time employment. A very small number of students served by special education (those who graduate with a modified or extended diploma) are eligible to continue receiving services from the school district until age 21.

In our district, as in many districts, we meet those students' needs through a program that we call Adult Transition Services. Our Adult Transition teachers and paraeducators are incredibly devoted to their students. They have created a menu of lessons and activities that allow young adults to build skills related to IEP goals and develop independence that will allow them to pursue productive employment and meaningful social interaction throughout their lives. Students spend a portion of the day on academic tasks. This includes functional mathematical and literacy skills, like managing a budget, reading a bus schedule, and writing a resume. Adult Transition also includes independent-living skills, like how to make a weekly menu, shop for groceries, and prepare lunch. And three days a week, students spend the afternoon in community-based work experiences, developing valuable employment skills on the job with local businesses.

This model has worked well to prepare students for postschool life. But we have also heard from students that it sometimes feels isolating. Remember Ben, the student from Chapter 7 who told a group of teachers about the amazing high school experience he had "when they let me out" of the self-contained classroom? When he moved on to our Adult Transition group, he immediately noticed that he was no longer among his peers without disabilities. His teachers did their best to get Ben and his classmates into community settings (like the public bus, grocery store, and community job sites). But Ben told us that for most of his day, he felt like he had returned to a self-contained class.

HOW TO MAKE TRANSITION SERVICES MORE INCLUSIVE

Inspired by Ben and other young adults who are craving natural, inclusive environments, we have been exploring how to make Adult Transition Services more inclusive. We can't just move our Adult Transition students into classrooms with other 18- to 21-year-olds in our schools because those age-level peers are no longer in public schools. So inclusion for Adult Transition won't look the same as it does for K–12 students. Instead, we realized that we need to find where other young adults are and provide our Adult Transition Services there.

In our community most high school graduates attend college, so we have been developing partnerships with local colleges and universities to create inclusive college experiences.

PARTNERSHIP WITH THE LOCAL UNIVERSITY

One of the exciting partnerships that we have been developing is with a local university's College and Community Studies (CCS) program. This is part of the national Think College movement, designed to provide a college experience for students with intellectual disabilities. Students enrolled in the four-year program earn a CCS certificate rather than a traditional bachelor's degree.

After developing a thorough memorandum of understanding with the local university, our district passes on state funding for students who attend the CCS program. According to this agreement, university staff provide the transition services outlined in the IEP, including specially designed instruction and related services in the areas of academics, employment, and independent living. The district does not pay the student's tuition. The student and family are responsible for tuition, just like for any other university student. And just like any other student, they may be eligible for a range of financial aid loans and grants to help them cover the cost.

In this particular program, academic supports are provided in two key ways. First, CCS program staff collaborate with university professors to modify the coursework. The students are enrolled in regular undergraduate classes, but they may have lighter reading assignments than their classmates, and they will be assessed with modified grading standards. In addition, CCS students have academic supports outside of class, including regular meetings with an academic counselor, who helps them understand assignments and complete their coursework.

The CCS program has a strong focus on preparing students for employment in a field that is connected to their interests and skills. For the first two years the university provides on-campus employment, including jobs in the athletic department, libraries, and cafeterias. In their third and fourth years the students move to off-campus jobs. CCS students have been employed in child care, food service, and office jobs in the neighborhood around campus.

The third key component of the CCS program is engagement in university life. Students are partnered with a peer navigator (usually a student studying social work or education), who helps them connect to the daily (or nightly) activities that make the college experience unique. CCS students have joined all kinds of community groups, including the frisbee club, the salsa dancing club, and ethnic identity groups. By their third or fourth year some students have developed the independence to move into on-campus housing. Moving out of the parents' house and into a dorm may be hard to imagine for families of students with intellectual or developmental disabilities. As with so many other elements of an inclusive society, it is important that we don't feel like we need to hold individuals with disabilities to a higher standard than their peers. There are many "typical" 18- to 21-year-olds out there who do not yet have the organization and time management skills that their parents would hope to see, yet they still manage to survive and thrive in dorms and apartments on campuses across the country.

Students enrolled in the CCS program are young adults with intellectual or developmental disabilities, so they are still eligible for other social services, including Vocational Rehabilitation, Developmental Disability services, and Supplemental Security Income. The CCS staff help the young adults and their families coordinate with these agencies to design braided funding to ensure that the right level of support is available for each student. This is particularly critical as students age out of "school-age" services when they turn 21. They are generally still enrolled at the university for their senior year, but the school district is no longer paying for transition services. So they need to bring in other sources of funding to ensure that they have the support they need to complete their university program.

There are many wonderful aspects of the CCS program and other Think College programs across the country. We are thrilled to be able to partner with our local university to provide this opportunity for the young adults in our district. But it is only for a limited number of students. First, the university does not have the capacity to provide robust transition services for every 18- to 21-year-old student in our district (and all of the other districts in the Portland metro area). And while the CCS program is designed for students with intellectual or developmental disabilities, there is still a threshold for admission. Students need to complete a thorough application and interview process and demonstrate a relatively high level of functional independence. There are many students receiving Adult Transition Services in our district who do not meet this threshold. As a result, we have been working to create another inclusive college opportunity for our students.

PARTNERSHIP WITH THE LOCAL COMMUNITY COLLEGE

Recently, we launched a new component of our Adult Transition program in partnership with our local community college. Two days a week, our Adult Transition Services would be provided at the college instead of at the alternative high school that had been the home base for the past eight years. District staff would continue to provide support for students' IEP goals in the areas of academics, employment, and independent living, but now this support would be based in the context of the community college—surrounded by other young adult peers.

For the academic component, we planned for all students to enroll in at least one community college class. The college has an introductory class called First Year Experience (FYE), which is designed to help new students transition to the expectations and rhythms of college life. This was a natural starting point for an inclusive academic experience. Nearly every new student takes FYE, so our Adult Transition students were entering on a relatively even playing field. The college had instructors who were committed to welcoming the full range of learners in their classes. And the pass/fail nature of the class was a natural fit for some modified coursework. During the winter term students branched out into a variety of courses based on their interests and strengths, focusing on courses that didn't require specific prerequisites. Students took classes in art, welding, theater set design, PE, automotive technology, and business. It was truly inspiring to hear students talk about their future career and personal possibilities now that they saw themselves as college students learning alongside other young adult peers.

> It was truly inspiring to hear students talk about their future career and personal possibilities now that they saw themselves as college students.

Another fundamental component of our Adult Transition Services is community-based work experiences. Our transition team has traditionally collaborated with local businesses to provide work experiences in the neighborhood around the alternative school where the Adult Transition program was based. This has been a powerful learning experience for students, so we wanted to make sure we were still finding ways for students to have these experiences.

Now that students were spending two full days on the community college campus, we partnered with college departments to find job experiences for our students. Some students helped departments with office tasks, tended plants in the Horticulture department's greenhouses, or stocked shelves in the food bank. Others worked in the cafeteria, counseling office, or Disability Resource Center.

The third component of our Adult Transition Services is focused on independent-living skills. The college provided a classroom space two days a week where our teachers could provide specially designed instruction that wasn't happening in the college classes or work experiences. This also served as a home base for our students if they needed a place to go between their classes and work experiences. Many students chose to spend their time in the cafeteria, student union, or other common spaces that are available for any community college student. This was a totally different way of providing services, but our Adult Transition teachers, paraeducators, and support specialists were remarkable in their creativity and flexibility.

Before the launch of this partnership with the community college, we held a student/parent information night with community college administrators and instructors, in addition to staff from our Adult Transition program. Young adults and their families were excited to hear our vision of an inclusive college experience. We launched with hopeful anticipation, knowing that we still had many details to work out and that there were many unknowns that we would discover through the process. Some of the complex details that we are continuing to work through include the following:

- How to provide academic and functional supports for students in a way that is appropriate in a community college setting—without having a paraeducator sitting beside the student in the classroom

- Variations in scheduling so that all of the Adult Transition students are not clustered in one or two FYE class periods—we don't want to accidentally create a self-contained classroom

- Transportation to meet the needs of students who want to take classes on other days: Students are growing in their functional independence and are able to ride on public transportation, but public bus routes from some areas of our district to the community college can be up to two hours each way. We are working to coordinate the district's bus contractor, two public transportation agencies, and the college's shuttle bus service.

- Opportunities/facilities to practice independent-living skills: In particular, our current Adult Transition facility (located at the district's alternative school) has a kitchen for students to practice preparing food, cleaning dishes, and so on. We are still looking for a suitable space at the community college for food storage and preparation.

- Navigating the different policies, regulations, and missions of two public education bureaucracies (a community college and a K–12 school district with an obligation to provide Free Appropriate Public Education)

Finally, we are hoping to partner with community college staff to design a menu of pathways for students. Some students may primarily take art or PE classes, while others may choose to pursue a certificate in welding or theater tech. We are also hoping that for some students, their work at the college may result in their attaining a National Career Readiness Certificate or other document to help demonstrate their knowledge and skills to future employers. These conversations are still in the early stages, so we do not yet know how this will look for students in the future.

Inclusive Teacher Education

For generations, education programs have had separate programs for special education and general education teachers. A student who is training to be a mathematics teacher may read a few chapters about learning disabilities. Or they may take an elective course in differentiation. But historically, there has been a tremendous disconnect in the education pathways for general education and special education teachers.

Recent graduates have more access to classes about inclusive education, but it is often still an elective course. Students pursuing a general education license may choose not to learn about teaching students with complex needs. And students pursuing a special education license may choose not to learn about delivering specially designed instruction in a co-teaching model.

And many student teaching programs for special education teachers still require experience in self-contained classrooms. A few years ago we noticed that we were not getting requests for student teacher placements from one of the universities in our area. We contacted a professor who is a strong advocate for inclusive practices to ask why their university hadn't been sending student teachers our way. They replied that one of the required components of the university's student teaching program was experience in a self-contained classroom, so they couldn't place students in our schools. We were stunned and a bit appalled. Promising young teachers were not getting the opportunity to embed themselves in an inclusive school community during the formative experience of student teaching. Instead they were required to intern in segregated classrooms. Happily, after we shared our concerns with the leaders of that program, they immediately adjusted their requirements.

We are partnering with others in advocating for inclusive special education experiences to be a required part of a student teaching program. We have recently joined a statewide task force that is addressing this issue, including university department chairs and staff from the state Department of Education and the teacher licensing board. This group receives technical assistance on structural change from the CEEDAR Center (Collaboration for Effective Educator Development, Accountability, and Reform), based at the University of Florida. We are excited to be part of the movement for long-term change to support inclusive schools by preparing the next generation of educators.

The Mental Health System

This book is not about reforming the mental health system to truly meet the needs of our youth. But we couldn't close without addressing the crucial role of mental health supports for all students. Anxiety, depression, and suicide rates are on the rise, which has a tremendous impact on students' ability to engage in their learning.

Districts across the country have acknowledged the importance of social-emotional learning. They are investing significant resources to help students learn these critical life skills. Our district has a long-standing commitment to meet the needs of the whole child by providing the circles of support that each child needs. We have added social workers, expanded the role of school psychologists, and explored schoolwide models to promote resiliency and social-emotional wellness among students.

With colleagues around our state we continue to support increased mental health care for children and families. Insurance barriers, language barriers, limited numbers of providers, and inability to access higher levels of care are all very real factors that affect children, families, and schools every day. We recognize that there is more for schools to do. And we acknowledge that school staff are not trained to be clinical mental health providers. States and local communities need to continue to invest in schools, and we believe they need to increase investment in mental health resources for students and their families.

Inclusive Practices in the Time of Distance Learning and COVID-19

We are writing the final drafts of this book in the spring of 2020, during the COVID-19 global pandemic. As we write, we are aware of the horrors of the disease, but we still do not know the full extent of the tragic loss of life and economic devastation that will result from the coronavirus. We are still trying to process what it means to continue to learn in a context where we cannot be together in a classroom.

Many things about how students and teachers experience school have changed dramatically, but we trust that we will all return to our schools again. We are hoping that we can use these unprecedented circumstances as an opportunity to learn new ways to help students connect in an inclusive setting.

The Oregon Department of Education (2020) seized the opportunity to make a bold statement for inclusion across all districts in our state:

> For many of our students who experience disability, this closure represents the first time in their educational history that they will be included to the same extent as their peers without disabilities. This reality presents an opportunity to think creatively and boldly. Harness this opportunity to lean into inclusive practices. Inclusion starts by considering the strengths each person brings to the educational process. What are the assets, talents, and specific strengths the student brings each day to the learning environment? ... Often it is the case that, as we evaluate services for students who have been identified for a disability, adult bias and historical patterns of instruction create limitations on student expectations.

In our district we have used this opportunity to place UDL at the center of our teaching practice. Teachers have been working on the concept of UDL for several years, particularly through co-teaching models. However, we have also seen that our amazing paraeducators will often provide accommodations and modifications "on the fly" during classroom lessons to make sure they are accessible for all students. Now that there are no paraeducators in the classroom, the responsibility for designing truly inclusive lessons falls on the classroom teacher (in collaboration with learning specialists, SLPs, and occupational/physical therapists).

Most districts are using some kind of online platform for posting lessons, gathering student work, and providing feedback. As we moved forward with virtual classrooms, each classroom teacher set up their own portal. In the early planning days, as we were all figuring out what distance learning looks like, some learning specialists proposed creating a separate virtual classroom for the students on their caseload, particularly those who have the most significant needs. The idea was that these students would not be accessing the same material as their general education peers, so it would be easier and more efficient to group them into a single virtual classroom for modified content.

We immediately sent a strong message to our special education staff and principals that we should not create separate virtual classrooms for students with complex learning needs. This would essentially be the same as creating a segregated self-contained classroom in the digital sphere.

Instead, we directed the learning specialists to partner with classroom teachers to help them develop lessons through a Universal Design lens. Some students might end up with different tasks (significantly modified coursework), but these things could still be assigned within the same virtual classroom with their peers.

Within the first week of distance learning, we heard a story from a teacher that confirmed we had made the right choice. The assignment in the second-grade classroom was to write a brief update called "Weekend News," record a video of themselves reading their weekend news, and upload it to the virtual classroom. One student, Alex, used his AAC communication device to write his story; then he made a video of himself reading the story aloud through the device. He said the highlight of his weekend was finding a dollar during an Easter egg hunt. After he uploaded the video, classmates posted comments. Some talked about how much they missed seeing Alex every day. One student said, "I like your haircut." Another said, "I found a dollar too, Alex!"

This assignment and comment thread created the opportunity for students to continue to engage in a natural and inclusive way. Alex commented on his friends' posts too. If he had been clustered into a separate virtual classroom for significantly modified coursework, he and his classmates would never have had the opportunity to maintain connections and find common ground.

Another parent reached out to us to share her child's experience. Parker is highly capable of engaging in all academic content. He has limited use of his arms and legs and uses an eye gaze device as his primary communication tool, so there are many activities that present barriers for him in our brick-and-mortar schools (e.g., building a mathematical model out of blocks). Yet in the virtual classroom, where all of the assignments are already in a digital format, most of his access issues have been resolved. We are excited about how his IEP team can incorporate what we learned from this virtual experience when we return to a more traditional school setting.

Many teachers are making short video recordings or voice-over slides to provide brief lessons in this virtual format. Jason is a student affected by attention deficit/hyperactivity disorder and dyslexia. In a video conference IEP meeting, Jason shared that being able to watch these short instructional videos repeatedly has increased his understanding of the material. It has also bolstered his confidence and given him more control over the pace of his learning.

We are learning many things during this strange time of social isolation and quarantine. Many things are new, and many of our understandings about the world may change. But one thing that we are finding remains true is that people belong together. People crave belonging. Inclusion is even more important now than ever.

Closing Thoughts

GUARDING AGAINST FADING MEMORY AND FALSE PROMISES

As we move toward our ninth year of fully inclusive schools, we recognize that we need to guard against the fading memory of segregated classrooms. Many of our classroom teachers, learning specialists, and administrators have been hired in the past eight years. As they operated within an inclusive model, they have witnessed (and contributed to) incredible student successes, but they have also experienced the challenging and complex realities that we describe in this book.

When working with a student who learns or behaves in ways that are unfamiliar, unexpected, or uncomfortable, it may be tempting to wonder if the child would be better off in a classroom staffed by "experts." Well-meaning adults who have never seen a segregated self-contained classroom may wonder if it makes sense to cluster students together to deliver services more efficiently.

As we have discussed throughout this book, there is overwhelming evidence from educational research that inclusive settings are more beneficial for academic and social-emotional learning for all students. And we have seen examples of those benefits throughout our schools. We recognize the critical importance of continuing to tell those stories and celebrate those successes to help us all remember that segregated classrooms were not better for the students in them or for the rest of the students in the school.

The same is true for the false promise of "expertise," which we addressed in Chapter 3. We have seen that building capacity in *all* teachers to support *all* students has created a positive, inclusive learning community where all students can succeed.

REVISITING THE CONTINUUM

In Chapter 2 we proposed a continuum of inclusive practices from separate schools to authentic belonging, meaningful student voice, and true friendships. We acknowledge that at any given time, the experiences that individual students have in our district will fall at various places along the continuum. There is no utopia: conflict and challenge will always be part of the human experience and part of schools. We know that there will always be more to learn and more work to do because we will always have students with unique strengths and diverse ways of learning. And we know that students in our schools now are experiencing opportunities to learn and belong in ways that are profoundly inclusive.

All students deserve inclusive schools, where they learn to respect one anothers' strengths and differences. All students deserve excellent schools, where they are deeply engaged in learning. The opportunity to attend inclusive and excellent

All students deserve inclusive schools, where they learn to respect one another's strengths and differences. All students deserve excellent schools, where they are deeply engaged in learning.

schools should not depend on your zip code or level of parent advocacy. We all want communities where people care, where they solve problems together, where they look at data and improve, where there are many pathways to success, and where hard work creates better outcomes.

As we stated in Chapter 1, inclusive education does require change. It requires uncovering assumptions and beliefs, it requires different roles, it requires trust, it requires innovation, it requires collaboration, and it requires capacity building. Becoming an inclusive school district requires intention. With intention, being an inclusive school district is a completely achievable goal.

The best practices for inclusive schools are also the best practices for excellent schools. *Improving instructional practices*, *creating inclusive cultures*, and *increasing student voice* are the keys to developing the scholarship, character, and community that we want for all children.

Our purpose in writing this book is simply to lay out the ideas and structures that are working for us on this messy, imperfect, and joyful journey. You may do things differently. You may discover more effective ways to move forward. We look forward to learning from you. What is important is that we commit to schools where everyone belongs and everyone learns, that we take action, that we get better, and that we *lead for all*.

Our children, all children, deserve inclusive and excellent schools.

References

Oregon Department of Education. (2020). *Oregon's extended school closure guidance: Special education* (Specially Designed Instruction Toolkit). https://www.oregon.gov/ode/educator-resources/standards/Documents/Specially%20Designed%20Instruction%20Toolkit.pdf

Index

A SAGE Publishing Company

Helping educators make the greatest impact

CORWIN HAS ONE MISSION: to enhance education through intentional professional learning.

We build long-term relationships with our authors, educators, clients, and associations who partner with us to develop and continuously improve the best evidence-based practices that establish and support lifelong learning.

Made in the USA
Las Vegas, NV
29 September 2022

56198038R00125